Winds of Doctrines

The Origin and Development of Southern Baptist Theology

W. Wiley Richards
Professor of Christian History, Missions, and Philosophy

*Florida Baptist Theological College
Graceville, Florida*

UNIVERSITY
PRESS OF
AMERICA

Lanham • New York • London

Copyright © 1991 by
University Press of America®, Inc.
4720 Boston Way
Lanham, Maryland 20706

3 Henrietta Street
London WC2E 8LU England

All rights reserved
Printed in the United States of America
British Cataloging in Publication Information Available

Library of Congress Cataloging-in-Publication Data

Richards, W. Wiley, 1932-
Winds of doctrines : the origin and development
of Southern Baptist theology / W. Wiley Richards.
p. cm.
Includes bibliographical references and index.
1. Southern Baptist Convention—Doctrines—History.
2. Baptists—Doctrines—History. I. Title.
BX6462.7.R53 1991
230'.6132'09—dc20 91-2780 CIP

ISBN 0–8191–8254–0 (alk. paper)
ISBN 0–8191–8255–9 (pbk. : alk. paper)

 The paper used in this publication meets the minimum requirements of American National Standard for Information Sciences—Permanence of Paper for Printed Library Materials, ANSI Z39.48–1984.

To My Grandchildren

Melissa, Jason, Jeremy
Trey, Mandy, and Bo

Acknowledgement

Manuscripts have a way of taking on a life of their own. Authors tinker, refine, enlarge and edit as they try to make the clearest and most accurate presentation possible. I am deeply indebted to Mrs. Sue Diehl for her patience with my constant revisions and for her diligence in deciphering my handwriting as she typed and re-typed the manuscript. My wife, nee Betty May Hargrave, and my son, W. Glen Richards, spent long hours on the word processor in preparing the manuscript for publication.

CONTENTS

PART I: CALVINISTIC EVANGELICALISM, 1609-1800

Overview 3

Chapter 1. Nurtured in Calvinism 5
    Historical Beginnings 6
    The Calvinistic Background 9
    The Major Baptist Groups 10
    Gaining a Consensus 11
    Summary 14
    Notes 14

Chapter 2. Calvinism on the Pinnacle 17
    The Bible, The Objective Source of Authority 18
    The Triune God 21
    Predestined and Quickened 23
    The Efficacy of the Cross 24
    The Local Church, The Objective Authority 25
    The Ordinances, Rites for Believers Only 27
    The Rise of Postmillennialism 32
    Missionary Zeal 34
    Summary 37
    Notes 38

PART II: ECCLESIOLOGICAL EVANGELICALISM, 1800-1899

Overview 43

Chapter 3. Calvinism on the Defense 45
    The Authority of the Bible Assumed 45
    Explicating the Trinity 47
    A Less Radical Depravity 50
    Sufficiency Versus Efficiency 51
    Summary 59
    Notes 59

Chapter 4. Baptist Church Successionism 63
   Baptist Ecumenism 63
   Baptist SuccessionISM 65
   The Supper, For Churches Only 69
   Alien Immersion and the Watery War 71
   Looking for the Millennium 74
   Molding the Missionary Spirit 78
   Proclaiming the Gospel 80
   Summary 81
   Notes 82

Chapter 5. Of Higher Critics and Calvinists 85
   The First Battle for the Bible 86
   Two Approaches to Infallibility 89
   The Benefits of Textual Criticism 91
   Restating Trinitarian Theology 92
   Searching for a Doctrine of the Atonement 94
   Trying to Understand Depravity 96
   The Origin of the Soul 97
   Summary 98
   Notes 98

Chapter 6. Landmarkism on the Rise 101
   Adopting a Name 101
   The Cotton Grove Resolutions 103
   The Local Church of Landmarkism 105
   Landmark Impact on the Ordinances 108
   The Ascendancy of Amillennialism 110
   The Necessity of the Resurrection 112
   Organizing for the Cause of Missions 113
   Summary 115
   Notes 116

PART III: EVANGELISTIC EVANGELICALISM, 1899-1960

Overview 121

Chapter 7. Committed to Evangelism 123
   Election Becomes Foreknowledge 125
   Psychology and the Soul 127
   Creationism and Traducianism 128

Contents   ix

Body, Soul, and Spirit 130
Christ's Substitutionary Death 131
Last Vestiges of Successionism 132
The Ordinances: Church Rites 134
De Facto Amillennialism 135
Summary 136
Notes 137

Chapter 8. Contending with the Critics 139
The Development of Form Criticism 139
Fundamentalist Reactions Against Liberalism 141
Southern Baptists and the Fundamentals 142
Further Attacks Against the Critics 145
Mullins on the Benefits of Higher Criticism 146
Uproar over Biological Evolution 146
Summary 147
Notes 148

Chapter 9. E. Y. Mullins and Neoorthodoxy 151
The New Orthodoxy 151
The Appeal to Experience 153
Revelation and the Bible 154
Election 155
The Sin-Death Principle 155
Summary 156
Notes 157

PART IV: INERRANTIST EVANGELICALISM VERSUS NEOORTHODOX EVANGELICALISM, 1960-1989

Overview 161

Chapter 10. At War Over the Word 163
The Theological Parameters 164
Defining the Positions 165
The Growing Popularity of Higher Criticism 167
Disagreement over Reliability 170
Hindrances to Defining Inspiration 173
Common Grounds 179
Summary 180
Notes 181

Chapter 11. The Last Stages of Calvinism 183
    Jesus and the Trinity 184
    The Holy Spirit Rediscovered 186
    Election Based on Free Will 187
    Body and Soul Versus Body-Soul 188
    Substitution Versus Example 190
    Eternal Security 193
    Political Liberation 194
    Summary 195
    Notes 196

Chapter 12. The Church Alive 199
    The Church, A Spiritual Entity 200
    The Ordinances: Free of Landmarkism 201
    Grudging Acceptance of Premillennialism 204
    Continuous Resurrection Versus Future Event 206
    Existence Beyond the Grave 208
    Summary 208
    Notes 209

Chapter 13. Whence and Whither 211
    The Bible 211
    Human Nature and Sin 212
    The Church 213
    Evangelism and Missions 214
    The Ordinances 215
    The End Time 216
    Living with the Controversy 217
    Notes 220

Index 221

INTRODUCTION

Southern Baptist theology developed out of evangelicalism. It holds the Bible in high esteem as the objective source of authority and maintains a firm commitment to trinitarian theology, the depravity of sinners, the substitutionary death of Christ, the centrality of the local church, the visible return of Christ, and heaven and hell as eternal abodes. Yet, that theology has evolved through the years in a distinctive way for Southern Baptists. Their theology has gone through three pronounced stages: Calvinistic evangelicalism, ecclesiological evangelicalism, and evangelistic evangelicalism. It now stands at the crossroads as inerrantist evangelicalism vies with neoorthodox evangelicalism for the right to direct the course of Southern Baptist theology.

The Calvinistic phase began in America with the founding of the Baptist church in Providence, Rhode Island, in 1639, and ended about 1800. Calvinists comprised a part of that original Baptist fellowship in the colonies. The process took a century and a half for Calvinism to triumph over its competitors, but by the end of the seventeenth century, it claimed the formal allegiance of most of those churches, which became the constituent elements of the Southern Baptist Convention. The conflicting and coalescing theologies that contributed to the rise of Calvinism are recounted in chapters 1 and 2. Analysis of the theology of prominent Baptists like Isaac Backus and influential confessions like the Philadelphia Confession of Faith form a significant segment of the study, but to guard against the tendency to ascribe an inordinate role to the few, citations from lesser individuals, pamphlets, and books render a measure of balance to the interpretation of a given era of thought. The account in these chapters chronicles the routes by which divergent theologies finally came together in the Calvinistic synthesis.

The second major phase in the development of Southern Baptist evangelicalism, the ecclesiological, began about 1800 and closed with the firing of William H. Whitsitt in 1899. Revival fires had broken out about 1800, which resulted in the influx of large numbers of converts joining Baptist churches. Coincidentally with this Second Great Awakening or Frontier Revival—the first Great Awakening having occurred following the preaching of men like Jonathan Edwards and George Whitefield—Regular Baptists in the United States began focusing their attention on the doctrine of the church. Their obsession to defend Baptist historical credibility by establishing its origin in the New Testament era lasted nearly a century. The conviction in 1800, that Baptist churches are the true churches, crystalized into a doctrine of Baptist church succession about the time that the Southern Baptist Convention was organized in 1845. Vestiges of Baptist church succession still remain in the convention, but it peaked with the Landmark movement, leveled off about 1900 and began declining in influence. Although the nineteenth century was the "Century of the Church" for Baptists in the South, for ease of presentation the four chapters devoted to that century have been evenly divided. The first two cover the period to 1845 and the other two, the latter half.

Southern Baptist evangelistic evangelicalism began taking shape at the beginning of the twentieth century. The firing of Theodore R. Clark at the New Orleans Baptist Theological Seminary in 1960 is taken here as signaling the end of that era. In this third phase of the development of evangelicalism, ecclesiastical evangelicalism softened as Southern Baptists became less patient with Landmarkism's abrasiveness. A new threat was already on the horizon. Fundamentalist Christians saw the rise of German rationalism as a threat to the concept of biblical inerrancy. Southern Baptists made tentative contact with the transdenominational fundamentalist counterattack but then withdrew into their own brand of denominational evangelicalism in education, evangelism, and polity as they forged an evangelistic program. Neoorthodox tenets arising out of the works of Karl Barth, Emil Brunner, Rudolph Bultmann, Paul Tillich, and others found few receptive ears among Southern Baptists during this period. Chapter 7 shows the gradual softening of the edges of both Calvinism and Landmarkism as they gave way to evangelism. Chapters 8 and 9 give an overview of the fundamentalist and neoorthodox reactions to liberalism and to E. Y. Mullins's impact on the future development of Southern Baptist theology.

Southern Baptists are now embroiled in a bitter fratricidal strife, the outcome of which will chart the direction of the convention for decades to come. A precursor of the controversy over the Bible and related doctrines began with the firing of Clark. It gained prominence when Broadman Press published Ralph H. Elliott's book *The Message of Genesis* and intensified with Broadman's publication of Genesis in *The Broadman Bible Commentary*. A new dimension to the ongoing controversy has come about since 1979 as conservative leaders orchestrated a plan to change the theological direction of the convention.

By what name shall the opposing factions of the controversy be known? At the outset, the pastors and others who led the assault dubbed their opponents liberals. The ones launching the counterattack labeled the opposition fundamentalist-independents. Neither designation is apt because theological liberalism, in the historical sense of denying the uniqueness of the Bible and interpreting God as an impersonal Force, is almost non-existent in the Southern Baptist Convention. Conversely, their opponents are not fundamentalist-independents. Most of the men so accused are products of Southern Baptist colleges and seminaries who have chosen to remain in the Southern Baptist Convention. The two factions are labeled inerrantist evangelicals and neoorthodox evangelicals. Fundamentalism is a loaded word with negative connotations as used by convention leaders. Because the issue of inerrancy has been a central theme in the controversy, it seems best to continue the use of that term because both words, inerrancy and evangelical, are more easily defined.

Neoorthodoxy, like fundamentalism, is a theologically definable word. This faction in the convention can be called neoorthodox evangelicals. For those on both sides, each designation represents a continuum and no attempt is made in this book to locate a given theology on the continuum. Once the axioms of inerrantist evangelicalism and neoorthodox evangelicalism are established, theologies can fall anywhere on the line. Chapters 10 through 13 attempt to establish these parameters of thought.

Southern Baptist theology continues to be in a state of flux. Nevertheless, a substratum of doctrines has remained intact through the years. Baptist understanding of the doctrine of election, for example, has varied through the years, but not their commitment to trinitarian theology. To give continuity of thought as well as standards of comparison, seven major doctrines are featured. Because of the esteemed status the Bible enjoys in Southern Baptist theology and life, attitudes toward biblical inspiration and authority stand in the forefront of the study. The other doctrines viewed both comparatively and historically in their development are beliefs about God, human nature and sin, salvation, the church, the ordinances, and the end of time. Subsidiary themes like preaching, evangelism, the role of women, and the importance of missions are injected when relevant. More extensive treatment is given those issues which confronted Baptists as their history unfolded.

Any effort to say what another person believes is risky. Inevitably, some thinkers will have been misrepresented, but not deliberately. Researchers can never divorce their deepest convictions from their task, but to paraphrase a concept learned from one of my history teachers, W. Morgan Patterson, I have striven for sympathetic objectivity, especially when analyzing the theology of those with whom I closely agree and of those with whom I deeply disagree. A historian is most likely to give an unobjective and slanted presentation of these two classes of writings.

Because my purpose is to present the origins and development of Southern Baptist theology, I have tried to show the historical context in which they grew. The cultural antecedents, though important, I have only touched at various points. More extensive treatment can be found in the writings of interpreters like W. W. Sweet, Sam Hill, Rufus Spain, and John Lee Eighmy.

I have quoted extensively from writers whose rules of spelling, punctuation, and grammar differ from those of the twentieth century. To catch the flavor of these styles, no attempt was made to modernize them.

PART I

CALVINISTIC EVANGELICALISM, 1609-1800

Chapter 1. Nurtured in Calvinism
Chapter 2. Calvinsim on the Pinnacle

OVERVIEW

From their modest numbers in England, scattered between the General Baptists who believed in a general atonement and Particular Baptists with their Calvinistic commitment to an atonement only for the elect, Baptists gradually gained their self-identity as a viable denomination. In the colonies, the theological parameters were broader at the beginning of Baptist work in 1639, when Roger Williams founded the first Baptist church in the New World. Calvinism nevertheless prevailed by 1800 with the beginning of the Frontier Revival, sometimes called the Second Great Awakening. Chapters one and two are devoted to that story.

CHAPTER 1

NURTURED IN CALVINISM

The people named Baptists surfaced in England at the beginning of the seventeenth century, at a time when the revolutionary principle of individualism and its social expression—voluntary association—would help break up existing social structures. As to the significance of free or voluntary associations, William Ebenstein wrote:

> Democratic theory sees in the principle of *voluntarism* the very lifeblood of a free society. Fellowship can most deeply be experienced in small, voluntary groups. Such groups were first formed in seventeenth-century England on a religious basis, and to this day the English-speaking world abounds with thousands and thousands of religious sects that are small in size and entirely voluntary in nature.[1]

People committed to the principle of individualism, when it was applied to religious matters, were no longer willing to grant civil and religious authorities the right to prescribe what one should believe or how one should worship. Baptists seemed to have an innate propensity for this underlying principle of democracy in small voluntary groups.

They surfaced at a propitious time. James VI of Scotland ascended the English throne as James I at the death of Queen Elizabeth in 1603 and inherited, in addition to the throne, a volatile religious situation. Dissension had been building for decades as men like Henry Barrows, Francis Johnson, Thomas Cartwright, John Field, and Thomas Wilcox tried to purge the Church of England of objectionable Roman Catholic rituals. Some of them, tiring of the struggle, broke with Anglicanism and began a separatist faction. Purportedly one thousand of these dissenters presented a formal request to the king in 1603, listing many of their complaints. James I rejected nearly all of the requests of this Millinary Petition but granted in 1604 the plea for a new translation of the Bible. The outcome was the celebrated King James, or Authorized, Version of 1611.

HISTORICAL BEGINNINGS

Baptists originated in England about 1600 as a part of a group of separatists who saw no hope of purifying Anglicanism and had begun private meetings of their own. Out of one of these small gatherings at Gainsborough, John Smyth, an Anglican clergyman, Thomas Helwys, a lawyer, and John Murton, a furrier, began a fellowship of General Baptists, so named because of their belief that Christ's atoning death was sufficient for the whole world. After the group sought refuge in Holland, Helwys returned to England, formed a church at Spitalfield in 1612 (which later clearly became a Baptist church) and almost immediately began agitating for religious liberty. He wrote his renown pamphlet *A Short Declaration of the Mistery of Iniquity* in which he contended that the king is mortal, not divine, and that no civil authority has the right to coerce anyone's conscience. With more courage than tact, he mailed an autographed copy to the king. When Helwys was imprisoned, Baptist individualism had taken its first toll. Helwys died sometime prior to 1616, perhaps while in prison, but his compatriots took up the cause of religious freedom. Leonard Busher, allegedly a member of Helwys's group at Spitalfield, published a tract entitled *Religious Peace or a plea for liberty of conscience* in 1614.[2]

The religious atmosphere in the American colonies in the seventeenth century was but little improved over that in England, as Roger Williams learned. Congregationalists from England had sailed to North America to escape religious strictures in England, but not with the purpose of gaining and guaranteeing religious freedom. Instead, they intended to make Congregationalism the official religion of their colony and did so. When Roger Williams wrote his book *The Bloudy Tenet of Persecution* and agitated openly for freedom of religion, leaders of the colony banned him. His subsequent establishment of Providence Plantations in Rhode Island "was the first civil government in the world to achieve complete religious liberty."[3] Baptist commitment to soul freedom claimed its first victory.

Victories were few and spasmodic. W. W. Sweet incisively noted, "The principles of the Baptists and the Quakers struck at the very foundation of the seventeenth century state and ecclesiastical organization, and were considered in the more conservative colonies, such as Virginia and Massachusetts, as dangerously radical."[4] As far as historical accounts go, no Baptists in the colonies suffered martyrdom at the hands of civil authorities; persecution took other forms. Henry Dunster, the president of Harvard College from 1642 until 1654, was forced to give up his presidency and the house he built because, although not a Baptist himself, he espoused believer's baptism and refused to have his daughter sprinkled.[5]

Baptists fought hardest in Virginia for religious liberty. The aristocracy in Virginia were deeply committed Anglicans who viewed the Baptists with suspicion. No Baptist church survived in Virginia until well into the seventeenth century, over a century after the Jamestown Colony was founded in 1607. It was perhaps inevitable, then, that Virginia provided the stage where the fight for religious freedom was most heated, beginning at least by 1767, when authorities in Virginia fined Lewis Craig for preaching. Between 1768 and 1775, other men like John Waller, James Childs, James Read, William Marsh, Allen Wyley, John Corbley, Elijah Craig, and John Pickett either were imprisoned or beaten for preaching. The experience of James Ireland, a young man of twenty-two years, indicates the Baptist tenacity as well as any. After being imprisoned in the Culpepper, Virginia, jail, his keepers tried to kill him by burning sulphur outside the jail, exploding gun powder under the jail and attempting to poison him.[6] Once released from prison, he promptly began another missionary tour.

On another occasion, John Waller, Lewis Craig, and James Childs were arrested for preaching. The court prosecutor charged, "May it please your worships, these men are great disturbers of the peace; they cannot meet a man upon the road, but they must ram a text of Scripture down his throat."[7] Waller defended himself and his colleagues, but, nevertheless, the court imprisoned them for 43 days. Imprisonment did not cool their ardor. While in jail the three "preached through the grates" in spite of a noisy mob outside.[8]

The Baptist cause did not go unnoticed by everyone in positions of authority. James Madison, a friend of John Leland, helped formulate the American Bill of Rights at the insistence of Leland and other Baptist leaders. Patrick Henry gave his talents and influence toward gaining civil relief for them. In a tribute to him, historian Robert B. Semple penned these words:

> It was in making these attempts that they were so fortunate as to interest in their behalf the celebrated Patrick Henry. Being always the friend of liberty, he only needed to be informed of their oppression, when, without hesitation, he stepped forward to their relief. From that day until the day of their complete emancipation from the shackles of tyranny, the Baptists found in Patrick Henry an unwavering friend.[9]

Other men with Baptist sentiments left their marks on seventeenth-century America. Roger Williams pioneered in establishing a colony founded on the principle of separation of church and state, a new experiment in the search for religious freedom. A hundred years later those of kindred spirit, like Isaac Backus and John Leland, helped coerce the founders of the fledgling nation to write a guarantee of religious freedom into its constitution. These and lesser-known theological lights also bequeathed to the new nation a legacy that helped form a group that eventually became the largest evangelical body in the United States, the Southern Baptist Convention, with a membership of more than fourteen million adherents.

Individuals, not denominations, write theology, and Baptists can point to men who pioneered in the formulation of their heritage. Roger Williams indelibly marked history by his stand for a free church unencumbered by civil control. A century later, John Leland (1754-1841) and Isaac Backus (1724-1806) saw the fruition of Williams's principles when they fought successfully for constitutionally guaranteed religious freedom. W. W. Sweet gave them that kind of recognition.[10] After assessing the importance of Thomas Jefferson and James Madison in the fight for religious liberty, Sweet candidly admitted, "But justice compels the admission that Jefferson's part in this accomplishment was not so great as was that of James Madison, nor were the contributions of either or both as important as was that of the humble people called Baptists."[11]

Three other Baptists deserve notice in regard to the contribution of Baptists to the cause of religious freedom. Isaac Backus wrote extensively in opposition to religious oppression. Richard Furman (1755-1825) also made a profound impact. Converted under the preaching of Joseph Reese, Furman—just sixteen years old—began preaching almost immediately, and accepted the call to pastor the Baptist church of the High Hills of Santee, near Charleston, South Carolina, when he was only nineteen. In the words of W. J. McGlothlin, he "rapidly rose to a position of commanding influence and power."[12] After his fervent support of the American Revolution led Lord Cornwallis to put a price on his head, Furman fled Charleston for his own safety. When the war was over, he served as a delegate to the Constitutional Convention in 1790, but his influence was most deeply felt by Baptists in his lengthy service as the pastor of the First Baptist Church of Charleston from 1787 until his death in 1825. J. A. Reynolds notes that he was "regarded by many as the outstanding Baptist leader of his day."[13]

In an age when Calvinism was gradually supplanting Arminianism as a formal statement of Baptist beliefs, Furman prefigured those of subsequent generations who saw not quite so clearly in matters of theology. To quote from Charles G. Sommers:

> Though in his views of Scripture doctrine he followed no man exclusively, yet he was not unwilling to be found coinciding with such men as Doddridge, Fuller, and Dwight. He thought that many of the advocates of exact system in theology, had not deserved well of the cause, and that it accorded better with Christian wisdom to adopt an unmutilated revelation, than to press it by forced constructions into the service of a system.[14]

As Sommers noted, "He was rather of the doubting than of the strongly confident class of Christian."[15]

THE CALVINISTIC BACKGROUND

Theologically, who were the people whom history dubbed Baptists? At least in the first few decades of life in the colonies, their theology mirrored the beliefs of their compatriots in England. There, two distinct groups of Baptists emerged and began formulating theological statements and confessions of faith. The Particular Baptists gained their distinctiveness because of their view of a limited atonement. The General Baptists believed in a wider interpretation of the atonement. The two interpretations are known in a broader sense as theological children of Calvinism and Arminianism.

Calvinism takes its name from one of the principal theological figures of the Reformation in Europe. John Calvin (1509-1564), a French reformer who studied for the Roman Catholic priesthood before finally taking a degree in law, became caught up in the Protestant Reformation and eventually settled in Geneva, Switzerland. His most famous work is probably *Institutes of the Christian Religion*, a two-volume set first published in 1536. Calvinism is not readily simplified, but its main features are succinctly summarized in the Canons of the Synod of Dort of 1618-1619.[16] However, if Calvinism could be expressed in a single concept, it would be an emphasis on the sovereignty of God. Even the salvation of believers has for its primary goal the glory of God rather than the personal happiness of the redeemed.

Calvinism customarily is taught under five basic principles.[17] (1) God in his sovereign grace and power, and apart from any precognition of faith in the redeemed, foreordained all those who were to be saved. (2) God actually and not just potentially reconciled to himself only the elect for whom Christ died and for whom he made satisfaction for sin. (3) Those whom God foreordained and for whom Christ made satisfaction will be drawn irresistibly to Christ by the Holy Spirit. (4) Those thus drawn cannot fall away and lose their salvation. (5) Human nature is depraved or corrupted to the extent that one cannot repent and believe until being drawn and regenerated by the Holy Spirit. Salvation, therefore, is totally by the grace of God and is not predicated upon anything the unregenerate do, including repenting and believing.

Calvinism's great protagonist came in the person of Jacob Arminius (1560-1609), a Dutch pastor who became disillusioned with the teachings of Calvinism and openly attacked the doctrine of predestination. After his death, his followers stated in five concise articles, known as the *Remonstrance*, the essence of his views.[18] The theological debate which Arminius and his followers precipitated finally culminated in the Synod of Dort in 1618-1619, at which time the Calvinists debated and then condemned Arminianism. The animosity generated in Europe between the two systems of thought wound its way across the Atlantic Ocean and lodged itself among the fledgling denomination called Baptists. Southern Baptist theology developed historically from a strong Calvinistic base which was subsequently eroded by the inroads of Arminianism.

THE MAJOR BAPTIST GROUPS

Historians credit Roger Williams with founding the first Baptist church in the colonies, a Particular Baptist church, with the formation of the church at Providence, Rhode Island, in 1639. From that beginning with one church and 24 members, Baptists in the colonies grew to number 986 churches and 67,475 members in 1790.[19] From 1639 until 1790, the identifiable Baptist groups were the Particular (later known as Regular) Baptists, General Baptists, General Six Principle Baptists, Seventh Day Baptists, New Light (or Separate) Baptists, and Freewill Baptists. The most dominant of these Baptists was the Particular Baptists as is indicated by the fact that 57,306 of the 67,475 Baptists were members of Particular Baptist churches by 1790.[20] Most of the General and Separate Baptists merged with the Particular Baptists by that year. The remaining Baptist fellowships were less influential in the formation of Southern Baptist theology, but their presence entitles them to a brief introduction in the order of their historical development.

General Six Principle Baptists came early to the colonies, perhaps as early as 1639.[21] They were in the Arminian tradition, but gained their distinctiveness by preaching the six basic principles in Hebrews 6:1-2. As one would expect of an Arminian Baptist, they rejected unconditional predestination and limited atonement. According to Robert G. Gardner, they practiced the laying on of hands by all believers at one's baptism rather than just by pastors and deacons.[22] By 1790, they numbered only 1,778 members and 22 churches.[23]

The Seventh Day Baptists owe their origin to John Crandall (1612-1676), an Englishman from Monmouthshire who immigrated to Massachusetts in 1634 after being disowned by his family in England when he espoused Baptist sentiments.[24] He joined the Williams group in 1637, gravitated to the John Clarke church in Newport,[25] and espoused sabbatarian views by 1669.[26] Since Seventh Day Baptists were drawn from both the Particular and General Baptist traditions, their distinctive beliefs come from their worship on Saturday rather than Sunday. They had 14 churches and 946 members in 1790.[27]

The Rogerenes split off from the Seventh Day Baptists. John Rogers (ca. 1648-1721) and two of his followers left the Seventh Day Baptists and organized a church in New London, Connecticut, in 1674.[28] Gardner lists some of their peculiar practices as opposition to long, audible prayers; marriage without benefit of the established clergy; refusal to be treated by a physician; prayer for the sick; and anointing with oil. They had only two churches in 1790.[29]

Gardner classifies another group, the Keithians, as Baptists even though they divided originally from the Quaker movement in Philadelphia about 1691. They emphasized the role of Christ in salvation while minimizing the Quaker belief in the sufficiency of a subjective leaning on the Divine Inner Light. Fewer than 50 members ever united with the four churches. All eventually reunited with Seventh Day and Particular (Regular) churches.[30]

Another group of General Baptists sprang up in Rhode Island in 1721. Arminian in doctrine, they rejected the laying on of hands and practiced open communion. Only 36 churches and 2,274 members existed in 1790.[31]

A second group of Seventh Day Baptists, the German, originated in 1728. John Conrad Beissel (1690-1728) left the German Baptist Brethren, or Dunkards, and formed a group of Seventh Day Baptists. Their group claimed five churches and 222 members in 1790.[32]

The Freewill Baptists came into being in 1780 at New Durham, New Hampshire, under Benjamin Randall (1749-1808). They believed in a general atonement but were most widely known for their teaching that believers could fall from grace, i.e., lose their salvation if they lapsed back into a life of sin. The Freewill Baptists apparently never had much influence in the formation of Southern Baptist theology. They had 18 churches and 401 members in 1790.[33]

GAINING A CONSENSUS

Although the lesser known Baptist groups conceivably could have had some bearing on the development of Southern Baptist theology, the most important sources of their theology are three: Particular (Regular) Baptists, General Baptists, and New Light (Separate) Baptists. As already discussed, Arminian Baptists of the Helwys group emigrated from England and settled in the colonies. South Carolina particularly enticed dissenters because of its reputation for openness toward people who diverged in doctrine from beliefs held by the establish denominations.

A second type of Baptist also left England, the Particular or Calvinistic Baptists. The church formed by Roger Williams was composed of both Particular and a few General Baptists, but Particular Baptists made their strongest inroads in Philadelphia. Baptist associations were formed in Philadelphia (1707), Rhode Island (1729), and Charleston (1751).[34] The Philadelphia and Charleston associations adopted the Second London Confession of 1677 as the expression of their doctrinal sentiments. The Second London Confession (also called the Assembly Confession) was essentially the Westminster Confession which the Presbyterians had published in 1646, and, in adopting the Second London Confession Baptists in Philadelphia and Charleston committed themselves to Calvinistic theology.

A third element in the formation of Baptists in the colonies arose out of the Great Awakening in the eighteenth century which broke out under the preaching of Jonathan Edwards, George Whitefield, and Gilbert Tennent, to name a few of the more prominent men whose personalities and preaching brought it about. They proclaimed the necessity of experiential religion entered by spiritual birth which must transcend a church membership arising from civil convenience. Many of the new believers found that their experience in Christ could not be contained in the old wineskins of Congregational and Presbyterian ecclesiastical polity. They claimed to have seen a "new light" and by the name "New Light" history knows them. When joined to a Baptist church, they were called New Light Baptists or Separate Baptists. Fanning out from New England and the Middle Colonies, they made their zeal felt southward into Virginia and the Carolinas. Two of the most significant pioneers for Baptists in the South—Shubal Stearns and his brother-in-law Daniel Marshall—settled in Randolph County, North Carolina, and formed the Sandy Creek Baptist Church. Stearns began with only 16 members, but the membership soared to nearly 900 during his sixteen-year pastorate . Ultimately forty-two other churches and 125 ministers ultimately sprang from that church. With justification, an inscription on the site of the original building calls it the "Mother church, nay a grandmother and a great grandmother" of all the Separate Baptists in the South. The merging of the zeal of the Separate Baptists with the associational tendencies of the General (Arminian) Baptists and the doctrinal strength of the Particular (Calvinistic) Baptists helped form the theological personality of Baptists, especially in the South.[35]

The three traditions of the Particular Baptists, General Baptists, and Separate Baptists lost most of their uniqueness in the South by the end of the eighteenth century as a result of two circumstances. First, the General Baptists seem never to have built a strong doctrinal base in the local church and consequently were no theological match for the evangelistic zeal of the Particular Baptists. Between 1750 and 1760, many General churches succumbed to the theological pressure of the Particular Baptists and adopted Calvinistic beliefs. Second, Calvinistic preachers deliberately helped churches make the change. The method by which some of those metamorphoses came about has been preserved. John Gano, a missionary sent out by the Philadelphia Association, would visit a General Baptist church, call it into business session, inquire about the conversion experience of the members, exclude the unregenerate, and reconstitute the purged membership into a Particular Baptist church. Robert Williams of South Carolina also was influential in bringing about the transition.[36] Within a few decades, the name Particular Baptists dropped out in favor of a new designation, Regular Baptists.

The transformation of General to Particular Baptist churches engendered by Gano and others would be castigated today as a high-handed and unwarranted interference in local church polity. It was possible in part in the eighteenth century because of the great esteem enjoyed by the Philadelphia Association; churches sought it for advice. Historian David Benedict recounts that a group of Arminian Baptists moved to Virginia from Maryland in 1743. When their minister succumbed to licentious living, the members petitioned the Philadelphia Association for guidance. It dispatched James Miller and David Thomas of Virginia to investigate the cause of the inquiry. With John Gano accompanying the other two as a spectator, the ministers arrived at the church, interviewed the members, and reorganized the church as a Particular Baptist church.[37]

The number of General Baptist churches thus reorganized into Particular Baptist churches between 1750 and 1760 is uncertain. George Washington Paschal said the change could more accurately be called a revolution.[38] According to Paschal, two mitigating factors allowed this transformation. (1) Only a small number of the previous membership actually formed the nucleus of the new one. For example, in the transformation of the Great Coharo Church around 1750, only about twelve of the original membership changed. (2) The preacher was usually converted first to Calvinism. To quote Paschal's analysis, "The method of reorganization was first for the church in conference to disband whatever organization had previously existed, which in most cases, if we may believe Burkitt and Read, had been very loose. It was the preacher's church, though he had his deacons also in some instances."[39]

A second circumstance which contributed to the merging of the Separate with the Particular Baptists is the evidence that the theological gulf between the two was not nearly as deep or wide as one might assume. Shubal Stearns, a member of the Congregational Church in Tolland, Connecticut, was converted by George Whitefield, a Calvinist. Further, the experience of Daniel Marshall, Stearns's brother-in-law, tied Separate Baptist doctrine directly to Calvinism in North Carolina and Georgia. Marshall served as a missionary among the Mohawks in Connecticut and then migrated into North Carolina via Virginia. In Winchester, Virginia, Marshall became acquainted with and joined a Particular Baptist church belonging to the Philadelphia Association. In the words of Abraham Marshall, Daniel's son: "And as the result of a close, impartial examination of their faith and order, he and my dear mother were baptized by immersion in the forty-eighth year of his life."[40]

Marshall's formal induction into the Opekon Church, a Calvinistic church,[41] was not therefore a conversion of convenience. When he established the Kiokee Baptist Church in 1792 near what is now Augusta, Georgia, that church become the mother church of Calvinism in Georgia. Jesse Mercer's chronicle of that work in *A History of the Georgia Baptist Association* shows how deeply Calvinism was embedded among the Baptists of the old Georgia Baptist Association. For example, Calvinists minced no words when they encountered Arminian sentiments. In a brief biographical sketch of James Matthews, Sr. (1755-1828), his biographer states that the "great Jeremiah Walker" had been guilty of the "most shameful apostasy," and almost led Matthews into "delusive errors." Only the "works of Providence and grace" prevented him from embracing the errors of Arminianism.[42]

The animosity, though somewhat muted, continued into the next century. Note an anecdote printed in 1824 under the intriguing title "No Arminians in Heaven":

When Dr. T. Goodwin was told of the death of his nephew, John Goodwin, he answered, "Then I trust there is another soul gone to heaven;"—"Gone to heaven, Sir!" replied the person, "Why he was a rank Arminian." "True," replied the Doctor, "but he is not a rank Arminian now."[43]

Calvinism appeared to be the victor at the end of the seventeenth century, but the appearance was misleading. Within fifty years, Calvinism among Baptists in the South would be diluted by infusions of Arminianism.

SUMMARY

Baptists from England found a difficult political environment in the American colonies. Led by Roger Williams and Doctor John Clarke, they pioneered in the growth of a new politico-religious relationship. They advocated separation of church and state, soul freedom, and the right of every individual to worship according to the dictates of his own conscience without interference by civil authorities.

Baptists experimented with various theological distinctives to the extent that some even chose to worship on Saturday rather than Sunday. However, three strong influences gradually dominated: Calvinistic, Arminianism, and New Light expressions of Baptist theology. By the end of the eighteenth century, Calvinism gained the ascendancy. At that time, its Baptist adherents took the name Regular Baptists.

NOTES

1. William Ebenstein, *Today's Isms: Communism, Fascism, Capitalism, Socialism* (New York: Prentice Hall, Inc., 1954), p. 93. Voluntarism is used here in the general sense of voluntary acts rather than in the philosophical senses occurring in ontology, ethics or philosophical theology.
2. Robert G. Torbet, *A History of the Baptists*, 3rd ed. (Valley Forge: Judson Press, 1963), p. 38.
3. William W. Sweet, *The Story of Religion in America*, rev. & enl. ed. (Grand Rapids: Baker Book House, 1983), p. 67.
4. Ibid., p. 2.
5. Torbet, *A History*, p. 203.
6. Robert A. Baker, *The Southern Baptist Convention and Its People, 1607-1972* (Nashville: Broadman Press, 1974), p. 65.
7. Robert B. Semple, *A History of the Rise and Progress of the Baptists in Virginia*, rev. & ext. ed. G. W. Beale (Richmond: Pitt and Dickerson, Publishers, 1894), p. 30.
8. Ibid., p. 32.
9. Ibid., p. 41.
10. Sweet, *The Story*, p. 190.
11. Ibid., p. 193.
12. W. J. McGlothlin, *Baptist Beginnings in Education: A History of Furman University* (Nashville: Sunday School Board of the Southern Baptist Convention, 1926), p. 28.
13. J. A. Reynolds, "Richard Furman, A Study of His Life and Work," (Th.D. dissertation, New Orleans Baptist Theological Seminary, 1962), p. 13.

14. Charles G. Sommers, *Memoir of the Rev. John Stanford, D.D., Late Chaplain to the Humane and Criminal Institutions in the City of New-York, by Charles G. Sommers, Pastor of the South Baptist Church in New-York Together with an Appendix, Comprising Brief Memoirs of the Rev. John Williams, the Rev. Thomas Baldwin, D.D., and the Rev. Richard Furman, D.D.* (New York: Swords, Stanford, and Company, 1835), p. 414.

15. Ibid., p. 412.

16. Philip Schaff, *The Creeds of Christendom with a History and Critical Notes*, 4th ed., rev. & enl., 3 vols. (New York: Harper and Brothers, 1919), 3:581-597.

17. Theological students long have learned the five points by a simple acrostic, TULIP, standing for Total depravity, Unconditional election or predestination, Limited atonement, Irresistible grace, and Perseverance of the saints.

18. Schaff, *The Evangelical Protestant Creeds*, pp. 545-549.

19. Robert G. Gardner, *Baptists of Early America: A Statistical History, 1639-1790* (Atlanta: Georgia Baptist Historical Society, 1983), p. 21. Gardner also lists Massachusetts with one unorganized church and five members in 1639.

20. Ibid., pp. 34-35 with pp. 20-21.

21. Ibid., p. 36.

22. Ibid.

23. Ibid., p. 37.

24. Paul E. Crandall, "John Crandall and the 17th Century Seventh Day Baptists," *Baptist History and Heritage* 2 (July 1967):114.

25. Ibid.

26. Ibid., p. 115.

27. Gardner, *Baptists of Early America*, p. 45.

28. Ibid., p. 48.

29. Ibid., pp. 50-51.

30. Ibid., pp. 51-52.

31. Ibid., p. 53.

32. Ibid., p. 53.

33. Ibid., p. 57.

34. Walter B. Shurden, "The Development of Baptist Associations in America, 1707-1814," *Baptist History and Heritage* 4 (January 1969):34.

35. Baker, *The Southern Baptist Convention*, p. 57. Walter B. Shurden takes issue with the theory of Baker, W. W. Barnes, and W. L. Lumpkin "that Separate Baptist associationalism initiated a process of centralization in Baptist ecclesiology." He argues that Separate Baptist emphasis on individualism caused them to repudiate associational relationships in which church autonomy might be compromised. He views the "patriarchal influence" of Stearns as the source of the strong influence of the Sandy Creek Association (Shurden, "The Development of Baptist Associations in America, 1707-1814," p. 36). The thrust of Shurden's complaint is somewhat muted, however, when one remembers that the Sandy Creek Association was the most influential of the Separate Baptist associations in the South. That association became normative for the South even though it may not have been normative for all Separate Baptists. The effect on the churches was the same.

36. Baker, *The Southern Baptist Convention*, p. 45.

37. David Benedict, *An Abridgement of the General History of the Baptist Denomination in America, and Other Parts of the World* (Boston: Lincoln and Edmands, 1820), pp. 313-314.

38. David Benedict, *An Abridgement of the General History of the Baptist Denomination in America, and Other Parts of the World* (Boston: Lincoln and Edmands, 1820), pp. 313-314.

39. George Washington Paschal, *History on North Carolina Baptists*, 2 vols. (Raleigh, North Carolina: The General Board of the North Carolina Baptist State Convention, 1930) 1:214.

40. Jesse Mercer, *History of the Georgia Association, Compiled at the Request of that Body, by Jesse Mercer* (Washington, Georgia, 1838. Reprinted by Georgia Baptist Association, Washington, Georgia, 1980), p. 371.

41. Baker, *The Southern Baptist Convention*, pp. 43-44.

42. Mercer, *History of Georgia*, pp. 403-404.

43. "No Arminians in Heaven," *Christian Watchman* 5 (February 24, 1824):48.

CHAPTER 2

CALVINISM ON THE PINNACLE

Colonial Baptists, few in number and lacking political power, diverse in origins and fragmented in doctrines, nevertheless possessed enough features to unite them around common interests. They, along with the Quakers and other sectarian dissenters, forged an identity in their struggles against the oppression of established churches.

The eighteenth century treated them much better. It is true that in a few of the colonies—Virginia is a good example—they struggled against civil oppression, but they still found sufficient latitude of action to grow new churches and organize themselves into associations. It was during that century that the zeal of the New Light Baptists under the impetus of men like Shubal Stearns and Daniel Marshall infused new life into the staid orthodoxy of the Calvinistic Baptists. Nevertheless, by the end of the century, Calvinism reigned virtually supreme in the formal pronouncements of the confession of faith adopted by the associations. On some points, such as the doctrines of the church and ordinances, Baptists sketched beliefs peculiar to themselves. In others, such as the doctrine of the Trinity, they followed traditional views.

Baptists during the colonial period produced not one book of systematic theology. Their energies instead were expended in struggling to gain religious freedom on the one hand and to establish indigenous churches throughout the colonies on the other. Their theology developed mainly out of fratricidal feuds between Calvinists and Arminians. An example of the impact that their fight for religious freedom made on theology can be seen in the works of Isaac Backus (1724-1806) as he tried to dissociate Baptists from the odious reputation of radical Anabaptists in Europe who arose during the second quarter of the sixteenth century. Hezekiah Smith and Richard Furman (1755-1825) also wielded wide influence, but the paucity of their extant writings precludes a thorough documentation of their beliefs. Apparently, they were Calvinists. As discussed previously, Furman could be classed as a moderate Calvinist. Smith was closely associated with men of Calvinistic beliefs, being a close friend of noted Calvinists like John Gano, James Manning, and Samuel Stillman. The theology of the period, then, can best be seen in the confessions of faith. These, when coupled with the thought of Isaac Backus and further insight offered by Richard Furman, offer insights into the theology of that period.

The confession that contributed the most to molding and codifying early Baptist doctrine was the Second London, or Assembly, Confession of 1672.[1] Later modified by Benjamin Keach and Elias, his son, the confession was adopted by the Philadelphia Association in 1742, an event of far-reaching significance. David Benedict says of the Philadelphia Confession that it "was regarded as the emporium of Baptist influence"[2] and a "document of high authority . . . throughout the South and West, when I first travelled in those regions."[3]

The Charleston Association also adopted the Philadelphia Confession in 1767. The most influential association in the South provided a clearing-house for advising churches about polity practices, and theology.[4] It also provided a forum and base for Calvinistic doctrines. Some of the other associations which adopted the confession were the Ketockton of Virginia in 1766, Warren of Rhode Island in 1767, Elkhorn of Kentucky in 1785, and Holston of Tennessee in 1788.[5]

The document known as the Philadelphia Confession is more correctly called the Second London Confession. Baptists in England had suffered persecution along with other dissenters during parts of the second half of the seventeenth century, and to show their essential agreement with the main tenets of Presbyterian theology, Particular Baptists met in a general conference and constructed the Second London Confession using the Westminster Confession as the basic document. They followed the general order of the Westminster Confession and often copied its words verbatim. They also altered it to suit their needs. As representative examples, they accepted the articles dealing with the Bible, altered the section on the church to accommodate Baptist polity, and appended articles on the laying on of hands and the singing of hymns. It is to these sources that attention is now turned.

In the following sections, the theology of the confession is cited to indicate the broad outlines of Baptist theology as it was developing by the end of the eighteenth century. Citations from Backus, Furman, and others provide a theological perspective from which to evaluate pertinent ideas in the confession.

THE BIBLE, THE OBJECTIVE SOURCE OF AUTHORITY

Baptist attitudes toward the Bible in the eighteenth century gave no hints of the storm that would break out among Southern Baptists over the issue of inspiration in the twentieth. The mechanism for it, unknown to them at the time, was already being set in motion in the forms of biblical criticism. Textual, or lower, critics were studying the ancient manuscripts in an attempt to get as close as possible to the biblical autographs (i.e., the original writings). There work has been invaluable in view of the fact that none of the first century writings are extant. The *Textus Receptus*, the Greek text popularized by Erasmus, was based upon tenth century and later manuscripts.[6] Biblical researchers attempted to uncover and compare more ancient writings to arrive at the original content as closely as possible. The earliest manuscript fragments date no further back than 135 A.D.[7]

Higher critics focused their attention on the content of the text by taking into account such factors as the style of writing, parallel structure, and the cultural background of the writers. Frederic W. Farrar, in his old but still serviceable *History of Interpretation*, cites the significance of Ludovicus Cappellus and Robert Stephens in redirecting the understanding of biblical inspiration with the publication of the *Critica Sacra* by Cappellus in 1650. Farrar called it the marking of a epoch:

> Among the extravagancies of reformed theology had been an assertion as to the miraculously perfect integrity of the text. . . . After the publication of his book no reasonable man could doubt that the Jewish notion of a correspondence of the Holy Books with the supposed autographs of Moses or Ezra down to the very apices of the letters, was a preposterous fiction. Robert Stephens said that he had found 2,384 variations in the oldest MSS. of the New Testament. It was admitted on all sides that these variations did not affect a single matter of faith. . . . But since these facts tended to show how untenable was the theory of verbal dictation, they were met with strange absurdities.[8]

Other names could be added. John James Wetstein, a professor at Basle, Switzerland, emphasized the human and literary side of the Bible along with its divine. Farrar also refers to the work of John Koch (1602-1669), a scholar who "emancipated exegesis from a dull tyranny, but subjected it to an extravagant typology."[9]

The name of Jean Astruc (1684-1766), a French physician, is irrevocably linked to the popularization of higher criticism. He studied the Genesis accounts and noticed two types of passages, those using the Hebrew word *Elohim* and those using the Hebrew *Jehovah* (i.e., YHWH) for God. From this evidence he deduced that the book of Genesis was composed of two separate creation accounts, a theory he espoused publicly in 1753.[10] Johann G. Eichhorn (1752-1827) applied higher critical methods to other Old Testament books and concluded that, in addition to Genesis, Exodus through Joshua also were composite books. He published a three-volume introduction to the Old Testament in 1780-83, a work which extended his influence in spite of its questioned accuracy in regard to certain issues.[11] He was also one of the earliest to hypothesize that the Synoptics were based on a "lost Aramaic gospel."[12] This unknown source was later given the identification of *Q*. According to Earle E. Cairns, Eichhorn "gave such studies the name of higher criticism."[13]

Most Regular Baptists in North America during the seventeenth and eighteenth centuries were blissfully unaware of speculations being raised by the higher critical school. Few of their preachers laid claim to having the benefit of a college education and relied instead on their own ability to glean from the Scriptures the beliefs that made them distinctively Baptist. The eminent leader Richard Furman, for example, received little in the form of public schooling, but what he received, he developed. Blessed with a precocious intellect, he memorized most of the First Part of the *Iliad* when he was only seven, learned the rudiments of Latin during his brief stint in school, but later become proficient in Latin and gained a working knowledge of Greek and Hebrew.[14] With the tools at hand, he mined the Bible for its truths.

Furman, Backus, Gano and a host of others seem to have accepted the authority of the Bible apart from critical evaluation. They believed and preached its contents. Having been reared in a theological world predicated upon the dogmas of the Westminster Confession of a hundred years ago as filtered through Baptist consciousness, they found little fault with the formulations of the Philadelphia-Charleston confessions as they pertain to the Bible. Those beliefs are stated in the confessions in Chapter I, "Of the Holy Scriptures." Section two lists the sixty-six books of the Bible and says they are the "Word of God written," thus allowing a distinction which became vital in neoorthodoxy in the twentieth century, namely, that Christ is the Living Word and the Bible is the Written Word. The section concludes with these words, "All [of] which are given by the inspiration of God, to be the rule of Faith and Life."[15] Section four asserts that God is the Author of Holy Scripture.[16]

The framers of the confession acknowledged that the assurance of infallible truth comes from the internal witness of the Holy Spirit within one's heart. Sections five and six recognize the ministry of the Holy Spirit in imparting "saving understanding of such things as are revealed in the Word."[17] The dual emphasis upon a reliable, objective revelation and a necessary, subjective experience served as a check against bibliolatry on the one hand and unbridled subjectivism on the other. The belief that every believer has the right and obligation to interpret the Bible also witnesses to the individualism that helped form the Baptist spirit.

One other teaching of the confession is pertinent at this point. Section eight notes that the Old Testament was written in Hebrew and the New Testament in Greek. The original manuscripts are lost, of course. Nevertheless, the Testaments were "inspired by God, and by his singular care and Providence kept pure in all Ages"; they "are therefore authentical."[18]

THE TRIUNE GOD

The theistic concept of God suffered assaults from a newcomer to the world, the scientific revolution, which developed in and as a result of a Christian theology of nature. In the Genesis story, God created the human race and vested in it the obligation to subdue the earth and have dominion over the fish, fowl, and every living thing that moves upon the earth (Genesis 1:28). A nature created by God could be studied, subdued, harnessed, or exploited without fear of transgressing upon the essence of God as is true in Eastern pantheism. Well did Alan Richardson observe that "the scientific revolution of the sixteenth and seventeenth centuries is, historically, the supreme achievement of the human intellect," but even more to the point, it "is, in truth, the achievement of Christian civilization."[19]

The achievement was not purchased without price, however, because the very principles being enunciated by science had a devastating effect on Christianity. As Copernicus, Kepler, Galileo, and Newton discovered the laws which describe the motions of the planets around the sun, the old geocentric explanation or the solar system succumbed to the heliocentric. Galileo was forced by the Roman Catholic Church to deny that the earth rotated around the sun, but papal fiat had no impact whatsoever on the movement of the earth.

Roman Catholicism was not the only loser. The feeling grew among scientists that the universe itself was a closed system in which the amount of energy is constant. No room was left for God to act. The celebrated written debate between Samuel J. Clarke, defender of Newtonian physics, against the criticisms of G. W. Leibniz, both of whom were committed Christians, was a foreshadowing of events to come. With unerring, prophetic insight Leibniz understood and stated the historical impact of the issues being debated. To the question, How shall one explain God's intervention in nature? he stated the dilemma:

> If it be done supernaturally, we must have re-course to miracles, in order to explain natural things: which is reducing an hypothesis *ad absurdum*: for, everything may easily be accounted for by miracles. But if it be done naturally, then God will not be *intelligentia supramundana*: he will be comprehended under the nature of things; that is, he will be the soul of the world.[20]

Leibniz attempted to reconcile the dilemma with his theory of a preestablished harmony in the universe, but his efforts had little lasting impact. Those who tried to harmonize science with belief in God first became seekers who firmly believed in a God of creation and redemption. That generation of thinkers gave way to deism, the theory that God created the world and then withdrew from its inner workings. By the nineteenth century, the concept of God became pantheistic in the world as Will and Idea of Schopenhauer, the Universal Mind or Spirit of Hegel, and similar concepts. By the twentieth, atheism supplanted pantheism for many thinkers.[21]

In spite of these portentous developments in the seventeenth and eighteenth centuries, most Baptists lived in a different cultural and intellectual world. Only rarely did arguments about the nature and existence of God impinge upon their discussions. Around the end of the eighteenth century and at the beginning of the nineteenth, a few ministers lapsed into Unitarianism.[22] The vast majority of their contemporaries contented themselves with traditional statements about God.

Beginning with the Philadelphia Confession of Faith and extending until the middle of the nineteenth century, Calvinistic Baptists expounded relentlessly on the sovereignty of God. Their commitment to Calvinism led to a theistic theology in which, when applied to daily life, was almost scholastic in its impact. Their trinitarian theism balanced the immanence of God with his transcendence. This balancing can be seen in a definition of theism proffered by E. Y. Mullins, when he wrote, "The Christian theistic view is that God is the infinite Spirit, personal, holy, loving, purposive, immanent in the world, and transcendent."[23]

Regular Baptists of the seventeenth century would have agreed. Chapter II of the Philadelphia Confession described God as infinite, spirit, immutable, immense, eternal, incomprehensible, and almighty. Further, God possesses life in himself and is therefore self-sufficient, the fountain of all Being. The essential features of trinitarian theology are either stated or implied. God is one in himself, but three in person. God the Father proceeds from neither, but the Father eternally generates the Son.[24]

The essential features of trinitarian theology are either stated or implied. God is one in himself, but three in person. God the Father proceeds from neither, but the Father eternally generates the Son. This statement obviously precludes the Arian belief that Sonship implies that the Father precedes the Son in sequence and time. Since the Father eternally generates the Son, the Son is subordinate in office or person, but not in essence and being. In a tacit adoption of the famous Filioque Clause,[25] the Holy Spirit is said to proceed from both the Father and the Son. In function, but not in essence, he is subordinate to the Father and Son, but in essence, the three are one.

Regular Baptists of the eighteenth and nineteenth centuries unequivocally worshiped Jesus Christ, God in the flesh, as the one who came to redeem. Chapter VIII of the Philadelphia Confession calls Christ "very and eternal *God*, the brightness of the Fathers glory, of one substance and equal with *him*: who made the World, who upholdeth and governeth all things he hath made."[26] Isaac Backus, that stalwart who labored so long for religious freedom, pointed out that one of Christ's names, Immanuel, "signifies GOD with us," and this "could never be true of any mere creature."[27]

Jesus Christ, fully God and fully man, came into the world on a redemptive mission. To effect redemption, God became incarnate in the person of Jesus, who was born the son of Mary. The incarnate Christ was very God and very Man, yet without sin. He lived; he was crucified. One of the most firmly held Baptist beliefs has been that Christ was resurrected from the dead; further, the body which died is the body that was raised.[28] In the words of the confession, Christ "arose from the dead, with the same body in which he suffered."[29]

The clear affirmation of the deity of the Holy Spirit goes back to the very beginning of Baptist creedal formulations. Chapter II of the Philadelphia Confession describes the Holy Spirit as one of the "three subsistences," the divine and infinite Being, "of one substance, power, and Eternity, each having the whole Divine Essence, yet the Essence undivided."[30] Further, the Holy Spirit proceeds from the Father and the Son. The confession has no separate article devoted to the work of the Holy Spirit, but the work may be inferred from various statements. Chapter I states that the Holy Spirit bears witness within believers to the infallible truth of the Holy Scriptures, inwardly illuminates believers, and brings them to a saving understanding of truths revealed in the Bible.[31] Chapter XVII adds further that the Holy Spirit sanctifies believers and prevents them from falling from a state of grace.[32] Other acts are ascribed to the Holy Spirit, such as conceiving Christ in the womb of Mary and anointing Christ when he began his public ministry.[33]

PREDESTINED AND QUICKENED

A. T. Robertson wrote, "One's theory of God and sin decides his theology and his life. Tell me your view of God and sin and I can fill out the rest."[34] That principle, when applied to the doctrine of human nature as seen by evangelical Southern Baptists, offers an incisive insight into a fundamental attitude. Having been brought into the world historically at a time when seventeenth-century England was beginning to question the divine right of kings to rule, Baptists exemplified the individualism of that century. Their perception of human nature grew out of their exegesis of the Scriptures rather than from philosophical postulates or from empirical observations. In so doing, their belief most closely approximates that of John Locke rather than the morbid pessimism of Thomas Hobbes or the unbridled optimism of Jean-Jacques Rousseau. Evangelical Baptists see people as made in the image of God—and therefore with worth and potential—but as fallen into sin—and therefore in need of a radical, ontological change. They have never believed that any society can be altered in a continuous and positive direction by altering the social structures only. Righteousness is primarily personal and only secondarily social. People must be changed at the core of their being by a personal encounter with God. This change is described by such expressions as "born again," "reborn," "born of God," "regenerated," or simply "saved." This initial encounter with God preempts all other considerations for them because without it one cannot live eternally with

God. For most evangelical Baptists, the world is divided into two classes, saved and unsaved.

Regular Baptists in the South, during the colonial period, matured under a strong and regular diet of Calvinistic theology. The doctrine of God as taught in Calvinism, especially the definition of predestination, seemed to leave little room for freedom of the will. The Philadelphia Confession asserts unequivocally that God has decreed "all things whatsoever" that come to pass, yet so as not to be the author of sin.[35] The confession further states that even though God knows all things that shall come to pass, predestination was not based upon God's foreknowledge of the future. On the contrary, the predestinating decree comprehends both the human and angelic realms to the extent that the number predestined to life can neither be increased nor diminished.

Such a fatalistic interpretation would seem to vitiate evangelistic endeavors if, as the doctrine stated, the number and identity of the elect has been decided before creation. On the contrary, it infused new zeal on the premise that victory was assured. Isaac Backus wrote a treatise in which he defended the teaching that God chose only a particular number to salvation without any regard to a foreseen faith and obedience.[36]

Unconditional predestination had its counterpart in the doctrine of total depravity. Sinners, because of their depraved nature inherited from Adam, are completely dependent for salvation upon the grace of God. According to the confession, they must be effectually called before they can repent and believe. The Holy Spirit quickens, renews, and enables the elect to answer the divine call and embrace the grace conveyed in it.[37]

Notice that the unregenerate cannot answer the "call" until they have been "quickened and renewed" by the Holy Spirit. Calvinistic preachers argued that the saving encounter began with regeneration and then proceeded to repentance and faith rather than, as Arminians contended, that the saving encounter began with repentance and proceeded through faith to regeneration. Isaac Backus cited two reasons often used to prove that regeneration precedes repentance and faith. First, he believed that the will of the Creator cannot be dependent upon the will of the creature.[38] To do so would remove salvation from the grace of God and make it contingent upon something the creature did, namely, repent and believe. Second, depravity precludes the capacity for one to repent and believe. Backus argued that to speak of repentance before faith was absurd because "who ever was sorry for any action, before he believed it to be some way disagreeable!"[39] The unsaved are utterly depraved prior to regeneration.

THE EFFICACY OF THE CROSS

The belief of Calvinists as reflected by Backus suggests the knotty problem of the extent of the efficacy of Christ's death on the cross for sin. Theories of the death of Christ can be classified in the broad categories of subjective and objective. On the one hand, advocates of the subjective view, popularly known as the moral influence theory, see no moral barrier between God and sinners except one's refusal to obey God. Sin as such needs no sacrifice. Abelard, a contemporary of Anselm in the twelfth century, is generally considered the first advocate of the view. "God saves us by revealing his love" is the summary of Abelard's view given by Robert H. Culpepper.[40]

On the other hand, proponents of objective atonement severely criticize the moral influence theory as giving inadequate emphasis to the death of Christ as an atonement for sin. They admit that the cross must have a subjective effect, but they see the total work as going beyond mere example or influence. The objective theories have this much in common, they define the atoning work of Christ in such a way that without it no one could be reconciled to God.

The crucial issue in constructing a theory of the cross can now be seen. It revolves around the question, How does the work of Christ relate to later generations? Calvinism left no doubt about the cruciality of the death of Christ as an actual, not potential, payment for sin. In the Philadelphia Confession, the atonement is placed in the framework of covenant theology in which a covenant of grace exists between the Father and Son. By an eternal covenant transaction, the elect obtain life and immortality.[41] The nature of the transaction rests on the perfect obedience and sacrifice of Jesus in which he satisfied the justice of God.[42] In the covenant of grace, Christ made satisfaction to the justice of God for the elect *only*, those whom God ordained to salvation. Although the effecting of salvation is wrought in the elect by the Holy Spirit, the accomplishment is certain. This is the view of limited atonement.

How widely held were these beliefs and how deeply were they believed is reflected in the writings of the day. In the latter part of the eighteenth century, Isaac Backus dealt extensively with the subject of salvation. He argued that life was forfeited by sin and could only be recovered by blood. Christ gave himself upon the altar of sacrifice. Backus then concluded, "And he says, *I lay down my life for the sheep*; a chosen number, and not for all mankind."[43] His views correspond to that of the Philadelphia Confession that Christ's death was the actual, objective basis without which personal salvation is impossible.

THE LOCAL CHURCH, THE OBJECTIVE AUTHORITY

Individualism finds full expression in Baptist life in the local church. Abhorring all ecclesiastical hierarchies, Baptists exalt the local church as a democratic and autonomous congregation of believers who voluntarily assemble for worship, spiritual training, and evangelistic outreach. Baptists, in their infancy, defined the church as both particular and universal. Of the latter, the Philadelphia Confession describes it as an invisible entity, the elect, and the spouse of Christ.[44]

However, the local church has been the abiding obsession of most Baptists, and the amount of discussion devoted to it in the Philadelphia Confession foreshadowed the relative importance of the local church; thirteen of the fifteen articles of Chapter XXVI concern it. The local assemblies are variously called particular congregations, particular societies, and a particular church.[45] A completely organized church consists of officers (bishops or elders and deacons) and members. Little latitude was left for a serious consideration of the mystical church.

Baptists of later generations would eventually drop the term *society* as a description of the church, but for several decades it was a serviceable word, used interchangeably with *church*. Hezekiah Smith, one of the founders of Brown University, "accepted the call of the Baptist Society in Haverhill [Massachusetts]" after he had "first united with the Church, by letter from the Baptist Church in Charleston."[46]

Whatever the term used, Baptist church polity offered a viable alternative to people who were disillusioned with established churches during colonial times in America. Joseph Biggs, a Baptist historian who published his work in 1834, gave three reasons why dissenters often surrendered their Presbyterian affiliation and became Baptists. First, they considered Presbyterian members "too extravagant in their apparel." Second, they did not believe the Presbyterian form of church to be right. Third, they resented the policy of the Presbyterians to "admit none to the ministry only men of classical education," many of whom seemed to be unconverted.[47] Isaac Backus recorded another practice "which was a principal reason" for the "separation from the church of England," that is, "having the worthy and the unworthy partake together at the Lord's Supper."[48] The complaints thus were against the existing church polity and practice. To gain ecclesiastical differentiation from the Presbyterians with whom they had so much in common theologically, Baptists like Isaac Backus attacked the Presbyterian covenant theology which saw in the Christian church a spiritual continuity between Jewish and Christian ritual. Presbyterian covenant theology posited a parallel between the two in that baptism was prefigured by the Jewish rite of circumcision. Backus demurred on theological grounds when he charged, "These ministers *confound* the constitution of the Jewish and Christian churches together, and shuffle and shift from one to the other, as occasion suits, and then charge us with not distinguishing between the *visible* and *invisible* church."[49] He countered that there is a difference between the materials and forms of the Jewish and Christian churches. As far as New Testament emphasis is concerned, the only "visible church-state instituted in the gospel" is a *"particular* one" to which a brother "can *tell* his grievance."[50]

Other factors helped mold the Baptist emphasis upon the local church. One was that Baptists often suffered at the hands of denominations aligned with governmental powers. They frequently identified the Pope of Rome as the Antichrist and the Roman Catholic Church as the Great Harlot of Revelation 17.

Throughout the eighteenth and nineteenth centuries, such allusions are too frequent to need documentation.

Another factor was the emergence of the doctrine of the "priesthood of believers," that every believer is a priest before God. Therefore, each person has the right of direct access to God. Most Baptists believed, and believe, that "soul liberty" is best preserved and practiced in an atmosphere where church is separated from state and where churches are independent of each other. All ecclesiastical hierarchy was automatically excluded. Baptist individualism found free expression in the democracy of the local church.

THE ORDINANCES, RITES FOR BELIEVERS ONLY

Baptists in the American colonies easily embraced the spirit of Zwinglianism in their doctrine of the Supper. In Chapter XXX of the Philadelphia Confession, the composers of the confession state that Christ gave the Supper for a perpetual remembrance to show forth the death of Christ.[51] Furthermore, the Roman Catholic doctrine of the supper is explicitly rejected in Chapter XXX.[52] The writers believed that the doctrine of transubstantiation was repugnant not only to Scripture, but even to common sense and reason.

The confession gives attention to the ordinance of baptism in Chapters XXVIII and XXIX, which state that baptism symbolizes the believer's fellowship with Christ in his death and resurrection; the only proper subjects are those who exercise repentance towards God, coupled with faith in, and obedience to, Christ; the only mode is by immersion.[53] The confession does not, unlike beliefs of nineteenth-century Landmark Baptists, state that only properly baptized candidates can partake of the Supper.

Baptists in the seventeenth century saw the close connection between the two ordinances. The historical setting which focuses attention on this issue was precipitated by the Half-way Covenant in Congregationalism. The Massachusetts Bay Colony established Congregationalism as its official religion, but in the course of history, younger members objected to public professions of faith as a requirement for membership. The denomination eventually reached an agreement which allowed both sides of the disagreeing factions to hold membership. A regenerate church membership was not required. According to Alvah Hovey, defenders of the covenant saw a spiritual value in having non-believers participate in the Supper; for instance, those who had received "grace" would receive more grace in the Supper, and those who had not received grace should be under proper advantage to receive peace.[54] Germane to the practice was the assumption that there was a continuity between the Christian church and the Jewish.

Given those circumstances, men with convictions like those of Isaac Backus began breaking with the established churches. These New Lights began the arduous task of establishing their own theological premises. Backus, who was reared as a Congregationalist, told of his own struggle to find an acceptable theological standard. He recounted:

> By these distressing trials, I was brought to see that we had made Christians our rule, instead of the Word [of] God; for his word required a credible confession of saving faith in order for baptism, and if we came to the holy Supper with any who were only sprinkled in infancy, we communed with unbaptized persons; and pedobaptists will never commune with any who are such in their view [that is, unbaptized]. Yet for fifty years past, I have been censored by them for refusing to wrong my conscience in that respect.[55]

He continued his argument by showing the discontinuity between the covenant of circumcision and the covenant of grace and wrote repeatedly to disprove the connection between the two.[56]

Polemically, Backus used accepted pedobaptist arguments for a limited participation in the Supper. Nearly all denominations, he noted, required baptism before allowing anyone to participate in the Supper. Backus believed that the real issue revolved around one's definition of baptism. Further, he realized that he must contrast the differences between the Old and New Covenants. His opponents vocally argued for infant baptism on the basis of similarities between the doctrines of baptism and the Jewish rite of circumcision. Just as the Old Covenant involved families, so must the New. Not so, said Backus, because the "covenant of circumcision is as different from the covenant of grace, as Hagar was from Sarah, as Ishmael from Isaac; and we are solemnly called to view the difference in that light."[57] Backus thus began the arduous task of differentiating Baptist theology from the older covenant theology of Congregationalism and Presbyterianism. His Calvinism had its limits.

Morgan Edwards (1722-1795), a Baptist contemporary of Backus and member of the Philadelphia Association, recorded for posterity the type of communion service observed by many Baptists in 1774. The account also offers insight into their theology of the Supper which had evolved by that time. Edwards wrote:

> The Lord's supper is a rite of divine institution and perpetual continuance. The direct end of it is, the remembrance of Christ's death. The materials are, a loaf of bread, and a cup of wine. The implements a table, a dish, a cup or more if needs be, candles & c. The administrator is, a minister. The posture is sitting. The frame of mind, serious and examinatory. The time is every Lord's day evening. The place generally is the church. The celebration of the rite, consists of a suitable exordium; taking the bread; blessing it and giving thanks; breaking it; giving it to the people; uttering the words of distribution; taking it; and eating. Likewise taking the wine; blessing it, and giving thanks; pouring the wine; giving it to the people;

uttering the words of distribution; taking and drinking the wine; singing a hymn; collecting for the necessities of saints; a benediction.[58]

Not all Baptist churches, however, observed the Supper every Sunday. Historian Morgan Edwards recorded that the supper was "generally" held at the church; however, exceptions were allowed. A church asked the Kehukee Association in 1786, "Is it legal to administer the Lord's Supper to a single person, in case of inability to attend public worship?" The answer came, "We believe it may be lawful in some cases."[59]

Baptists in the eighteenth century grasped the significance of the connection between the ordinances and the administrator of the ordinances, but their refusal to stipulate a definite link between the two shows an openness that gave way to rigidity of thought in the nineteenth century. Associational pronouncements indicate some latitude in the matter of a proper administrator for baptism. A church in 1783 questioned the Kehukee Association whether a baptism was legal if performed by an "unauthorized minister." The answer was given, "It is our opinion, that the person who administered the ordinance was very much out of his duty, and displeasure ought to be shown to such a practice: but as for the person's baptism, as it was done in faith, we esteem it right."[60] The Charleston Association reached the same conclusion. One Paul Palmer, described as a "disorderly person," had administered the ordinance of baptism. The association ruled that because he had baptized according to the Word of God, persons baptized by him were accepted into the churches "upon satisfactory examination as to principles and grace."[61]

The issue also arose whether a baptism was valid if performed by an unbaptized person. A man named James Hutchinson attempted to associate with Georgia Baptists in 1791. Hutchinson had previously been a Methodist, and his baptism was called into question because it had been performed by "an unbaptized person." Georgia Baptists decided his baptism was invalid.[62] The evaluation of Robert B. Semple, who wrote a history of Virginia Baptists, offers an insight of someone who lived during this time. He said that most associations left the decision to the person whether or not to be rebaptized. The question had been placed before most of them at one time or another, and they all deemed it unnecessary to rebaptize, or else they left it up to the conscience of the person. They declared that "the most important prerequisite to baptism was faith in the subject," although most of them appended the advice that fixed rules for qualifying an administrator should normally be followed.[63]

Before closing this section on the ordinances, a brief analysis of the virtually defunct rite of footwashing among Southern Baptists presents an example of their understanding of the role of the church in society. Although footwashing is never even mentioned in some confessions, many Baptists nevertheless have observed footwashing. One of the earliest descriptions of the rite was given by Morgan Edwards:

Washing feet is a rite of divine and perpetual obligation. The ends of it are, to oblige christians to be beneficially condescending one to another; and to signify to them a cleansing from the sins they are liable to after baptism. The performer of the rite is any christian. The place is, at home. The time, once a year, at least. The attendants of the rite are, supper or love feast &c. The requisites are, water, bason, towel, and a form of words expressive of the ends of the rite.[64]

Since the rite was performed in private, it could be classified as a Christian obligation, not a church ordinance.

Baptists during the eighteenth century experimented with a variety of ordained officers in their churches. In addition to ordaining ministers and deacons, some churches had ruling elders. Historian Robert B. Semple reported that Samuel Harris, pioneer Baptist evangelist in Virginia, "was ordained a ruling elder" in 1759.[65] Semple gave none of the qualifications for the office. Most Baptist churches eventually dropped the terminology.

Baptists ordained pastors of churches, but they differed in the way they handled the matter of ordaining evangelists or itinerants, as the traveling missionaries were called. Morgan Edwards implied that they were ordained, but in a special category:

The office of *missionaries* or modern *evangelists* is, generally, occasional and temporary; therefore their titles (like those of *pastors, bishops,* &c) are but relatives, which they lose when the relation, that giveth them rise, ceaseth: for which reason they must be chosen out of those that had been ordained *teacher*. Their work is, to itinerate on the special errands of the churches. They are put in their office by the choice of those churches; ordination; prayer; &c. with fasting and are to be paid by the same churches.[66]

Isaac Backus recorded an incident, however, in which a "minister at large" was refused ordination. A man named Job Macomber, a licensed preacher from Backus's church, had become associated with a small Baptist church which subsequently requested his ordination. Backus's journal for October 2, 1782, reads:

Elder Nelson and Jeremiah Bosset, from Taunton church, and elder Job Seamons and Jacob Newland, from Attleboro, met here with our church, to consider a request from the Baptist church in New Gloucester, that we would ordain brother Job Macomber as a gospel minister. Upon mature deliberation, we found that their request was not to ordain him as their pastor, and we had not clearness in ordaining him as a minister at large, and so did not do it.[67]

The most common designation for pastor was the title elder. Occasionally, as with Jesse Mercer, esteemed leaders were called father. Not until the post-Civil War period did the title *elder* give way to *reverend* in the minutes of the churches.

The New Light Baptists exhibited enough initiative in the matter of ordination that they even reinstated—for a while, at least—the office of apostle after a careful investigation of Ephesians 4:11-13. Consequently, three apostles were elected: Samuel Harris, Elijah Craig and John Waller. To use Thomas Armitage's cryptic phrase, "And then three Baptist Bishops were let loose upon the churches."[68] The churches "put on their glasses and brought out their New Testaments to see where they could find this crochet," and, not finding it, gave the "apostles" a cold reception. The "chop-fallen" apostles reportedly "quit their high episcopacy at once." The General Association in embarrassment never passed an "act abolishing the apostolate, but let it die a natural death" although at a later date they declared the office was for New Testament times only.[69]

Some churches recognized other officers. A deacon was to care for the "secular" interests of the local church, "obliging him to the due care and management thereof: authorizing him to require, receive, and lay out money towards answering the church's worldly necessities."[70] Morgan Edwards described the office of the clerk ("called in Scripture the *occupier of the room of the unlearned*") as of apostolic origin in which the "*unlearned* or laity" led in "those parts of worship wherein they are to join, as in *prayers, singing, saying amen* & c; and also in being a scribe for the church."[71] Ruling elders assisted the minister in maintaining "rules of order and government."[72]

Women also held offices, according to Edwards. He declared the office of deaconess to be of "divine and original and perpetual continuance in the church" for the purpose of caring for "the sick, miserable, and distressed poor."[73] Likewise, the office of eldress consisted of

> praying, and teaching at their separate assemblies; presiding there for the maintenance of rules and government; consulting with the sisters about matters of the church which concern them, and representing their sense thereof to the elders; attending at the unction of sick sisters; and at the baptism of women, that all may be done orderly.[74]

The freedom allowed Baptist women in the eighteenth century never reached to the level of serving as pastors of churches. Leon McBeth cites three examples of women, however, who were gifted in speaking. Martha Stearns Marshall, the wife of Daniel and sister of Shubal Stearns, was noted for her prayers and exhortations; Margaret Neuse Clay and Hannah Lee in Virginia were female "preachers."[75] In spite of these gifted women and the latitude of service permitted in New Light Baptist churches, the role of women was drastically curtailed by the end of the eighteenth century when the Regular Baptist organizations overwhelmed those of the New Lights.

THE RISE OF POSTMILLENNIALISM

Many New Testament scholars subscribe to the maxim that one of the motivating forces which impelled first-century Christians to propagate their faith was their belief that Christ was to return in their day and bring history to its close. Convinced of his soon return, they shunned personal comfort on behalf of a higher calling to evangelize the world before that fateful event. Paul's admonitions in II Thessalonians, chapters 2 and 3, and Peter's apocalyptic exordium in II Peter, chapter 3, attest to the importance of the doctrine to them.

Later in history, apocalyptic zealots took advantage of the relaxed religious strictures during the Reformation era and proclaimed the dawn of a new era. They did more than proclaim. Believing that Christ was to set up his visible reign on earth—the seat of the divine government often coincided with the favorite town of the apocalyptist—they formed armies and marched in chiliastic zeal. Millennialism from that time forward earned an unsavory reputation. A definition of terms may be in order at this point. *Postmillennialists* believe that the world, as a result of the preaching of the gospel, will experience a time of moral renewal characterized by a decline in the forces of evil and an increase in the forces of good. This period of universal good will be a golden age on earth, the millennium. Christ will return at the close of that era to judge the world. *Amillennialists* disallow any golden age on earth. The Kingdom of God roughly coincides with the church. Christ's reign is a spiritual reign in the lives of believers. *Premillennialists* have many variant nuances, but generally they believe that before Christ returns to reign personally on earth, a time of great tribulation will engulf the earth, probably for a period of seven years. Some premillennialists believe that Christ will come secretly before the tribulation period (Pre-tribulationists) and take away believers in an event called the rapture of the church. Some believe Christ will come during the tribulation (Mid-tribulationists) and others believe he will come after the tribulation but before the millennial reign (Post-tribulationists). Dispensationalism is a further refinement of pre-tribulation, premillennialism.

Chiliasm was a form of premillennialism whose adherents believed the millennial reign must be brought in by force. Premillennialists contributed to the negative image earned by the chiliasts by their unsavory conduct under Oliver Cromwell. Seeking respite from Anglican oppressive measures, many dissenters saw in Cromwell the hope of deliverance. A group called the Fifth Monarchy Men joined his cause. Taking their name from the book of Daniel in the Old Testament, they believed that four great kingdoms on earth (the Babylonian, Medo-Persian, Greek, and Roman) would be followed by a fifth, the Kingdom of Christ. By identifying the Fifth Kingdom with the millennial reign of Christ, they, like the Anabaptist Chiliasts on the continent, saw the possibility of fulfillment in their day. The excessive zeal of leaders like Christopher Feake, Major-General Thomas Harrison, Major-General Robert Overton, John Rogers, and Thomas Venner offended many English Baptists. When Baptists in England drew up the

Second London Confession of 1688, they carefully avoided the use of chiliastic oratory, preferring a simple statement (Chapters XXXI and XXXII)[76] affirming belief in a resurrection of the dead and a general judgment.

The poor image of the chiliasts was doubtless an embarrassment for Baptists in the American colonies. Many of them went to great lengths to disallow any connection with the radical elements of millennialism. Isaac Backus also felt the impact. In a reply to Benjamin Lord's attempt to tie Baptists to the radical Anabaptists in Europe, Backus reveals his own estimate of the Anabaptists and of religious persecution in his day. He wrote:

> And in the next page, you refer to the Anabaptists in Germany, 240 years ago, who Mr. Dickenson calls "the madmen of Munster." But pray, Sir, why are we so often referred to them, in this controversy about baptism? when we have in no respect a whit more, if so much relation to them, as you have to the *pope of Rome*. Were they *anabaptists*?—so is he *pedobaptist*. Did they use violence to support their cause?—so does he, even imprisonment and death, to maintain:—and let every conscience judge which party has the greatest resemblance to such methods now. You know, Sir, that there have been numerous instances of late years among us, of imprisonments and confiscations of goods, for no greater crime than refusing to conform to, and support that worship which you are pleading for.[77]

By the middle of the 1700s, a period of great spiritual excitement and expectancy took root among dispirited people. Backus sensed that mood, capitalized on it, and began developing a postmillennial view of history. He disallowed Anabaptist chiliasm, but he also developed a rather complete philosophy of history that caught the attention of other Baptists. He believed in a general resurrection, a day of judgment, everlasting punishment for the wicked, and eternal life for the righteous, ideas which he condensed into a confession of faith in 1756.[78] That same year he wrote a more detailed confession.[79]

Other writings of Backus show that he had an elaborately developed philosophy of Christian history. He saw in the Book of Revelation "a prophecy of the great events which should take place, from the coming of Christ to the end of the world."[80] He identified the man of sin as the Pope, the two horns of Revelation 13:11 as the officers of church and state uniting their influence in schemes of power, and the "deadly wound" as the Reformation.[81] Some form of postmillennialism, with its optimistic view of history seemed to be in his mind. He wrote, "The Scriptures plainly represent that the Church of God in these latter Days, will get Victory over the Corruptions of Antichrist gradually, and by Degrees."[82] It would be a progressive victory in four steps. "They get Victory, first over the *Beast*; then over his *Image*; thirdly, over his *Mark*, and lastly over the *Number of his Name*. Rev. 15:2."[83] Absent is any reference to an earthly reign of Christ after his return at the end of the age.

The second coming of Christ was a vital doctrine among other Baptist contemporaries of Backus. That George Whitefield of England helped bring about the Great Awakening in America, church historians acknowledge; the force of his preaching was also felt among the Baptists. Robert B. Semple reported that Daniel Marshall "was one of the thousands, in New England, who heard that son of thunder, Rev. George Whitfield [sic], and caught his seraphic fire."[84] Semple then evaluated the effect on those who believed in the imminent return of Christ:

> Firmly believing in the near approach of "the latter day glory," when the Jews, with the fullness of the gentiles [sic], shall hail their Redeemer, and bow to his gentle sceptre; a number of worthy characters ran to and fro, through the eastern states, warmly exhorting to the prompt adoption of every measure tending to hasten that blissfull period. Others sold, gave away, or left their possessions; as the powerful impulse of the moment determined; and, without script, or purse, rushed up to the head of the Susquehanna, to convert the heathens; and settled in a town called Onnaquaggy, among the Mohawk Indians. One, and not the least sanguine, of these pious missionaries, was my venerable father.[85]

That zeal for preaching spilled over into other geographical areas as New Lights moved southward and began to establish new churches.

MISSIONARY ZEAL

A survey of the origins of Southern Baptist theology would be incomplete without including the development of their missionary enterprises and missionary zeal. Concerning their enterprises, the profound impact made on world missions by William Carey of England has been chronicled widely. The story of missionary organizations in the colonies is not so widely known, but Baptists in America were also establishing missionary organizations. The Philadelphia Association sent out missionaries like John Gano as early as 1755.[86] When the association established a permanent missionary fund in 1766 for the purpose of supporting its missionary enterprises, missions gained formal backing. Their courageous action was a model for Baptists across the land.

Other associations entered into missionary work. The Charleston Association began work in its neighboring counties about the time that Philadelphia sent out its first missionaries. It made extensive contact with the work of the Kiokee Baptist Church near Augusta, Georgia, through Elder Edmund Botsford and others. Also, the Shaftesburg Association in Vermont appointed a committee in 1802 to handle funds for missions, examine candidates for missions, and pay salaries. Missions was coming of age.[87]

The story of missions, however, finally devolves upon people who are committed to missions. Baptists in the colonies produced their stalwarts. Shubal Stearns and Daniel Marshall revolutionized parts of North Carolina and moved southward into Georgia with their tireless activities. Abraham Marshall, Daniel's son, said of his father, "He went from place to place, instructing, exhorting and praying for individuals, families and congregations, whether at a muster, a race, a public market, the open field, an army, or a house of worship—wherever he was able to command attention."[88]

Daniel Marshall developed sound methods for establishing new churches. As the work grew, he set aside a group of workers for future use by licensing men who seemed capable of being developed as ministers. From these licentiates, as he called them, he had a pool of qualified men from which to draw as needs for pastors arose. Abraham Marshall credited this as being the route by which Alexander Scott, Sanders Walker, Samuel Cartledge, Silas Mercer, Abraham Marshall and many others "passed, all of whom became active, able and influential ministers."[89] The Calvinism most of them professed deterred not from their missionary exploits.

The successes of Marshall and Stearns in evangelism, and the establishment of new churches, grew out of the dedication of unique men called and blessed of God. Stearns especially was endowed with a magnetic, almost mesmerizing personality. Tidence Lane, one of Tennessee's "pioneer Baptist preachers," to use J. J. Burnett's language, traced his conversion to an encounter with Stearns. Lane heard about Stearns and traveled forty miles on horseback to see the famed preacher. The impact was profound. Note the effect of Stearns's eyes as they affected Lane:

> When the fame of Mr. Stearns' preaching reached the Yadkin, where I lived, I felt a curiosity to go and hear him. Upon my arrival I saw a venerable old man sitting under a peach tree with a book in his hand and the people gathering about him. He fixed his eyes upon me immediately, which made me feel in such a manner as I had never felt before. I turned to quit the place, but could not proceed far. I walked about, sometimes catching his eyes as I walked. My uneasiness increased and became intolerable. I went up to him, thinking that a salutation and shaking of hands would relieve me, but it happened otherwise. I began to think he had an evil eye and ought to be shunned, but shunning him I could no more effect than a bird can shun the rattlesnake when it fixes its eyes upon it. When he began to preach, my perturbations increased, so that nature could no longer support them, and I sank to the ground.[90]

Those pioneer evangelists often preached under less than ideal conditions and sometimes humor was at their expense, as Elder Edmund Botsford from the Charleston Association could confirm:

> At a certain time, Mr. Botsford ascended a barrel. He had made some progress in his sermon, then, whether in consequence of some radical defect in the barrel, or the vehement emphasis of the foot, with which he accompanied his address, (a thing quite common with our zealous fathers) all at once the head of the barrel gave way, and the preacher descended with it. It does not appear, however, that he was diverted from his upright posture, or that his misfortune essentially deranged the thread of his discourse.[91]

The aplomb of the preacher and the self-control of his hearers were sorely tested on an occasion when the congregation was assembled in a grove. As the sermon unfolded, one hearer became drowsy and began to nod.

> A large surly goat, that was nibbling grass hard by, happened to notice the sleeper, and interpreted the nodding of his head as a challenge for battle. The animal approached and retired; approached again, and again retired, as though doubtful whether the gentleman was in earnest. But the sleeper continued to nod, and the animal at length became seriously enraged. He took a martial position, shook his head in anger, and then darted forward with fury, and laid the sleeper low. Many of the congregation smiled; and the preacher, who was so situated as to be obliged to witness the whole transaction, could not find it in his heart to reprove them. There can be no doubt that the drowsy gentleman was more impressed by the assault of the goat, than by the sermon of the preacher.[92]

Occasional incidents of humor should not detract from the fact that revivals were serious business. People in Virginia, for example, were powerfully moved by the mood of the meetings. Semple reported:

> It was not unusual, to have a large proportion of the congregation, prostrate on the floor; and, in some instances, they have lost the use of their limbs: No distinct articulation could be heard, unless from those immediately by: Screams, cries, groans, songs, shouts, and hosannas, notes of grief and notes of joy, all heard at the same time, made a heavenly confusion, a sort of indescribable concert.[93]

Semple added, somewhat regretfully, that the confusion also allowed hypocrites to come into the churches.

By the end of the century, the preachers lapsed into doctrinaire sermons dedicated to the search for biblical truths. Benedict states that it was their custom in preaching to dive deep "into the plans of Jehovah in eternity, and to bring to light, as they supposed, the hidden treasures of the gospel, which they, in an especial manner, were set to defend."[94] His characterization of the content of sermons preached at the beginning of the nineteenth century attests to the dogmatism of the day. He wrote:

> The kind of preaching now much in vogue, at the period and among the people here had in view, would have been concluded the quintessence of Arminianism, mere milk and water, instead of the strong meat of the gospel. Then, and with our orthodox Baptists, a sermon would have been accounted altogether defective which did not touch upon Election, Total Depravity, Final Perseverance, etc.[95]

Nevertheless, the brand of Calvinism of the eighteenth century gave way to a decidedly modified version in the nineteenth, as Baptists in the South began releasing themselves from their Calvinistic moorings in favor of a theology more suited to the needs of a denomination starting to grasp the vision of a worldwide program of evangelization.

SUMMARY

Baptists during the seventeenth and eighteenth centuries gradually gravitated theologically to the stately maxims of the Westminster Confession modified to meet Baptist nuances of thought. Its statements about the infallible teachings of the Bible, about the nature of the triune God, and the belief that Christ's atoning death was a satisfaction to God which procured salvation for the elect they accepted. The doctrine of the church was a different matter. While adhering confessionally to belief in a church universal, their practical emphasis was given to the church particular and local. Baptism by immersion constituted the biblical mode for them. Participation in the Supper was restricted to believers who had been immersed, as Isaac Backus argued.

Baptists also allowed for divergencies of opinion about ordination. Men alone were permitted to be pastors, but women held the offices of deaconesses, eldresses, and exhorters. The laying on of hands was applied to officers of the church as well as, in many instances, to believers immediately following baptism. Even ruling elders were allowed in some churches although the office eventually dropped out among Southern Baptists.

The belief in Christ's soon return nurtured in many a zeal to win people to Christ. The chiliasm of the Anabaptists in Europe found little sympathy among Baptists in America. Postmillennialism gained ground.

Zeal for preaching to all classes of people wherever people congregated led to conversions and church growth. Following a lull after the Revolutionary War, a new period of rapid expansion gave new impetus to a languishing work. The stage was set for a Second Great Awakening.

NOTES

1. William L. Lumpkin, *Baptist Confessions of Faith*, 1st ed. (Philadelphia: The Judson Press, 1959), pp. 241-295.
2. David Benedict, *Fifty Years Among the Baptists* (Glen Rose, Texas: Newman and Collins, [1913]), p. 234.
3. Ibid., pp. 36-37.
4. H. Leon McBeth, *The Baptist Heritage* (Nashville: Broadman Press, 1987), p. 219.
5. Lumpkin, *Baptist Confessions*, p. 352.
6. H. E. Dana and R. E. Glaze, Jr., *Interpreting the New Testament* (Nashville: Broadman Press, 1961), p. 111.
7. Ibid.
8. Frederic W. Farrar, *History of Interpretation: Bampton Lectures, 1885* (Grand Rapids: Baker Book House, 1961), p. 387.
9. Ibid., p. 386.
10. Earle E. Cairns, *Christianity Through the Centuries: A History of the Christian Church*, rev. & enl. ed. (Grand Rapids: Zondervan Publishing House, 1981), pp. 411-412.
11. *New International Dictionary of the Christian Church*, s.v. "Eichhorn, Johann Gottfried."
12. Ibid.
13. Cairns, *Christianity*, p. 412.
14. *The Baptist Encyclopedia*, s.v. "Furman, Richard, D.D."
15. Lumpkin, *Baptist Confessions*, p. 249.
16. Ibid., p. 250.
17. Ibid.
18. Ibid., p. 251.
19. Alan Richardson, *History, Sacred and Profane* (Philadelphia: The Westminster Press, 1964), p. 20.
20. H. G. Alexander, *The Leibniz-Clarke Correspondence, Together with Extracts from Newton's Principias and Opticks* (New York: Barnes and Noble: Manchester University press; Philosophical Classics, 1956), p. 20.
21. For a popularized description of this development, see James W. Sire, *The Universe Next Door: A Basic World-view Catalog* (Downers Grove, Illinois: Intervarsity Press, 1976). Nietzsche hints at the same thought with his God-is-dead proclamation.
22. Benedict, *Fifty Years*, p. 109.
23. E. Y. Mullins, *The Christian Religion in Its Doctrinal Expression* (Philadelphia: The Judson Press, 1917), p. 122.
24. Lumpkin, *Baptist Confessions*, p. 253.
25. The Filioque Clause continues to be a divisive issue between Greek Orthodox and Roman Catholicism. At the Council of Constantinople in 381, bishops from all parts of the world gathered to discuss the person of Jesus Christ. One of the confessional statements they adopted states that the Second Person of the Trinity proceeded from the Father. It seems that the Greek element left the Council after which the Roman branch emended the doctrine to say that the Holy Spirit proceeded from both the Father and the Son.
26. Lumpkin, *Baptist Confessions*, p. 260.
27. Isaac Backus, *Spiritual Ignorance Causeth Men to Counter-act their Doctrinal Knowledge: a Discourse from Acts XIII, 27*, (Providence: W. Goddard, 1763), p. 5.
28. Lumpkin, *Baptist Confessions*, pp. 260-261.
29. Ibid., p. 262.
30. Ibid., p. 253.
31. Ibid., p. 250.
32. Ibid., pp. 272-273.
33. Ibid., p. 261.
34. A. T. Robertson, *Keywords in the Teaching of Jesus* (Philadelphia: American Baptist Publication Society, 1906), p. 43.
35. Lumpkin, *Baptist Confessions*, p. 254.
36. Isaac Backus, *The Doctrine of Sovereign Grace Opened and Vindicated and Also the Consistency and Duty of Declaring Divine Sovereignty and Men's Impotency while yet We Address Their Consciences with the Warnings of Truth and Calls of the Gospel* (Providence: J. Carter, 1771), pp. xii, 71.
37. Lumpkin, *Baptist Confessions*, p. 265.
38. Backus, *The Doctrine of Sovereign Grace*, pp. 12-13.
39. Ibid., p. 35.
40. Robert H. Culpepper, *Interpreting the Atonement* (Grand Rapids: William B. Eerdmans Publishing Co., 1966), p. 91.
41. Lumpkin, *Baptist Confessions*, p. 260.

42. Ibid., p. 262.
43. Isaac Backus, *The Atonement of Christ Explained and Vindicated Against Late Attempts to Exclude It Out of the World* (Boston: Samuel Hall, 1787), p. 8.
44. Lumpkin, *Baptist Confessions*, p. 285.
45. Ibid., p. 286.
46. Reuben Aldridge Guild, *Chaplain Smith and the Baptists; or, Life, Journals, Letters, and Addresses of the Rev. Hezekiah Smith, D.D., of Haverhill, Massachusetts* (Philadelphia: American Baptist Publication Society, 1885), p. 110.
47. Joseph Biggs, *A Concise History of the Kehukee Baptist Association from It's Original Rise to the Present Time* (Tarborough, North Carolina: Printed by George Howard, 1834), p. 34.
48. Alvah Hovey, *A Memoir of the Life and Times of the Rev. Isaac Backus, A.M.* (Boston: Gould and Lincoln, 1859), p. 46.
49. Isaac Backus, *A Discourse Concerning the Materials, the Manner of Building and Power of Organizing of the Church of Christ, with the True Difference and Exact Limits Between Civil and Ecclesiastical Government and also what are and what are not Just Reasons for Separation Together with an Address to Joseph Fish, Pastor of a Church in Stonington, Occasioned by His Late Piece Called the Examiner Examined* (Boston: J. Boyles, 1773), p. 3.
50. Ibid., p. 17.
51. Lumpkin, *Baptist Confessions*, p. 291.
52. Ibid., pp. 291-292.
53. Ibid., p. 291.
54. Hovey, *A Memoir*, pp. 44-45.
55. Isaac Backus, "An Account of the Life of Isaac Backus," Unpublished manuscript on microfilm, Historical Commission, Southern Baptist Convention, pp. 83-84.
56. Isaac Backus, *A Short Description of the Difference Between the Bond-Woman and the Free, As they are Two Covenants* (Boston: Edes and Gill, 1770), pp. 34-35.
57. Backus, "An Account," pp. 84-85.
58. Morgan Edwards, *The Customs of Primitive Churches; or a set of Propositions relative to the same, materials, constitution, power, officers, ordinances, rites, business, worship, discipline, government, & c. of a church; to which are added their proofs from scripture; and historical narratives of the manner in which most of them have been reduced to practice* (Philadelphia: n.p., 1774), pp. 83-84.
59. Biggs, *A Concise History*, p. 74.
60. Ibid., p. 55.
61. Wood Furman, *A History of the Charleston Association of Baptist Churches in the State of South Carolina; with an Appendix Containing the Principal Circular Letters to the Churches* (Charleston, South Carolina: J. Hoff, 1811), p. 37.
62. Semple, *A History*, p. 302.
63. Ibid., p. 303.
64. Edwards, *The Customs*, p. 93.
65. Semple, *A History*, p. 378.
66. Edwards, *The Customs*, p. 45.
67. Hovey, *A Memoir*, p. 283.
68. Thomas Armitage, *A History of the Baptists; Traced by Their Vital Principles and Practices, from the Time of Our Lord and Saviour Jesus Christ to the Year 1889*, rev. and enl. ed. (New York: Bryan, Taylor & Co., 1889), p. 732.
69. Ibid.
70. Edwards, *The Customs*, pp. 36-37.
71. Ibid., p. 43.
72. Ibid., p. 32.
73. Ibid., p. 42.
74. Ibid., p. 41.
75. Leon McBeth, *Women in Baptist Life* (Nashville: Broadman Press, 1979), pp. 43-44.
76. Lumpkin, *Baptist Confessions*, pp. 293-295.
77. Isaac Backus, *A Letter to the Reverend Mr. Benjamin Lord, of Norwich; Occasioned by Some Harsh Things Which He Has Lately Published Against Those Who Have Dissented from His Sentiments About the MINISTRY, the CHURCH, and BAPTISM* (Providence, New England: Printed by William Goddard, 1764), pp. 9-10.
78. Hovey, *A Memoir*, p. 336.
79. Isaac Backus, *The Testimony of the Two Witnessed Explained and Vindicated with a Few Remarks Upon the Late Writings of Dr. Hemmenway and Dr. Lathrop*, 2d ed. imp. (Boston: Samuel Hall, 1793), p. 5.
80. Ibid., pp. 21-22; also, see Backus, *The Infinite Importance of the Obedience of Faith and of a Separation from the World Opened and Demonstrated; Second Edition Corrected and Improved* (Boston: Samuel Hall, 1791), p. 26.

81. Isaac Backus, *All True Ministers of the Gospel Are Called into That Work by the Special Influence of the Holy Spirit; a Discourse Shewing the Nature and Necessity of an Internal Call to Preach the Everlasting Gospel, Also Marks by Which Christ's Ministers May Be Known from Others, and Answers to Sundry Objections; together with some Observations on the Principles and Practices of Many in the Present Day Concerning These Things, to which Is Added Some Short Accounts of the Experiences and Dying Testimony of Mr. Nathanael Shepherd* (Boston: Fowle, 1754), p. 76.
82. Ibid.
83. Semple, *A History*, p. 369.
84. Ibid.
85. Ibid.
86. Baker, *The Southern Baptist Convention*, p. 97.
87. Ibid., p. 98.
88. *History of the Baptist Denomination in Georgia: with Biographical and Portrait Gallery of Baptist Ministers and Other Georgia Baptists.* Compiled for *The Christian Index* (Atlanta: James P. Harrison & Co., 1881), p. 23.
89. Ibid., pp. 23-24.
90. J. J. Burnett, *Sketches of Tennessee's Pioneer Baptist Preachers, Being, Incidentally, a History of Baptist Beginnings in the Several Associations in the State Containing, Particularly, Character and Life Sketches of the Standard-Bearers and Leaders of Our People*, 2 vols. (Nashville: Marshall and Bruce Company, 1919) 1:319.
91. Charles D. Mallory, *Memoirs of Elder Edmund Botsford* (Charleston, South Carolina: W. Riley, 1832), p. 54.
92. Ibid.
93. Semple, *A History*, p. 37.
94. Benedict, *Fifty Years*, p. 103.
95. Ibid.

PART II

ECCLESIOLOGICAL EVANGELICALISM, 1800-1899

    Chapter 3. Calvinism on the Defense
    Chapter 4. Baptist Church Successionism
    Chapter 5. OF Higher Critics and Calvinists
    Chapter 6. Landmarkism on the Rise

OVERVIEW

By the start of the nineteenth century, Baptist theology in the fledgling nation was securely ensconced in the arms of Calvinism, or so it seemed. Churches surrendered their Arminian sentiments, associations professed their loyalties, and preachers exhorted predestination from countless pulpits. Nevertheless, these developments could not prevail against a rising missionary fervor, the challenge to basic assumptions about the extent of the atonement, the meaning of depravity, and a refocusing of theological perspective. Regular Baptists, especially in the South, turned their attention to ecclesiology, an obsession that kept their doctrinal apologists occupied for all of the nineteenth century. It was to be the century of the church and its ordinances as Landmarkism arose and took the South by storm. The century of ecclesiological evangelicalism had begun. It closed in 1899 when the trustees of The Southern Baptist Theological Seminary fired its president, William H. Whitsitt, for questioning the New Testament origins of Baptist churches. However, Landmarkism as a distinct movement was dying, and the withdrawal in 1905 of a large faction of Landmarkers to form their own association attested to that fact.

Chapters 3 and 4 cover the first half of the century with chapter 3 given to an investigation of the reasons for the decline of Calvinism. Chapter 4 describes the origin and beginning stages of Baptist church successionism. The next two chapters, restricted to the second half of the century, feature the further break-up of Calvinistic doctrines, first encounters with higher criticism, and the beginning of the decline of Landmarkism.

CHAPTER 3

CALVINISM ON THE DEFENSE

The Revolutionary War dissipated evangelistic zeal as Baptists, Quakers, and other dissenting groups supported the American Revolution in the belief that true religious freedom would come in no other way. Their hopes were confirmed in the American Bill of Rights. However, evangelistic work languished following the war until a spiritual awakening about 1800 kindled new flames of soul-winning fires. Baptist churches in the South boasted a membership of 110,514 by 1814, the year the General Missionary Convention of the Baptist Denomination in the United States for Foreign Missions was formed, and increased to 365,346 in 1845 when the Southern Baptist Convention was founded.[1]

Some of the most far-reaching developments, however, originated away from the American shores. In England, Andrew Fuller significantly altered the doctrine of the atonement and helped break the hold Calvinism exerted over the Baptists. In Germany, the seeds of higher criticism took firm root in the area of biblical interpretation. Some of these developments would pass by Southern Baptists in the nineteenth century only to find a lodging among them in the twentieth in the form of neoorthodoxy. Their consuming theological passion for most of the nineteenth century would be the church and the ordinances. Their love affair with Calvinism had reached its most intense fervor by the first few decades, soon to decline.

THE AUTHORITY OF THE BIBLE ASSUMED

The Philadelphia Confession lost some of its luster in the nineteenth century as associations and individuals drew up confessions more consonant with the new mood engendered during the time of missionary expansion. Two later confessions began to wield wide acceptance among Baptists in America, the Principles of Faith and Practice of the Sandy Creek Association (1816) and the New Hampshire Confession of Faith (1833). William L. Lumpkin says the Principles of Faith and Practice reflects the outlook of the most influential Baptist association in the South during the eighteenth century.[2] In its statements about the Bible, the word infallible drops from use. Article two states simply that the Scriptures of the Old and New Testaments are the Word of God, the only rule of faith and practice. The other confession of wide influence was the New Hampshire Confession of Faith (1833), the most widely disseminated creedal declaration of American Baptists.[3] Article one contains no direct reference to inerrancy or infallibility. Instead, the Bible, a perfect treasure of heavenly instruction, presents truth without any mixture of error.[4]

The composers of the nineteenth century confessions assumed, but did not define, inspiration. The writers of numerous essays, articles, and letters published in periodical literature were equally imprecise. They turned their energies toward more practical matters. Campbellism and antimissionism threatened and then decimated Baptist ranks in several Southern states. As denominationalism developed, Baptists wrestled with the doctrine of the church and its ordinances. Biblical authority was assumed, not argued. Without apology, the Scriptures were quoted to buttress theological positions. A study of the Baptist periodicals[5] of the early nineteenth century reveals the same uncritical attitude toward biblical inspiration. A Baptist magazine ran two articles in 1820 which dealt with the Bible. The author discussed two reasons why the Bible should be studied. First, the Bible is the Word of God. "Its sacred pages came not by the will of man; but by the inspiration of the Holy Ghost."[6] Second, the figurative language compels careful study and analysis.[7] The content of the material indicates that Baptists were becoming conscious of critical problems in the Bible.

A discussion in the *Baptist Chronicle, and Monthly Monitor* in 1841 indicates the trend of thinking at that time. Almost predictably, the author described the Bible as the unerring rule of faith and practice. A significant statement follows: "In interpreting the word of God, the original Scriptures must necessarily be the ultimate appeal." This statement is a tacit admission that translations have limitations; it signifies a distinct divergence from the efforts of earlier European theologians who tried to defend the text of various translations. The article in *The Baptist Chronicle* pointed out that God used languages *"as they existed"* to communicate the revelation. The writer of the article drew two conclusions: The import of any word can only be solved by reference to the common usage of the day; and "secondly, lexicographers do not constitute a supreme tribunal from which there is no appeal."[8] The writer left open the need for contextual analysis as interpreted by the reader.

By the time the convention was organized in 1845, Baptist writers were already at work defining the way the inspiration of the Bible was accomplished.

For example, *The Christian Review* ran a lengthy discussion in 1844 on the subject of inspiration. The author reviewed several definitions of inspiration and concluded, "Or we may say, more briefly, that the sacred penmen were completely under the direction of the Holy Spirit, or, that they wrote under a plenary inspiration."[9] After proffering several possible proofs of inspiration, such as the excellence of the doctrines and the agreement with each other of the different parts, the writer then declared that the "most direct and conclusive evidence that the Scriptures were divinely inspired, is found in *the testimony of the writers themselves.*"[10] The biblical writers authenticated their divine commission by miracles and thereby established their "authority and infallibility" as teachers of divine truth.[11]

Another facet of the problem of inspiration was touched upon by Andrew Broaddus (1770-1848), whom William Cathcart called the foremost preacher of his generation.[12] This concerns the relationship of Christ to the Bible. Broaddus made no attempt to correlate how Christ the Living Word relates to the Bible the Written Word, but he did note the centrality of Christ in the biblical account. Noting that the Bible is "the all-sufficient instrument of our salvation, without popish tradition, without human additions of any sort," he then observed that "we are not thus made wise, even by this source of wisdom, without 'faith in Christ Jesus.'"[13] Broaddus continued, "He is the great governing object, the animating principle of the holy oracles, the focal point whence the heavenly light radiates through all the sacred pages—through all the departments of religion."[14]

At this stage of their theological development, Baptist theologians generally accepted the authority of the Bible and its inspiration although they were not unaware of critical problems relating to language and the historical transmission of the text. The *American Baptist Magazine* in 1820 carried an article on the necessity of making a critical study of the Bible a part of theological education.[15] Baptists in the South, however, were far removed geographically and academically from those who felt the need to subject the Bible to critical evaluation. Their time would come later.

EXPLICATING THE TRINITY

As Baptists in the southern United States continued to formulate their own confessional statements, they invariably included trinitarian doctrines. The Principles of Faith of the Sandy Creek Association, adopted in 1816, declared belief in a trinitarian Being consisting of Father, Son and Holy Ghost, the three being one God, not three.[16]

Tucked away in the minutes for 1816, the Cumberland Baptist Association included a summary of the interrelatedness of the Godhead which shows a theological development doubtless beyond that of the majority of its constituents. The minutes state:

Dear brethren, we believe there is one and only one God, (a) and that there is [sic] three divine persons in the Godhead; Viz. Father, Son and Holly [sic] Ghost; this is a mystery we cannot fully comprehend, yet it is the truth we sincerely do believe. Nothing can be true of the infinite creator that can be fully comprehended by the capacity of a creature, (b) hence those ideas of God, are the trust [truest] which are incomprehensible; we therefore believe this mystery of mysteries, to be revealed in the gospel of Christ; viz. the Unity in Trinity, & trinity in Unity, in the Godhead; that God, the father, is one perfect God of, and in himself, that God the son, is one perfect God, of and in himself, and that God the holy ghost, is one perfect God, of, and in himself; and yet these three are but one perfect God, of, and in himself, (c) is the mystery on which we propose to treat, viz. the being of all beings, is but one in essence, yet three in person, and that those three persons in the one essence, are absolutely distinct from each other, (d) and yet but one eternal God, and these three divine persons in the one essence are to each other as related in the word of God, viz. that the first is a father to the second, and the second a son to the father, (e) and that the third proceeds from them both; and yet there is neither first, second nor third, as to nature, viz. he that begat was not at all before him that was begotten, nor he that proceeds from them both, any later than them from whom he proceeded, and we therefore believe that God is not called father, son and holy ghost, as if the divine nature of the one did beget the divine nature of the other, or that the divine nature of the third did issue forth and proceed from the first and second; for then these would be three divine natures; whereas there is but one divine nature, and three divine persons, in that divine nature, and not three distinct Gods in person, in that divine nature, and not three distinct Gods in nature, but one God, and three distinct persons in that one God, we do not believe that it was the divine nature of the father, but the divine person of the father that did from eternity beget, not the divine nature, but the divine person of the son, and from the divine person of the father, and the son did, from eternity proceed the divine person of the holy ghost, and so one is not before the other as to nature, but as to persons they are first, second, and third, in order from eternity; as they are three distinct persons, but one eternal God, father, son, and holy ghost.[17]

A more comprehensive theological sentence would be difficult to find. It affirms trinitarian theology, the Filioque Clause, and the deity of the three Persons of the Trinity.

The New Hampshire Confession of 1833, in a similar vein of thought, relates the redemptive activity to the triune God.[18] The work of redemption was accomplished by the three Persons of the Trinity, all of whom are truly God.

The person of the Holy Spirit as understood by evangelical Baptists can be learned from other writings. For example, an essay attributed to Robert Hall was published in *The Christian Watchman*. Hall described the Holy Spirit as a free agent who may withdraw himself if slighted, neglected, or opposed.[19] Two years later, in 1844, the *Biblical Recorder* set forth the Holy Spirit as one who leads and guides, having the attributes of personality. The author then said, "We affirm, then, that the Spirit is a *distinct* and *divine* person; and not, as Socinians contend, 'a mere power, or attribute.'"[20] These kinds of evidences were admirably enumerated and classified by Boyce in his *Abstract of Systematic Theology*.[21]

As a Person of the God-head, the Holy Spirit has a vital role in the redemptive process. A discussion in the Cumberland Association in 1816 delineated the respective roles of Father, Son, and Holy Spirit in redemption. The Minutes read:

> Hence if the third person had been my redeemer, who should have been my sanctifier? Not the father nor the son, for as the first person is first in the divine economy of grace; and redemption is first in order before sanctification in the work of grace: so the divine person who redeems should be first in order before the divine person who sanctifies. Hence the first person in the God-head saves; the second redeems; and the third sanctifies, and it follows that the first person gave us to Christ, before time; the second redeemed us in his time, and the third sanctifies us in our time.[22]

The subject of the baptism of the Holy Spirit appears occasionally in the writing of this period. It was usually understood to refer to the event at Pentecost as recorded in chapter two of Acts. In 1819, Pentecost was discussed in the *American Baptist Magazine and Missionary Intelligencer*.[23] The author recounted features of the Pentecostal experience: It was obviously upon believers and therefore not regeneration; it was the baptism of the Holy Ghost; and it was to qualify the apostles for usefulness as well as to declare the apostles and others as the people of God. The writer saw the baptism as a bestowal of external gifts "such as were necessary at that age of the church, for the confirmation of believers and the conviction of infidels."[24] He concluded that Christians cannot now properly pray that they might be baptized with the Holy Ghost.

Baptists living in the Charleston area also watched as some of their numbers wavered in their Christology. The Arian teaching that the Son was created by the Father has never gained wide acceptance among evangelical Baptists, but one of the few exceptions occurred in 1735. Some of the members of the Baptist Church of Charleston, the citadel of Calvinism in the South, became convinced that Christ was less than God. Wood Furman, chronicler of the Charleston Association, reported that they withdrew and formed their own church which became extinct after a period of fifty years.[25]

Unitarianism also made small inroads among the Baptists in Charleston, in spite of the Calvinism taught there. David Benedict wrote of a previous schism: "Forty years ago, a small company of our strong men, mostly ministers, began to falter in their course, and eventually went over to the Unitarian side."[26] The split occurred about 1810. Defections since then have been rare, and even then only on an isolated basis.

Predictably, the Unitarian controversy evoked discussion about the nature of God. Able men rose to the defense of the faith. William T. Brantly, for example, preached a sermon before the First Baptist Church of Augusta, Georgia, in which he earnestly contended that God is one but has personal distinctions.[27]

But the Unitarian contention was cut short by other pressing issues. Alexander Campbell raised the question of salvation by grace versus baptismal regeneration. Opponents of missions bitterly denounced the trend toward missions and a more structured organization. Unitarianism was cut off before it could take root among Baptists in the South.

A LESS RADICAL DEPRAVITY

Few Baptist writers in the early nineteenth century doubted that a person is composed of both body and soul or that a sinner is born depraved. Joseph A. Warne wrote a tract entitled "Human Depravity Considered", in which he discussed the extent of depravity. He argued that sinners must be totally depraved, if they are depraved at all, "for there are no degrees of destitution."[28] Depravity is negative in its nature and "admits of no degrees."[29] Such a definition of depravity necessitates that God act initially in the salvation experience. Half a century after Warne, Alvah Hovey wrote that faith "presupposes the effectual call or regenerating work of God by his Spirit."[30]

In spite of the fervency with which the Calvinists defined total depravity, innovative thinkers voiced their discontent with the received doctrine. Particular atonement, the teaching that Christ died only for the sins of the elect, was being replaced by the teaching of a more general atonement, especially the interpretation of Andrew Fuller of England.[31] Likewise, depravity was being re-defined. An article in the *Columbian Star* in 1822 is indicative of the change. The author observed that depravity could be defined in such a way as to render it obnoxious to the taste and understanding. He categorically denied that human nature offers "one unvaried and unalleviated mass of deformity."[32] A better way to assert depravity "is to fasten on the radical element of depravity, and to show how deeply it lies incorporated" with one's moral constitution.[33] Depravity would eventually be understood as affecting every facet of personality with no one facet being utterly corrupted.

The *Christian Review* carried an article about infant salvation in 1836. The writer, like so many others of his day, assumed the unity of the race in Adam. He interpreted the fall of Adam as affecting all mankind, but he defined depravity in a different sense than did his Calvinistic brethren. An infant, he wrote, inherits "a bias toward sin, which must be removed," but infants by birth are not actual

Calvinism on the Defense

transgressors.³⁴ Strictly speaking, then, an infant which dies has need of "sanctifying grace," but not of "pardoning mercy." Southern Baptists generally have followed that analysis. They would say that infants are *safe*, not *saved*.

The pens of other influential men helped break up the rigid Calvinism. The writings of William T. Brantly, Sr. (1787-1845), popular preacher and former editor of Georgia's *Christian Index*, show his conflict with the Calvinistic doctrine of total depravity. He explained depravity as a consciousness of internal moral evil which no human power can subdue or eradicate.³⁵ That he did not accept the Calvinistic definition of total depravity can be determined from his ideas about predestination and irresistible grace. Of the former, he claimed ignorance: "I know not what it is."³⁶ Nevertheless, he went on to say that predestination never made a unity of the human race by necessity. Neither has it ever interfered with perfect liberty of thought or action, nor deducted "one iota from the absolute freedom of any intelligent and responsible agent."³⁷ Of irresistible grace, he stated flatly that "the grace of God as put forth and exerted in the salvation of sinners, is not irresistible."³⁸ Further, election teaches nothing "inconsistent with the idea" that salvation may be accepted or rejected.³⁹

Dissatisfaction with Calvinism can be inferred from the number of articles devoted to election, depravity, and atonement during the second quarter of the nineteenth century as opposition came into the open. Questions were being raised about the role of preaching if the salvation of the elect is determined by predestination. The editor of the *American Baptist Magazine* replied that preaching is an ordained end by which God accomplishes his purpose.⁴⁰ Calvinism was on the defense.

SUFFICIENCY VERSUS EFFICIENCY

The Calvinistic belief about Christ's death on the cross had powerful and influential voices in the South between 1800 and 1845, such as P. H. Mell (1814-1888), W. B. Johnson (1782-1862), and Jesse Mercer (1769-1841). Nathaniel M. Crawford (1811-1871), president of Mercer and Georgetown colleges, minister, and theologian, typifies their group (with the possible exception of Jesse Mercer in his later years, as discussed below). To Crawford, belief in a general atonement casts doubt on the purpose and power of God in history. These are protected by the doctrine of limited atonement. He wrote:

> If God's purpose was universal while his work is limited, he has failed to accomplish his purpose: and this failure must be either because he changed his mind, or had not wisdom to contrive, or power to execute, a plan that would accomplish his purpose. . . . The effect of God's purpose of salvation through the death of Jesus, is limited and special: his purpose failed in no point; therefore that purpose was limited and special.⁴¹

To accomplish the elect's salvation, Christ assumed human flesh, rendered obedience to the law and fulfilled its righteousness, and suffered "that justice might be satisfied, and a propitiation rendered to God."[42] Crawford's views are an accurate expression of the attitude of many Calvinistic Baptists of the first half of the nineteenth century.

Voices like those of Mell, Crawford, and, later, James Petigru Boyce, could not stem the tide. The sharp edges of Calvinism gradually were rounded off to a less abrasive structure. As already cited, historian David Benedict alleged that the kind of preaching in vogue at the middle of the century would have been judged the quintessence of Arminianism.[43]

There are several reasons for this decline. First, the organization of churches into associations based on Calvinistic tenets was more apparent than real. Of the three types of Baptists which had been drawn together in America,[44] two groups had come from England. These two were the Regular Baptists (Calvinistic type), and the General Baptists (Arminian type). A third group originated in America. These Baptists were called Separates, or New Lights (mildly Calvinistic). They had separated from other churches in New England after the Great Awakening. How these three theological strands of thought were woven into a Calvinistic fabric already has been recounted above. Suffice it to say that the pastors were usually won over to Calvinism first, and then the churches.[45]

That the theology of the General Baptists in the South had been overpowered but not silenced is reflected in two confessions. The Terms of Union Between the Elkhorn and South Kentucky, or Separate, Associations, adopted in 1801, eliminated the preaching of general atonement as a hindrance to communion.[46] To say that Christ tasted death for every man was a long step from saying that he died only for the elect. Another confession, and one that was widely circulated, also favored a general atonement. Article VI of the New Hampshire Confession, 1833, says, in part, that the blessings of salvation are made free to all by the Gospel.[47] The assertions in these two confessions are but small indicators of a latent sentiment that was re-emerging among Regular Baptists in the South.

A second factor in the decline of Calvinism can be traced to the temper of the times. It was an era of evangelistic and missionary fervor, and during the great Frontier Revival of 1800 large numbers of converts joined Baptist churches. The Calvinistic definition of limited atonement, coupled with a view of man's nature that said he could not repent and believe until after regeneration, left little room for an invitation for personal commitment. True, Calvinists went to great lengths to attempt harmonizing limited atonement with a general invitation to all men, but their intricate theological distinctions were lost upon preachers who possessed little or no formal education. Benedict reports that about 1800 little more than thirty Baptist ministers in all the country "had been through a course of collegiate training."[48]

A third contributing factor in the breaking up of Calvinism among Baptists revolves around the rise, development, and schism precipitated by Campbellism.

Alexander Campbell (1788-1866), a Presbyterian from Scotland who immigrated to the United States, eventually joined the Baptists. In the 1820s, his theology had developed along lines not compatible with the beliefs of the Baptists with whom he had aligned himself. Specifically, he advocated a form of baptismal regeneration. Through his periodical, *The Millennial Harbinger*, Campbell had a powerful and influential tool to disseminate his views. Before Campbell was identified as being at variance with the Baptists, his magazine and teachings reached across the South and caused entire associations to leave the Baptist ranks and join the Reformers, a movement which crystallized into the Disciples of Christ in 1832.

Campbell tapped reservoirs of sentiment among Baptists in 1829 and 1830 that had lain untouched. For one thing, the Reformers, as Campbell called them, resented the adoption of any creedal statements by churches or associations. They capitalized on the fear "that a creed is something pertaining to the inquisition, or some monster of the days of yore, whereby men were made, by the dint of the word, flames and the like, to adhere to certain opinions."[49] The adoption of a creed presupposed the authority to enforce it.

Campbell also attacked the prevailing idea of total depravity. Robert B. Semple wrote a letter to Campbell posing seven questions covering Campbell's doctrines. Campbell subsequently published Semple's letter in *The Millennial Harbinger* with Campbell's explanations. On the question of depravity, Campbell took strong issue with the description of mankind as being uniformly depraved. He agreed that in one's natural state a person is alienated from the life of God and therein is without hope, but he disagreed with the doctrine of total depravity because depravity "cannot designate a state: for in states there are no degrees."[50] Campbell continued:

> He that affirms that all men are *totally* depraved, makes all men alike depraved, and as depraved as Satan; for Satan is no more that *totally* depraved. If, moreover, every child be *totally* depraved, there is no possibility of any person becoming worse than another, nor worse at any period of his life than he was when he first saw the Sun.[51]

His description of depravity as experiential rather than a condition or state of being, left room for a new emphasis on faith which divorced it from the prior requirement of regeneration. His view of faith most closely approximated what may be called *historical faith*, i.e., faith about the truth of an event or statement, as contrasted with *saving faith*, i.e., faith as a dynamic commitment to Jesus Christ. To quote Campbell, "So faith is neither more nor less than the belief of testimony, whatever that testimony may be. The testimony of God is all that any Christian believes, when he has the faith of a Christian."[52] In so arguing, Campbell took faith from the realm of theologians and gave it back to the common man. Laying aside subtle nuances about effectual and ineffectual calling, one could read the Bible and *believe* it. To Campbell that kind of faith was Christian faith.

Another aspect of the saving act as understood by Campbell relates to the moment of regeneration. Calvinists believed that the Holy Spirit regenerates the elect who afterwards repent and believe. Many devout believers confidently argued that they were a part of the elect, but many others lacked that full assurance. A reading of deathbed accounts as given in the diaries and periodicals of that era shows that many "died in hope." Ministers or concerned friends not uncommonly read Scriptures of assurance to the dying. The problem was, How could the dying be sure of their election and regeneration? They could assume that because they were repenting and believing they must have been regenerated, but how could they know that their repenting and believing were genuine? Campbell gave the doubters an experience by which to know when they had been saved: baptism. One of Semple's questions and Campbell's answers was directed to the time and method of regeneration in Campbell's system:

> *Query 4*—"I understood you to assert that immersion, or baptism, is the act of regeneration, and the medium of forgiveness of sins: and that the scriptures do not authorize us to assert or believe that any are regenerated or forgiven until immersed. In other words, that the blood of Christ is never applied but through the medium of baptism. Is this a correct statement of your views?"
> *Answer*—It is very nearly a correct statement of my views.[53]

As a corollary to the above, Campbell believed that baptism demands a proper administrator.[54]

Campbell's definition of Christian faith as belief in a testimony, and his identification of the nexus of regeneration with baptism in water, created a furor among Baptists in the South. Nathaniel M. Crawford wrote his book *Aphesis Amartioon* in an attempt to refute Campbellism. As early as 1825, Andrew Broaddus, a man of gentle spirit and quiet nature, began to earn the reputation of a polemicist against Campbell.[55] W. T. Brantly, editor of *The Columbian Star, and Christian Index*, tried a combination of ridicule and reconciliation in an article published in 1829:

> If friend Campbell will discontinue his attacks upon the Ten Commandments, upon Christian Baptisms, Predestination, and other doctrines of Grace, and will direct all his *smartness* against the Free Thinkers, we will forgive him the past, and will shake hands with him for the time to come, as a useful colleague in the common cause.[56]

Aside from the fact that Brantly grossly underestimated the differences between Campbell and his erstwhile Baptist brethren, "Friend Campbell" had other ideas.

He ripped the denomination asunder. Men like W. C. Buck (1790-1872) salvaged some churches and associations,[57] but Campbellism eventually resulted in hundreds of Baptist churches leaving the denomination to follow Campbell.[58] Campbellism split the Baptists, but it also made them rethink the salvation experience and resulted in their reemphasis upon experiential religion and especially the importance and nature of the new birth in Christ.

Probably the most significant single factor in the break-up of Calvinism was the work of Andrew Fuller of England. Baron Stow penned words in 1826 about Fuller's importance that showed almost uncanny foresight. He wrote, "The history of Fuller may be said to consist of a three-fold division, under each of which he will command the admiration and esteem of future generations. We allude to him, as the corrector of false Calvinism, the impugner of deistical and Socinian heresy, and the advocate of missions."[59]

How accurate Stow's analysis was can be seen in the testimonies of prominent Baptists from succeeding generations. Francis Wayland wrote that "Gill's Divinity was a sort of standard" until "a change commenced upon the publication of the writings of Andrew Fuller."[60] Jeremiah B. Jeter voiced almost the same sentiments as Wayland;[61] J. M. Pendleton admitted his own theological indebtedness to Fuller.[62] James P. Boyce also traced the change in Baptist understanding of the atonement to the work of Andrew Fuller.[63]

Fuller rejected one of the fundamental assumptions of the Calvinistic system. While he saw the death of Christ as a "propitiatory sacrifice"[64] and a way for mercy to be exercised "consistent with the honor of God,"[65] he was impatient with the idea that sin was a debt which Christ paid.[66] Calvinists had proclaimed that the death of Christ was an actual satisfaction which secured the redemption of the elect. Fuller saw the atonement as sufficient for all sinners but efficient in its application. He hesitated to say that Christ satisfied divine justice to open the way of salvation,[67] but the death of Christ did make an atonement for sin in which "*sin was expiated*" and "*a way opened for God to draw near to the sinner, and the sinner to God.*"[68] He admonished, "View it as a glorious expedient devised by infinite Wisdom for the reparation of the injury done by sin to the divine government, and for the consistent exercise of free mercy to the unworthy. . . ."[69] Fuller explicitly stated his belief about the substitutionary death of Christ:

> The sufferings of Christ in our stead, therefore, are not a punishment inflicted in the ordinary course of distributive justice, but an extraordinary interposition of infinite wisdom and love; not contrary to, but rather above the law—deviating from the letter, but more than preserving the spirit of it. Such, as well as I am able to explain them, are my views of the substitution of Christ.[70]

At this point, Fuller's language closely resembles that of the Dutch writer, Hugo Grotius, who propounded what is known as the Governmental Theory of the

Atonement, i.e., Christ's death for sin was necessary in order to maintain the integrity of the divine government.

W. T. Brantly, Sr., stated as early as 1830 the essential similarities and differences between Fuller and John Gill, the champion of orthodox Calvinism:

> Dr. Gill resolves election into the provisions and capacity of the atonement. Fuller resolves it into the Sovereign will and pleasure of God. Dr. Gill affirms that the atonement goes so far, and no further. Fuller denies that the momentous transaction which we call the atonement, is to be measured by the limits of calculation or number, alleging in illustration of his view, that the atonement must have been precisely what it is, had God designed the salvation of one individual only, and that it need be no more for the salvation of myriads.[71]

How serious a breach did Fuller make in the Calvinistic system? Thomas J. Nettles places Fuller in the Calvinistic camp. After quoting H. C. Vedder's statement that Fuller had adopted an Arminian interpretation of the atonement, Nettles affirms, "Such statements could be misleading and make Fuller appear less Calvinistic than he was."[72] Nettles admirably expounds those points in Fuller's theology that show Fuller's orthodox Calvinism. He also notes that Fuller's exposition of the sufferings of Christ as sufficient for all but efficient in the elect is "in precise harmony with the canons of the Synod of Dort."[73] The critical fact remains, however, that Fuller shifted the limitation in the effect of Christ's death from the sufferings per se to the decree of God. The net result is the same as far as the elect are concerned, but one of the crucial five points of Calvinism, was seriously jeopardized. Baptists in the South already were questioning the Calvinistic definition of the depravity of human nature. When coupled with Fuller's exposition of the atonement, two of the five basic points were weakened.

Fuller's view of the atonement found sympathetic ears among Baptists in the South. While holding firmly to the cardinal points of God's election and grace, they gravitated toward Fullerism. His views of Christ's death were more compatible with a free offer of salvation to all sinners.

W. T. Brantly apparently had studied the works of both John Gill and Andrew Fuller. At times, Brantly sounded as thoroughly Calvinistic as Gill himself. Brantly defended objective atonement when he said, "Now what is it that gives to the blood of Christ its atoning efficacy? Not merely divine appointment. There must have been an intrinsic virtue—something, which in the nature of things was adapted to answer the demands of *absolute justice*, or it could never have received the divine approbation."[74] He saw the efficacy in the "ineffable and incomprehensible *union* of divinity and humanity."[75] Limited atonement is implied when he avowed that the work of Christ could not "be frustrated by contingency"; furthermore, "we love to think of that stable purpose of mercy," he wrote, "which marks out by designations peculiar to itself, the candidates for future bliss. . . ."[76]

On the other hand, Brantly's thought ran close to that of Anselm of Canterbury (1033-1109), who explained the atonement in his famous work *Cur Deus Homo?* as being effected by the God-Man who satisfied the offended honor of God by dying on the cross for sin. To quote Brantly:

> The blood of Jesus Christ cleanses from all sin. The expiation of all sin in them who believe, is found in the blood of Christ. . . . Their sin is atoned for, and pardon and justification secured, through the satisfaction rendered to Divine justice by the death of Christ. The blood which is thus available to atone, is the *blood of Christ*. He was both God and man; and though a divine nature could not bleed and die, yet a divine person could. . . . The union of the divine and human natures in Christ, is the foundation of that peculiar faith which is the medium of comfort to despairing souls.[77]

When addressing the specific issue of limited atonement as opposed to general atonement, Brantly argued that the death of Christ "has in itself sufficient efficacy to cleanse from all sin." He added further that if any "sin cannot consistently, with the divine government, be forgiven, it must be for other reasons than the inadequacy of Christ's sufferings."[78]

Brantly was not alone in his Anselmic description of the efficacious death of Christ. The Cumberland Baptist Association, in 1816, records, "The sum of all we have said is this; man can suffer, but cannot satisfy. But the second divine person, who was both God and man in one person, could both suffer and satisfy, and reconcile us to God, by his cross."[79]

The case of Jesse Mercer is somewhat enigmatic. Nettles correctly classifies him with the Calvinists,[80] and that assessment is certainly true of the Mercer of 1830. That year, W. T. Brantly, who at that time was the editor of *The Columbian Star, and Christian Index*, ran a notice that Cyrus White, the pastor of the Bethlehem Baptist Church in Jasper County, Georgia, had written "a pamphlet of about 20 pages, which labors to prove the unlimited scheme of atonement."[81] The periodical then ran a series of ten articles by Jesse Mercer entitled "Mercer's Letters to White on the Atonement," in which Mercer defended limited atonement. A quotation from Letter IX for the November 13, 1830 issue typifies Mercer's argument:

> But if I have respect to the purpose of the Father in giving his Son to die, and to the design of Christ in laying down his life, I should answer it was *for his elect only*.
>
> . . . .
>
> If the substitution of Christ consists in his dying *for, or instead of others, that they should not die*, this, as comprehending the designed end to be answered by his death, is strictly applicable to none but the elect; for, whatever ground

there is for sinners, as sinners, to believe and be saved, it never was the purpose or design of Christ to impart faith to any other than those who were given him of the Father.[82]

However, fifteen years later, Mercer moved to a position more aligned with that of Fuller:

> The fulness of the atonement is not to be measured by the *number saved*; but by its *competency to save one sinner*.... If it is capable *amply to save* ONE SINNER that believeth in Jesus, then it is *of the same capacity* to save to the uttermost all that come unto *God* by him. So that to talk of a limited atonement, is to talk of an atonement short of the requisitions of Justice, and which leaves sin partially atoned for![83]

His thought thus moved from the idea that the sufferings of Christ equaled the penalty of the sins of the elect to the idea that whatever was sufficient for one sinner was sufficient for all. Fullerism prevailed.

Mercer and Fuller were not alone in their view of general atonement. Andrew Broaddus already had been preaching a similar doctrine. "And here I take occasion to say," he proclaimed, "that a consistent and scriptural view of this subject appears to lead to the conclusion, that the atonement is *general* in its *nature* and *extent*."[84] His sermons resounded with ideas that would become standard expression among later generations. He represented the Father as guarding the "rights of Deity and the honor of the eternal throne" and "requiring, on behalf of Divine justice, a propitiatory sacrifice."[85] The Son, "equally disposed to vindicate all the claims of Deity, and actuated by the same Divine benevolence," assumed the role of Redeemer and "became a willing sacrifice."[86]

Gillites and Fullerites took sides and launched tirades against each other splitting churches and associations in the process. J. J. Burnett tells of one East Tennessee preacher, Ephraim Moore, who was put on trial in his church for preaching free salvation for all who believe and for advocating world-wide missions.[87] Moore won the debate at his heresy trial, as Burnett called it, until he was forced to admit having read and endorsed a book written by one Garrett Dewees, suspected of leaning toward Arminianism. Moore was excluded, but when many people followed him, he was later reinstated.[88] As an outgrowth of this "battle of the giants," the representatives of Holston, Tennessee, Nolachucky, and East Tennessee Associations met in 1843 and adopted an article which stated in part that "the blessings of salvation are made free to all by the gospel, and that nothing prevents the salvation of the greatest sinner on earth but his own voluntary refusal to submit to the Lord Jesus Christ." The associations further added that none of the articles adopted were to be "construed in their meaning as to hold with the doctrine of particular, eternal and unconditional election and reprobation."[89]

Hosea Holcombe, the historian of Alabama Baptists for that period, probably best caught the spirit of the age with his astute observations. He noted that confusion reigned on all sides. What some called Calvinism, others denigrated as Arminianism. The New Test party took sides against the orthodox, or Old School party. The doctrines of election and predestination, so loved by the Old School preachers, were feared by the younger preachers. Holcombe put his finger on one redeeming feature when he said, "Examine any Christian on his experience, and he is sound in faith; his wise heart, as Mr. Davis remarks, contradicts his blockhead."[90]

SUMMARY

The nineteenth century began in an exciting way as the great Frontier Revival broke out and resulted in the rapid growth of Baptist churches. In their evangelistic ardor, evangelical Baptists accepted the authority of the Bible and gave little thought to critical problems relating to its composition. Calvinism also had ascended to the top and ostensibly claimed their allegiance.

By 1845, the situation would change. Their acceptance of the Bible remained firm, but they began maturing in their awareness of critical developments in the world of Christian scholarship. At the same time, they took a second look at their Calvinistic heritage and modified it in two significant areas. They began to see depravity in a new light. No longer did it presuppose the necessity of regeneration before one could repent and believe.

The doctrine of the atonement suffered a similar fateful decision. Andrew Fuller of England irrevocably placed the debate on new footing when he attacked Calvinism's tenet of an atonement sufficient only for the elect. Two of the five fundamental Calvinistic tenets were thereby qualified. A third, belief in irresistible grace, found itself falling before a developing Baptist evangelistic zeal. Calvinism was on the pinnacle for many Baptists in the South, but its hold on them was loosened.

NOTES

1. Robert A. Baker, *The Southern Baptist Convention and Its People, 1607-1972* (Nashville: Broadman Press, 1972), p. 144.
2. William L. Lumpkin, *Baptist Confessions of Faith* (Philadelphia: The Judson Press, 1959), p. 357.
3. Ibid., p. 361.
4. Ibid., pp. 361-362.
5. The first American Baptist magazine, the *Massachusetts Baptist Missionary Magazine*, appeared in 1803. After the periodical was adopted by the Triennial Convention, the name was changed to *Baptist Missionary Magazine*. The *Christian Watchman* was begun in 1819, and *The Columbian Star*, now known as *The Christian Index*, in 1822 (*Encyclopedia of Southern Baptists*, s.v. "Newspaper, The Denominations," by E. C. Routh).

6. "The Importance of Studying the Scriptures," *American Baptist Magazine and Missionary Intelligencer* 2 (September 1820):389.

7. "Figurative Language of the Bible," *American Baptist Magazine* 2 (November 1820):421-423.

8. "For the Regulation of Theological Controversies," *Baptist Chronicle, and Monthly Monitor* 1 (January 1841):107-108.

9. "Inspiration of the Scriptures," *The Christian Review* 9 (March 1844):2.

10. Ibid.

11. Ibid.

12. *Cathcart's Baptist Encyclopedia*, s.v. "Broadus, Rev. Andrew." Note the variant spelling of Broaddus. The spelling adopted here is that of the biographer, J. B. Jeter.

13. J. B. Jeter, *The Sermons and Other Writings of the Rev. Andrew Broaddus, with a Memoir of His Life*, ed. A. Broaddus (New York: Lewis Colby, 1852), p. 150.

14. Ibid.

15. "The Importance of Studying the Scriptures," *American Baptist Magazine and Missionary Intelligencer* 2 (September 1820):389-392.

16. Lumpkin, *Baptist Confessions*, p. 358.

17. *Minutes of the Cumberland Baptist Association, Begun and held at Piney Meeting-House, Hickman County, on Saturday preceding third Lord's Day in September 1816, and days following* (Franklin, Tennessee: Printed by I. N. Henry, 1816), pp. 9-11.

18. Lumpkin, *Baptist Confessions*, p.362.

19. Robert Hall, "The Work of the Holy Spirit," *The Christian Watchman* (January 21, 1842), p. 9.

20. "The Deity of the Spirit," *The Biblical Recorder* 9 (March 30, 1844):1.

21. James Petigru Boyce, *Abstract of Systematic Theology*, rev. F. H. Kerfoot (Philadelphia: American Publications Society, 1899), pp. 130-136.

22. *Minutes of the Cumberland Baptist Association*, p. 12.

23. "The Baptism of the Holy Ghost," *American Baptist Magazine* 2 (November 1819):197-201.

24. Ibid., p. 198.

25. Wood Furman, *A History of the Charleston Association of Baptist Churches in the State of South Carolina; with an Appendix Containing the Principal Circular Letters to the Churches*, (Charleston, South Carolina: J. Hoff, 1811), pp. 6-7.

26. David Benedict, *Fifty Years Among the Baptists*, (Glen Rose, Texas: Newman and Collings, [1913]), p. 109.

27. W. T. Brantly, *Trinitarian Rationale: A Sermon, Delivered in the Baptist Church, Augusta, Georgia, on the Eighth of February, 1824* (Augusta, Georgia: Printed at the Chronicle and Advertiser office, 1824).

28. Joseph A. Warne, "Human Depravity Considered," *Tracts of the Baptist's General Tract Society* (Philadelphia: The Baptist General Tract Society, n.d.), p. 158.

29. Ibid.

30. Alvah Hovey, *Manual of Systematic Theology and Christian Ethics* (Boston: Henry A. Young and Company, 1877), p. 259.

31. See below, "Sufficiency versus Efficiency in the Death of Christ."

32. "From Chalmers' Discourses. Prudence in the Defense of Important Doctrines," *Columbian Star* 1 (March 30, 1822):4.

33. Ibid.

34. "Atonement for Sinner is Effected by the Intercession of Christ, With His Own Blood, in Heaven," *Christian Review* 1 (September 1836):346, footnote.

35. W. T. Brantly, "The Troubled Conscience, and the Peace-Speaking Blood of Christ," *The Tracts of the Baptists General Tract Society*, 7 vols. (Philadelphia: The Baptist Tract Society, n.d.) 7:257.

36. Brantly, *Themes for Meditation, Enlarged in Several Sermons, Doctrinal and Practical* (Philadelphia: C. Sherman and Co., Printers, 1837), p. 56.

37. Ibid.

38. Ibid., p. 52.

39. Ibid., p. 59.

40. "Difficult Subjects," *American Baptist Magazine* 8 (November 1828):332-339.

41. N. M. Crawford, *Christian Paradoxes* (Nashville: South-Western Publishing House, 1858), p. 184.

42. Ibid., p. 47.

43. Benedict, *Fifty Years*, p. 103.

44. W. W. Barnes, "The Development of a Denomination Consciousness Among American Baptists," *Southwestern Journal of Theology* 2 (October 1918):70.

45. George Washington Pascal tells how this transformation took place. He points out that the old group would be disbanded and a new one organized. The number in the group usually would be small. In one instance, only twelve existed out of a previous membership of more than two hundred. *History of North Carolina Baptists*, 2 vols. (Raleigh, North Carolina: The General Board of the North Carolina Baptist State Convention, 1930) 1:211-214.

46. Lumpkin, *Baptist Confessions*, p. 359.

47. Ibid., p. 363.

48. Benedict, *Fifty Years*, p. 50.

49. *The Baptist Chronicle, and Georgetown Literary Register* 1 (June 1830):86.

50. Alexander Campbell, *The Millennial Harbinger* 1 (August 2, 1830):54.

51. Ibid., p. 355.

52. Ibid.

53. Ibid., p. 357.

54. *The Columbian Star* 3 (October 9, 1824):461.

55. J. B. Jeter, *The Sermons and Other Writings of the Rev. Andrew Broaddus, with a Memoir of His Life*, Edited by A. Broaddus (New York: Lewis Colby, 1852), p. 23.

56. W. T. Brantly, "Alexander Campbell and Francis Wright, & Co.," *The Columbian Star, and Christian Index* 1 (October 3, 1829):215.

57. George R. Jewel, "Historic Old Kentucky Papers Revive Interest in Editor W. C. Buck," *Western Recorder* (February 19, 1931), pp. 4-5.

58. Baker, *The Southern Baptist Convention*, p. 150.

59. Baron Stow, "Sketch of Andrew Fuller," *The Columbian Star* 5 (December 23, 1826):204.

60. Francis Wayland, *Notes on the Principles and Practices of Baptist Churches* (New York: Sheldon, Blakeman and Co., 1857), p. 18.

61. J. B. Jeter, *Baptist Principles Reset, Consisting of Articles on Distinctive Baptist Principles*, new enl. ed. (Richmond, Virginia: The Religious Herald Co., 1902), pp. 12-13.

62. J. M. Pendleton, "The Atonement of Christ," *Southern Baptist Review and Eclectic* 2 (January-February 1856):46.

63. Boyce, *Abstract*, p. 317.

64. Andrew Fuller, *The Atonement of Christ, and the Justification of the Sinner*, ed. Joseph Belcher (New York: American Tract Society, n.d.), p. 126.

65. Ibid., p. 202.

66. Ibid., p. 68.

67. Ibid., p. 139.

68. Ibid., p. 132.

69. Ibid., p. 121.

70. Ibid., p. 71.

71. W. T. Brantly, Sr., "Gill and Fuller," *The Columbian Star and Christian Index* 2 (January 16, 1830):45.

72. Thomas J. Nettles, *By His Grace and for His Glory: A Historical, Theological, and Practical Study of the Doctrines of Grace in Baptist Life* (Grand Rapids: Baker Book House, 1986), p. 111.

73. Ibid., p. 123.

74. Brantly, "The Troubled Conscience," p. 258.

75. Ibid., p. 259.

76. Brantly, "The Doctrines of Grace," *The Columbian Star, and Christian Index* 1 (August 8, 1829):91.

77. Brantly, "The Troubled Conscience," p. 250.

78. Ibid., p. 259.

79. *Minutes of the Cumberland Baptist Association 1816*, p. 13.

80. Nettles, *By His Grace*, pp. 166-168.

81. *The Columbian Star, and Christian Index* 2 (May 22, 1830):332.

82. Jesse Mercer, "Mercer's Letters to White on the Atonement, Letter IX," *The Columbian Star, and Christian Index* 3 (November 13, 1830):307-309.

83. C. D. Mallary, *Memoirs of Elder Jesse Mercer* (New York: Lewis Colby, 1844), p. 290.

84. Jeter, *The Sermons and Other Writings*, p. 109.

85. Ibid., p. 107.

86. Ibid.

87. J. J. Burnett, *Sketches of Tennessee's Pioneer Baptist Preachers, Being, Incidentally, a History of Baptist Beginnings in the Several Associations in the State Containing, Particularly, Character and Life Sketches of the Standard-Bearers and Leaders of Our People*, (Nashville: Marshall and Bruce Company, 1913), p. 380.

88. Ibid., p. 381.

89. Ibid., p. 382.

90. Hosea Holcombe, *A History of the Rise and Progress of the Baptists in Alabama: With a Miniature History of the Denomination from the apostolic age Down to the Present Time, Interspersed with anecdotes original and selected, and concluded with an Address to the Baptists of Alabama* (Philadelphia: King and Baird, Printers, 1840), p. 51.

CHAPTER 4

BAPTIST CHURCH SUCCESSIONISM

The years between 1800 and 1845 witnessed momentous events for Baptists and other Christians as well. For Baptists committed to missions, missionary outreach fostered an antimissionary reaction which threatened to stultify the new mood. Antimasonry feelings affected some churches. Debates over the meaning and method of baptism honed Baptist perceptions of themselves as they confronted Campbellites and pedobaptists.

Baptists came of age as a vital force on the religious scene as some of their writers struggled to legitimize their origins to themselves and others. Believing themselves to be the possessors of New Testament truth and order, they searched for evidence that they were the historical embodiment of the New Testament church. Baptist church successionism was born. The interaction of their doctrine of the church with beliefs about baptism and the Lord's Supper paved the way for Landmarkism in the second half of the century.

Beliefs about the endtime contributed to Baptist evangelistic zeal. Millennialism embedded itself in their doctrine. J. N. Darby and the Plymouth Brethren in England would indirectly influence the beliefs of rank and file Southern Baptists with the then novel doctrine of a secret, pretribulation rapture of the church, a teaching later popularized by C. I. Scofield in the edition of the Bible by that name. The first five decades of the nineteenth century were crucial.

BAPTIST ECUMENISM

Emphasis on the local church prevailed in Baptist thought by the 1830s. The confession adopted in 1816 by the Sandy Creek Association has possibly an oblique reference to the invisible church when it calls Jesus Christ the head of the church. However, it had already defined the local church in terms of personal fellowship and an organization capable of exercising discipline.[1]

Seventeen years later, the New Hampshire Confession of Faith omitted any reference to the universal dimension; it defined the church solely as a local assembly.[2] When J. Newton Brown placed the New Hampshire Confession in *The Baptist Church Manual*, when J. M. Pendleton put it in his *Church Manual* and Edward T. Hiscox incorporated it into his *New Directory*,[3] the doctrine of the local church was given almost exclusive coverage among Baptists.

Just one year after the Baptist Convention of New Hampshire formally adopted its confession in 1833, Baptists in the Kehukee Association of North Carolina also formally defined the church as local:

> A church of Christ is a congregation of men and women, publicly professing faith in Christ Jesus, and being regularly baptized by immersion, who have covenanted together, given themselves up to one another in the Lord, to be governed by his word, and to be guided by a regular and prayer discipline, agreeably to the Holy Scriptures.[4]

Thus, Baptists from New Hampshire to North Carolina held a common conviction about the primacy of the local church.

Probably no one was aware of it at the time, but Regular Baptists in the South had reached a turning point in their doctrine of the church. Would the denomination develop in a non-sectarian, cosmopolitan, ecumenical direction, or would it move toward a provincial, narrowly-based fellowship? It followed the latter, although the ingredients for the former existed at the time of the Second Great Awakening. Beginning in 1800, when Baptist churches experienced unprecedented numerical growth, a mood of excitement, expectancy, and optimism pervaded many congregations. Missionary fervor and evangelistic zeal bloomed into a formidable expansion of churches and missionary enterprises. Some Baptist visionaries, as did concerned leaders in other denominations, investigated the possibility of a spiritual union of all denominations. As early as 1794, the Charleston Association recommended that a General Concert of Prayer to be held on the first Tuesday of January, April, July, and October of each year. The object was to "unite with a number of good men of different denominations, at home and abroad" to pray for a general revival of all Christians, for the evangelization of the heathen, and for the conversion of the Jews to Christianity.[5] The recommendation was renewed from year to year.

A more ambitious enterprise was attempted in Georgia in 1802. On May 2 of that year, a group of Baptist leaders composed of both laymen and ministers met at Powelton. The subject of union among all Christians was proposed for discussion by none other than Jesse Mercer. The proposal was received enthusiastically. Henry Holcombe, who had recently arrived from Savannah, moved that a committee be appointed "to concert a plan of promoting union, and communion" among all Christians.[6] Mercer, Holcombe, and Joseph Baker subsequently comprised the committee. After discussing the issue, the committee decided that Georgia Baptists were too disorganized "to concentrate their powers for any particular purpose." As an alternative, the committee recommended that each association appoint three representatives to meet annually in a central location with "individuals, and societies, of other denominations." The committee proposed to strengthen the bonds of a general union "until all who breathe the spirit, and bear the image of the meek and affectionate JESUS, shall enforce a strict discipline, and sit together at his table."

The desire among Baptists who sought to unite Christendom apparently was widespread. Articles on the subject appeared with increasing frequency. One writer lamented the fact that divisions existed among the denominations. He discussed why differences occurred: error, party spirit, personal interest, prejudice of education, and the influence of authority. He then proposed that all such considerations be relinquished and that Christians should "resort to that revered Volume."[7] He climaxed his essay with a proposal that one more society be formed, a "society for the promotion of union among all Christians." A branch should be formed in every country.

The writer quoted above incorporated one proposition that ecumenical Baptists insisted upon as a ground of union, i.e., union must be based upon truth as revealed in the Bible. This requirement evolved into a spirit of exclusiveness that helped turn segments of the Baptists toward a strong denominationalism. As one man expressed the idea in 1820, "Let prejudice be asleep, let the heart be candidly open to conviction, and the Bible would soon dispel the discordant errors and dangerous delusions of a benighted world, and introduce the predicted day when the church shall be one in sentiment, affection and practice."[8] Another wrote, "The edifice of union can be built on the basis of truth alone. No compromises, no half-way covenants, no sacrifices to expediency, can produce permanent concord."[9] The insistence that transdenominational union must be founded on truth, not compromise, guaranteed that Baptist ecumenicists would have no impact in forthcoming ecumenical discussions because truth meant truth as Baptists saw it. By the time the World Evangelical Alliance was organized in 1846 in London, Baptist zeal for union had been supplanted by other interests. Instead of moving toward cooperation with other denominations, they turned inwardly to denominational expansion as Baptist church succession killed any remaining vestiges of the Baptist ecumenical spirit.

BAPTIST SUCCESSIONISM

Baptist apologists at the beginning of the nineteenth century encountered a vexing problem in their debates with members of other denominations, namely, how to gain credibility for a denomination which its accusers said was formed in the seventeenth century. How could such people lay claim to being the New Testament church founded by Christ and his apostles?

Baptist historians took up the challenge, developing four basic theories to explain their origins.[10] (1) Some believed that Baptists have existed from the time of John the Baptist and his immersion of Jesus in the Jordan River. Therefore, Baptist churches have existed since the New Testament, but they have been known by the name Baptist since the seventeenth century. (2) Other historians held to a theory of succession of Baptist principles. That is, different groups from the time of Christ have adhered to distinctive Baptist principles, although not known by the Baptist name. (3) In the third explanation, Baptists are spiritually kin to the Anabaptist groups in Europe, which originated in the sixteenth century, but a direct connection between Baptists and Anabaptists is neither demonstrable nor desirable. (4) The fourth explanation located the origin of the Baptists among the Puritan-Separatist movement around London in the early seventeenth century. Variations of these four occur. For example, some Baptists hold to both (4) and (2) or (3). They say the name Baptist was first used in the early seventeenth century to describe a particular group but that Baptist principles have been held by various groups throughout the Christian era. Baptists are thus "spiritually kin" to those groups.

When and where Baptist churches arose historically deals with only part of the problem. The other part relates to the *manner* of succession of authority. Christians who hold to the doctrine of *apostolic succession*, as taught by Roman Catholics, Anglicans, Greek Orthodox, and others, see ecclesiastical authority stemming from an unbroken line of ordained clergy from Peter and the apostles to the present. Probably all Baptists reject this doctrine, but some favor *baptismal succession*, in which baptism by immersion by immersed administrators can be traced from Jesus and the apostles to the present. Others aver that the authority and validity of the local church comes from an unbroken line of churches extending from the Jerusalem church to the present. The Landmark Baptists preached both *baptismal* and *church* succession.

The conviction that true churches have always existed independently of Roman Catholicism arose early among English and American Baptists. The Philadelphia Confession recognized that all churches are subject to error and that some have degenerated so as to become synagogues of Satan. Nevertheless, Christ always has had, and continues to have a true Kingdom in this world.[11]

Baptists had an early champion in Thomas Crosby, an English Baptist historian who produced a four-volume work *The History of the English Baptists*, written between 1738 and 1740. Crosby traced Baptist principles all the way back to John the Baptist.

Baptist successionism in some form gained acceptance early among a segment of Baptists in the United States. Alexander Campbell published synopses of various denominations in 1830. Of the Baptists he wrote, "They claim an immediate descent from the Apostles, and assert that the constitution of their churches is derived immediately from Jesus Christ. Others affirm that they had their origin at a much later day, even as late as the 16th century."[12] Campbell did not identify "others," but some sixty-five years before the "Whitsitt Controversy" would shake the convention, Campbell averred that some people believed Baptists arose in the sixteenth century.

Baptist successionism had powerful adherents among Baptists in the South. No less a personage than Jesse Mercer published a circular letter in 1811 attempting to identify the true apostolic church. He penned the article in response to a furor stirred up by the question of whether or not pedobaptist denominations were "ORDERLY AND VALID."[13] His method of disproving the validity of the pedobaptists was to set forth the identifying characteristics of the true apostolic church, show that pedobaptists failed to meet the criteria, and then conclude that Baptist churches do. He gave four main theses. The first is that the "APOSTOLIC CHURCH *continued through all ages to the end of the world*, is the *only* TRUE GOSPEL CHURCH." Second, Christ is the only head and true source of authority for that church. Third, in the true apostolic church, all ministers are servants in the church, are equal, and have no power to "lord *it over the heritage of their Lord*." Fourth, "all things are to be done in FAITH, *according to the gospel pattern*."[14] Having established his criteria, he then demonstrated that pedobaptists, especially of the Roman Catholic variety, significantly fell short of the biblical pattern. It bothered him not that the succession could not be proved:

> But if it be said that the apostolic succession cannot be ascertained, and then [sic] it is proper to act without it; we say, that the loss of the succession can never prove it futile, nor justify anyone out of it.—The Pedobaptists, by their own histories, admit they are not of it; *but we do not*, and shall think ourselves entitled to the claim, until the reverse be clearly shown.[15]

If Baptists, he felt, could not demonstrate succession, they at least did not derive their authority "from the MOTHER OF HARLOTS," an allusion to Roman Catholicism common to Mercer's time.[16]

Baptist successionists of succeeding decades agreed with the sentiments of Mercer. Robert B. C. Howell, noted opponent of J. R. Graves and Landmarkism, preceded Graves in believing that Baptist churches existed from the time of Christ. This fact stands out in a statement by Howell, written when Graves was only seventeen years old. He wrote in 1837:

> In my former letters to you [the readers], I have shown that the true orthodox Baptist church has ever been, from the days of the Apostles until now, a missionary body; that the church was formed upon this principle by her great head, Jesus Christ; and that her whole government is based upon her character with relation to this subject.[17]

Just three years after Howell's letter, Hosea Holcombe published his history of the Baptists of Alabama. In it, he enunciated his ideas of Baptist history which may be called "spiritual kinship." By this term is meant that Baptist principles have been held by various groups beginning with the first Christians. In the words of Holcombe:

> It is concluded, from the details here given, that the first Christians were Baptists; that the baptism of infants commenced about the fourth century; that persons professing the peculiarities of the Baptists were found in different parts of the world; and that throughout all the changes which attended the progress of years, the reign of error, the usurpation of Antichrist, and the dominion of English episcopacy, they were marked by each dominant party in the ancient and later ages, as objects of persecution; their Baptist sentiments forming one of the charges brought against them.[18]

Holcombe did not quite endorse direct succession of the various groups. Instead, he believed that individuals "who possessed Baptist sentiments" were sometimes "mixed with the general body of Christians, and scattered over a wide surface to whom we assign the designation by which we are distinguished."[19] He admitted that those individuals did not necessarily maintain sentiments exactly the same as those now held by Baptists. The point of similarity was their "line of conduct with reference to baptism."[20]

Andrew Broaddus joined those who sought to prove the antiquity of the Baptists. He noted that Tertullian questioned infant baptism in the third century. Broaddus then asked rhetorically:

> And then, for the residue of the time, to fill up this period of a thousand years, where, let me ask, were the Anti-Pedobaptists going under different names, of whom Mosheim says, that "the true origin of that sect *is hid in the remote depths of antiquity*, and, of consequence, difficult to be ascertained," and Mosheim, be it observed, is far from being partial to the Baptists.[21]

The editors of the *Baptist Banner, and Western Pioneer* took up the cause of succession about 1840. Edited at one time or another by William C. Buck, W. C. Crane, R. B. C. Howell, J. M. Peck, and A. R. Brinkley, the periodical represented some of the most influential Baptists in the South. Crane wrote an article in 1841 defending the apostolic origin of the Baptists. He argued:

> We are in fact the *Apostolic Church*, what makes a church *the church*, but the fact that it embraces and defends, more of the doctrines and practices of primitive Christianity than another. This we claim—our government is the true scriptural mode, our baptism is the only proper mode, our worship is

more like the simplicity of apostolic days, than the pompous displays of Episcopacy, and other kindred branches of Zion."[22]

Two weeks later, another article appeared in the same publication which purported to be a quotation from "an Account of the Origin of the Dutch Baptists," by Dr. Ypeis and Rev. J. J. Dermont. The article identified Baptists with the ancient Waldenses, Anabaptists, and Mennonites and concluded that Baptists may be considered the only Christian group which has existed from the days of the apostles.[23]

A series of articles was printed in the *Baptist Banner, and Western Pioneer* the following year. They were written by G. H. Orchard, an advocate of what Robert G. Torbet called the apostolic succession of Baptist churches.[24] Orchard denied that Baptists originated with the Munster Anabaptists of the sixteenth century. Using the historian Mosheim and others as authorities, he traced the succession through such diverse groups as the Euchites, Novations, and Donatists.[25] In a subsequent article, he sought to show that true believers existed in England long before the seventeenth century.[26] Manifestly, the theory that Baptist churches have always existed—albeit under different names—did not originate with James R. Graves the founder of Landmarkism. He was its popularizer. As one of the editors of *The Baptist*, he had a forum from which to spread his ideas. J. J. Burnett wrote that "no man in the South was more widely known than its editor, or had a greater influence upon the denomination."[27] Graves would utilize the paper, which he renamed *The Tennessee Baptist* in 1847, to become one of the most vocal and able advocates of Baptist church succession.

THE SUPPER, FOR CHURCHES ONLY

Before Landmarkism helped restrict the observance of the Lord's Supper exclusively to the local church, some associations observed it at annual meetings. To illustrate, a small altercation developed in 1808 over the effort of some brethren to have the associational sermon and business session on Saturday in order to save time. The association rejected the move on the grounds that all associational exercises on Saturday should be preparatory to the observance of the Supper on Sunday. They should allow nothing which would divert the mind "from the great object which then claims its attention."[28]

Groups other than churches and associations assumed the legitimacy of an extra-church observance of the Supper. The Mississippi Baptist Association voted in 1820 to organize a "union, or Minister's meeting, on every fifth Sunday in the year; that the ordinance of the Lord's Supper be observed at these meetings."[29] Other associations hotly contested such actions as they tried to combat the creeping influence of Campbellism. When the Boone's Creek Association was being organized in Kentucky, three ministers who "were strong advocates of the doctrine of Elder [Alexander] Campbell, yet affiliating with Baptist churches and associations," proposed that a particular clause be inserted in the constitution which provided that the Lord's Supper be observed on the second day of the association. The association refused to insert the clause although it did observe the Supper that one time. According to S. J. Conkwright, that is the only recorded instance of the association's observance of the ordinance.[30]

Observance of the Supper by non-church assemblies was the exception rather than the rule. Baptists of that era came to believe that the Supper was given as a church, not a denominational, ordinance. This significance is implied in an official action by one of the churches in the Boone's Creek Association, the Boone's Creek Church. Deacon Squire Boone, a nephew of Daniel Boone, entertained a motion in 1814 to determine whether "the deacons should present the elements of the Lord's Supper to persons not in union with us. The church unanimously answered in the negative."[31]

Many churches, if not almost all, eventually adopted closed communion. In Alabama, the Antioch Baptist Church in Lafayette wrote into its articles of faith, "We believe no minister have [sic] a right to the administration of the ordinances only such as are regularly called and come under the imputation of hands by the Presbytery, and where administering the ordinances in full fellowship in the church where he belongs."[32] Closed communion, communion restricted to local members or else members of "like faith and order" of the church performing the rite, was widely practiced. Movements in the direction of associational observances were doomed from the start.

If the local church discouraged observance of the Supper beyond the local church, inter-denominational participation was unthinkable. Resolutions against it were passed by associations across the spectrum of Baptist life. The Charleston Association expressed its opposition as early as 1802. In answer to the question, "Is it consistent with Gospel order for the Baptist churches to commune with pedobaptists who appear to be truly pious?" the association gave a negative reply. The argument followed three general lines. Communing with pedobaptists would amount either to acknowledging the validity of infant baptism, or else to affirming the propriety of admitting unbaptized persons to the Lord's Supper. Also, the church would be assuming the power to alter the order that Christ established for the churches. The minutes concluded, "These are obstacles in our way to such communion, which we have not been able hitherto to surmount."[33] That same year, Richard Furman attended a camp meeting. When the Presbyterians and Methodists held a communion service, he said the Baptists abstained from participating, because of their beliefs about immersion and the Supper.[34]

A decade and a half later, the Red River Baptist Association in Tennessee opposed inter-denominational communion. A person who is a Baptist, they declared, is bound by the laws of Christ. When the unsaved make a public profession of faith in Christ and follow him in immersion, certain implications about the baptism of infants follow. The associations asserted:

He makes to believe that infant baptism is a vain and useless tradition, and one of the props and pillars of Anti-Christ's kingdom, and consequently, that all christians who believe in and practice it, are in an unbaptized state; that they are living in error, and daily neglect of a pointed command of our Lord Christ.[35]

For a Baptist to commune with such persons would "savor more of hypocrisy than Christian charity."[36] Other associations, such as the Hudson River Baptist Association, also favored restricted communion.[37] Even the prestigious periodical *The American Baptist Magazine and Missionary Intelligencer* ridiculed those who wanted to do "away with doctrine, creeds, and sentiments" in favor of "charity, fellowship, and union." The author of the article then launched into a defense of "Particular communion," as he called it. The apostles, he said, followed the order of winning and then baptizing. Also, to admit unbaptized persons to the Supper undervalues baptism, encourages a neglect of gospel institutions, and blurs the distinction between the church and the world. Since the observance of the Supper is a command of Christ and its requisites are established by him, Christians may not arbitrarily dispense with either out of regard for the esteem of other Christians.[38] The critical point focused on baptism.

ALIEN IMMERSION AND THE WATERY WAR

Baptist expositors in the early nineteenth century, as did their forebears, saw the necessary connections between baptism and the Supper. They likewise recognized the role that a proper administrator plays in the ordinance of baptism. They debated whether baptism administered by a non-immersed administrator qualified as biblical baptism. R. B. Semple thought so, as did J. B. Jeter (1802-1880). Jeter remembered an event occurring in the 1824 meeting of the Portsmouth Association, in which he tried to defend alien immersion and lost:

> Of the proceedings of the Association I recollect nothing, except a discussion of the validity of Pedobaptist immersions. In this conflict I fleshed my youthful sword, and was ingloriously defeated. I had associated with Semple, A. Broaddus and others among the fathers, who maintained the validity of such baptisms, and had adopted their views. . . . I remember but a single illustration of Elder Piondexter. "Roundness," he said, "is essential to a bullet; beat it flat, and it will cease to be a bullet. So certain things—an authorized administrator among them—are essential to baptism, and without these things it is not baptism." I made, so far as I can recollect, no attempt to reply. The Association decided by an overwhelming vote that Pedobaptist immersions are not valid baptisms. I was defeated, but not convinced.[39]

Others agreed with Jeter. A correspondent wrote to the editor of *The Columbian Star* attempting to refute Alexander Campbell's contention that baptism demands a proper administrator.[40] He noted that Roger Williams and others were not immersed by a proper administrator. Sincerity of the candidate was emphasized.

The supporters of alien immersion defended it on two premises. First, they declared baptism to be a gospel, not a church, ordinance. The right to baptize, therefore, arose out of the Great Commission and not out of church polity. Andrew Broaddus argued, "Baptism is a gospel ordinance, but not a church ordinance; it would seem, therefore, that a person, as a subject, or a possessor of the gospel faith, may, on that ground, claim the privilege of baptism."[41] Second, they contended that the theory that baptism required a proper administrator was nullified on the practical grounds that any break in the succession from apostolic times would make all subsequent baptisms null and void. Richard Fuller, writing when Landmarkism was at its zenith, addressed that question when a Baptist minister, who had recently married a Methodist woman, asked whether her immersion was valid even though performed by a Methodist minister who had been sprinkled. Fuller believed that her baptism was "informal," but not "null and void." He set forth his reasoning:

> Now there is one argument which, of itself, goes far to settle this question. It is that if no baptism be valid without an administrator, whose baptism is regular, then there can be no valid baptism. The validity of baptism would depend on an unbroken succession of regularly baptized administrators from the days of the Apostles; and if there be a defect in this chain, that defect violates all the subsequent baptisms. The oft exposed fiction of the Apostolic succession is ridiculous enough, but the baptistical succession is even more puerile.[42]

The controversy seethed. The Broad-River Baptist Association in South Carolina refused to accept members from the Seventh Day Baptists unless they were rebaptized,[43] stressing qualifications for administering baptism. The local association of the Old Waterlick Church in Shenandoah County, Virginia, recorded its understanding of scripturally valid baptism. They gave three essential elements. The candidate must be a professed believer; the administrator must be a member in good standing in a local Baptist church as well as one who had been regularly ordained according to the faith and practice of the church; and the subject must be immersed in water in the name of the Father, the Son, and of the Holy Spirit.[44] A consensus of opinion was gathering.

Disputes with other denominations over the mode of baptism vitally influenced the development of the Baptist doctrine of baptism. David Benedict called it "a water war, in which multitudes on both sides engaged for a long course of years."[45] Benedict credited Daniel Merrill of Maine with precipitating the conflict. Merrill had been a Congregationalist but gradually became convinced of the Baptist cause. In a letter published in 1805, Merrill described the agony of his own bosom as he wrestled over his decision.[46] The eventual association of Merrill and most of his congregation with the Baptists brought the issue into the open. Congregational churches in New York[47] and Massachusetts[48] also experienced tensions created by mixed communion. As the Baptists formed their own churches, the acrimony broke into the open.

For the next several years, the argument raged over the meaning of the Greek word *baptizein*. To illustrate, when a medical dictionary was published in 1814, the editors of the *Massachusetts Baptist Missionary Magazine* were quick to note that the first article supported the definition of *baptize*, "to plunge."[49] Word studies of the Greek word appeared in various periodicals. By 1836, at least one Baptist writer thought the war had been won. In language that showed more wishful thinking than historical insight he declared, "The ablest advocates of infant baptism admit that the scriptures do not teach it, either by direct precept or by plain example; and no responsible scholar would now venture to deny, that the leading and most obvious meaning of the words employed in the New Testament to indicate baptism, is immersion."[50]

The mode of baptism was not the only point which separated Baptists from other evangelical groups. The practice of infant baptism received its fair share of attention. Pedobaptists, particularly Presbyterians in the Charles Hodge tradition, strongly emphasized covenant theology. Baptists just as strongly attacked it. As discussed previously, Isaac Backus saw the implications of covenant theology for church membership and rejected it in his day. Men like W. T. Brantly and Richard Fuller were equally outspoken nearly a century later. Brantly wrote a tract whose very title stated his position: "The Covenant of Circumcision, no Just Plea for Infant Baptism."[51] Fuller also rejected the baptismal implications of the Abrahamic Covenant. Speaking of that covenant he grumbled, "Now I ask any candid reader, what has this to do with baptism? Had not men a system to defend, and were not people's minds confounded with a jargon about covenant mercies, no one could receive so many errors as are united in this argument."[52] Covenant theology became a prime feature of the theology of James P. Boyce, who founded Southern Seminary about ten years later, but even Boyce's position and prestige were insufficient to give covenant theology a secure niche in the thought of his denomination. Covenant theology among Southern Baptists virtually succumbed with Boyce.

Footwashing, as an ordinance, began dropping from favor among Baptists in the South. A query was sent to the Sandy Creek Association in 1807, "Is washing of feet an ordinance of God, to continue in his church until Christ's second coming?" The association answered, "We think it is."[53] George W. Purefoy, who wrote a history of the association to commemorate its centennial in 1858, disagreed. By that time, he said, very few Baptists believed the rite to be a church ordinance. Instead, it was to be observed by Christians only in their *social* intercourse.⁵⁴ R. D. Owen agreed in sentiment in 1842 in an article published in the *Baptist Banner, and Western Pioneer*.⁵⁵

Alabama Baptists were not so convinced. Hosea Holcombe reported that many churches there practiced footwashing in 1840, "particularly the New Test party."⁵⁶ The minutes of the Macedonia Baptist Church, organized in 1844 in Chilton County, Alabama, show that footwashing was a part of the church's Abstract of Principles: "Rule 10th—We believe that as our Lord and Master washed his disciples feet we also ought to wash one another's feet." The last recorded instance of footwashing at Macedonia was in the minutes for May, 1915.

LOOKING FOR THE MILLENNIUM

At the time of the Watery Wars between Baptists and their pedobaptist adversaries, other evangelicals delved into the mysteries of the second coming of Jesus Christ. J. N. Darby and the Plymouth Brethren in England focused their interest on prophecy and began propagating a form of premillennialism now called dispensationalism. Dispensationalists divide the whole of mankind's history into eras or dispensations in which they say God tests the human race in reference to a particular mode of conduct, such as innocence, conscience, or human government. Integral to the system is the belief in a secret coming of Christ, the Rapture, at the beginning of seven years of tribulation. During the tribulation, the church, already resurrected, receives its rewards and celebrates the Marriage Supper of the Lamb as the Bride of Christ. At the same time, the nation of Israel on Earth will accept Christ as the Messiah and will be His witnesses prior to the Second Coming. At an event dispensationalists call the Revelation, Christ will come triumphantly and visibly with his saints, judge the nations, and set up his millennial reign. All dispensationalists therefore, are premillennialists, but not all premillennialists are dispensationalists. At the time Darby was developing his system in England, Baptists in the South were mainly postmillennialists and premillennialists, but amillennialism gained a following.

The *Analytical Repository*, the first Baptist newspaper in Georgia and one of the first in the United States,⁵⁷ devoted part of volume one to a study of prophecy which it defined as "an anticipated history of interesting facts from the *beginning* to the *end* of time."⁵⁸ The method of interpreting the Book of Revelation was approximately that of Backus. The author wrote, "It contains the prophetic history of all the prominent events in which the church was to be concerned from her rise to her confirmation in glory."⁵⁹ Involved in that history were Mohammed, "the great sensual apostate"; the Pope, "the great idolatrous apostate"; and the "powers of Atheism, established by *revolutionary France*."⁶⁰ All of these were warring against the true church. The author saw a correlation between church history and the prophecies of the Revelation. For example, the seals show the church to the end of the fourth century; the last trumpet has been sounding since the commencement of the French Revolution. The author used premillennial language when he concluded that the world will probably "endure for 7000 years; namely 6000 before the first resurrection and second coming of CHRIST, and the remaining 1000 years during his reign upon earth; and that at the end of that period the second resurrection and end of the world were to succeed."[61] Hosea Holcombe was editor of the *Analytical Repository* at the time.

A spirit of revival and optimism characterized the first quarter of the 1800s. Missionary societies were formed; publications were circulated to encourage evangelistic fervor. The Savannah Baptist Society for Foreign Missions, of which William B. Johnson was president and William T. Brantly was corresponding secretary, sent out an appeal to surrounding states and pointed to prophetic fulfillment as an incentive to consecration. The appeal, which hints at their millennial propensities, said in part:

> Wars and rumors of wars, the overturning of the nations, the rapidly increasing destruction of the man of sin, and the growing spread of divine truth, events, predicted by the prophets, and represented by them as prelusive [prelude] to the general diffusion of the Gospel, clearly show that the universal triumph of Christ, the King of Zion, is not far distant.[62]

A year later, in 1815, Baptists in Mississippi appended a circular letter to the minutes of their annual meeting, a custom of the day. The letter noted that Baptists had long been praying for the destruction of Anti-Christ, for the fullness of the Gentiles, for the calling in of the Jews, and for the universal spread of the Gospel. Using apocalyptic imagery, the letter continued:

> Our God is pouring out the vials of his wrath and shaking terribly the nations of the earth:—while many are purified and made white; many are running to and fro, and knowledge is increasing. We have reason to believe that a glorious change is about to take place, in the moral and political world. For the kingdoms of this world, must become the kingdoms of our Lord and of his Christ.[63]

The same optimistic missionary optimism was included in the 1819 address of the Baptist Board of Foreign Missions for the United States. Concerning the work of the board, the report stated, "They are happy in the reflection that the events of another year serve to confirm the expectation and increase the joy of thousands who are *waiting for the consolation* of the latter day, and who, from the signs of the times, have concluded that the promised period cannot be distant."[64] The millennial overtones are strong.

Postmillennialism took firm hold among Baptists in Mississippi. The Mississippi Baptist Association, in its circular letter for 1823, began with terminology almost identical with that of 1815, quoted above. Then a significant statement is made. God "has used, is now using, and will continue to use. . . Bible Societies, Education Societies, Missionary Establishments, and Missionary Labours" to bring about his most holy purpose of judgment and mercy.[65] Premillennialists, by contrast, believe that the millennial reign of Christ will be ushered in by cataclysmic judgment and not by missionary labors.

The editors of magazines used their media to promote their eschatology. An article in the *American Baptist Magazine and Missionary Intelligencer* used the language of postmillennialism when it averred:

> The Bible should be studied, because it is the essential means of ushering in the glory of the latter day. Before the age of millennial peace shall bless a degenerate world, the doctrines of man and devils must be wholly exterminated. This great work must be effected by "the sword of the Spirit, which is the word of God."[66]

The *Christian Watchman* was less sure of the method, but equally emphatic about the outcome, when it proclaimed:

> According to the sure Word of Prophecy, allowing for the variety of interpretations, before the oak which was planted yesterday shall have reached its full maturity, the whole Earth shall have become the Garden of the Lord. The Fullness of the Gentiles, in every sense, is at hand. The earth will soon be full of people, and full of knowledge: the desert is beginning to bloom, and the darkness to disperse; and the minds of men are ripening for, and expectant of, the greatest change which, as yet, has passed over the earth.[67]

Premillennialism has had a more turbulent history among Baptists in the South. As already discussed, Isaac Backus felt constrained to disallow connection with Anabaptist chiliasts. Premillennialism, likewise, twice suffered set-backs in the nineteenth century. The first came with Alexander Campbell in the 1820s. Because of his view of baptismal regeneration, whole congregations left the Baptist ranks. Premillennialism was promoted by Campbell. The very title of his monthly publication, *Millennial Harbinger*, suggested his estimation of millennialism. Throughout the 1830s he printed separate series on the millennium and prophecy. To his credit, he gave space to opposing viewpoints, as for example, a long letter from an avowed postmillennialist in support of that interpretation.[68]

The rise of Campbellism was eventually interpreted as a sign of satanic agency which, along with other heretical groups, presaged the end. Note the following assessment by a contemporary of Campbell:

> The signs of the times are ominous, affording indications that we are to expect some uncommon event. . . . The Devil knowing that his time is short

and that the thousand years of his close confinement is near at hand, is employing all the agency, artful cunning, and devilish hate that his infernal rage and malice can send forth. Atheism, Deism, Unitarianism, Universalism, Campbellism . . . are pouring forth their filth and foam, flooding the land all over, by means of their periodicals and other publications.[69]

Premillennialism soon suffered another setback, this time because of William Miller, a Baptist from New Hampton, New York.[70] Miller predicted that Christ would come in 1843 to establish his millennial reign. Later, the date was changed to October 22, 1844.[71] There was widespread disillusionment among his followers when the predicted event failed to happen.

Not all Baptists could be classified as either postmillennialists or premillennialists. The third major interpretation, amillennialism, gained popularity among those who believe the millennium as taught in the Bible refers to a spiritual reign in the lives of believers. An article in the *Christian Watchman* in 1823 so stated:

The whole spiritual part of the millennium is nothing more than the principles of the Gospel operating with their full force upon the heart and life and character of the Christian, in his personal and social capacity. By many it must be confessed an idea is formed of the Millennium; as a supernatural state in which wonders without number will exist; and in which ordinary means of improvement will, because unnecessary, be superseded. The change in mankind I acknowledge will be great; but only and wholly—in Christians being entirely under the influence of the Gospel.[72]

The *Christian Watchman* took a skeptical attitude toward date-setting. In discussing the "prophetic number 1260 days, 40 and 2 months, time, times, and half time," the author observed "that out of fifty-four who have given their opinions of the commencement and end of the prophetic number, 1260 days, thirty-two have already proved false, and that the whole of the fifty-four disagree."[73]

Baptists of the amillennial persuasion identified the Kingdom of God with the church, although not in the sense that J. R. Graves and the Landmarkers later made that connection. Amillennial Baptists saw the Kingdom of God mainly as a present, spiritual reality rather than as a future socio-political event. Little need was seen for intensive study of eschatological implications. The "visible kingdom" was a phrase used frequently by Baptists in the nineteenth century. In discussing the importance of baptism, Andrew Broaddus wrote that it "is obviously requisite to an admittance into the visible kingdom."[74] As time went on, "visible kingdom" became synonymous with church; kingdom work became church work.

Most of the confessions adopted between 1800 and 1845 incorporated general statements about the fact of Christ's visible return at the end of the world and the reality of heaven and hell. The millennial question was ignored. In the Principles of Faith of the Sandy Creek Association 1816, Article V committed itself to belief in one resurrection, a general judgement, and the eternal state of both the righteous and wicked dead.[75] The *New Hampshire Confession* of 1833 affirmed essentially the same sentiments.[76]

MOLDING THE MISSIONARY SPIRIT

The nineteenth century began with a spirit of revival as the Second Great Awakening shook large numbers of Baptists from their lethargy following the American Revolutionary War. Less than half a century later missionary Baptists split irrevocably as Baptists in the South formed the Southern Baptist Convention in 1845. By that date Southern Baptists counted 9 state conventions, 4,395 churches, and 365,346 members.[77] A more complete description of the causes of the schism is deferred for now.

The rapid increase in membership was not achieved without adversity. In addition to facing the social, economic, and political changes in a newly-formed nation trying to chart its own course, Baptists had to surmount internal opposition and schisms. The issues of freemasonry and slavery were minor sources of internal tensions in the South. David Benedict traveled across the South during this period and reported that "Southern Baptists never had much disputing about masonry, and none about slavery among themselves."[78] Opposition to slavery centered in the North among abolitionists trying to rally the conscience of the nation against slavery. Even James P. Boyce, one of the founders and the first president of the Southern Baptist Theological Seminary, defended slavery as a scriptural institution.

The anti-mission conflict, however, threatened the very roots of missionary endeavors. Walter B. Shurden lists five factors that contributed to the rise of the anti-missions controversy: ministerial jealousy, fear of centralization, financial support of ministers, hyper-Calvinism, and strong personalities who opposed missions, such as John Taylor (1752-1835), Alexander Campbell, and Daniel Parker (1781-1844).[79]

A brief overview of the theology of Parker and Taylor shows the interaction of theology with missions. Parker, uncouth, untrained, and slovenly in dress but effective in debate, opposed missions, theological schools, tract societies, and religious newspapers. His views of predestinarian theology were based upon two-seeds-in-the-spirit theology. Since only the predestined, the seed of God in Adam, would be saved, he believed, it was unscriptural to send missionaries to Satan's children, those of the seed of Satan in Adam. In two books, *Views of the Two Seeds* and *The Second Dose of Doctrine on the Two Seeds*, he expounded on that theme. John Taylor, from Virginia, wrote his *Thoughts on Missions* in opposition to missionary activities. Alexander Campbell and many others joined the anti-mission chorus. Churches split over the issue and whole associations often voted to go one way or the other.

J. J. Burnett accurately portrayed the spirit of the 1820s and 1830s when he wrote:

> Among the biographies in this volume will be found a number of sketches of "Primitive or Old School" preachers; such they designated themselves in their minutes. . . . They, and their sires, had fought for civil and religious liberty, for the rights of the individual, the rights of the common people, and of the local church. They had thus either contracted or inherited a religious *bias* in the direction of individualism and local church independence, or Baptist democracy. They would naturally, therefore, look with suspicion upon ecclesiastical machinery or organization beyond the local church or district associations. . . . Besides, most of these preachers were Hyper-Calvinists, believing that the Lord could and would take care of his own affairs in his own good time. Neither had they learned by experience or observation the wisdom and necessity of cooperation in order to [accomplish] largest service and greatest results in the Lord's work. Little wonder, therefore, that in the presence of a new order of things among Baptists these men first hesitated, then opposed.[80]

Oppose they did. Some of the opposition arose from their utter commitment to individual competency in matters religious. Isaac Backus himself had argued cogently for "liberty of conscience," that no civil power had any right to coerce the human conscience.[81] The same kind of spirit that would defy the Congress of Massachusetts would not allow the establishment of ecclesiastical machinery that could also coerce the conscience. They relinquished ground grudgingly.

Untrained formally, but believing in the right of the individual to interpret the Bible for himself, frontier Baptists were prone to take the Bible literally. Implications drawn from the Scriptures created vexing situations for associational work. Basil Manly, clerk of the Sandy Creek Association, reported difficulty in 1816 in persuading some churches to forward statistics to him. "They had an idea," said Manly, "that God intended [to show] his disapprobation of that by his displeasure against David for numbering the people."[82]

Fortunately for the missionary faction, equally strong personalities considered a strong missionary outreach an imperative for Baptists. The contribution of Luther Rice (1783-1836), Adoniram Judson (1788-1850), William B. Johnson (1782-1862), and others need not be recounted here.

Lesser known preachers also profoundly influenced the missionary impulse of the Baptists. John Taylor, for example, recorded that over a period of fifty years he had "travelled at least one hundred thousand miles, . . . chiefly on the business of preaching."[83] Elijah Rogers in Tennessee was equally committed to the missionary cause. J. J. Burnett could say:

He was a pioneer in missions, and a John the Baptist preparing the way for a missionary movement, even while he was held in fellowship by his anti-mission and anti-effort brethren. While the leaders of the anti-mission school gave their time and energy to discussing "fixing fate, free-will and foreknowledge absolute," Elijah Rogers was one of the first to break the shell of fatalistic belief and declare for missions.[84]

Jeremiah Vardeman in Kentucky, described by his biographer as "a great revivalist," served as pastor of the Lulbegrud church in Kentucky from 1810 until 1817 and preached revivals. Services would begin "at eleven o'clock and after preaching would continue in exhortation, singing and prayer until admonished by the going down of the sun that it was time for dismissal."[85]

PROCLAIMING THE GOSPEL

The content of the sermons varied between two extremes. On the one hand there was the traditional, orthodox preaching. J. B. Jeter preserved an example of its contents. He remembered, "It was eminently controversial. Every preacher was a polemic. Whether his text was doctrinal or practical, historical or poetical, gracious or denunciatory, he could find in it a book on which to suspend his distinctive notions, and a club with which to defend them."[86] On the other hand stood those who spiritualized their texts in which "they would take plain, historical passages of Scripture, and, by fanciful resemblances, draw from them a lessons of which their authors never dreamed."[87] George Purefoy regretted that by 1858 no specimens of the spiritualizing sermons remained, but he attested to the popularity of the preacher who displayed the greatest ingenuity in giving what he conceived to be the spiritual meaning of the text.[88]

The style of delivery by those open-air preachers evolved into a distinctive "heavenly tone" or "holy whine." The "heavenly tone" was described by one hearer in the following way:

> It was made up of assumed intonations of the voice, expressive of great earnestness, and was composed of the cadence of whining, mourning, lamentation and wailing, and was intended to arouse the sympathies of both preacher and auditor. We seldom meet with "the heavenly tone" at this day; except as very imperfectly imitated by some of our colored brethren in their public prayers and exhortations.[89]

J. B. Jeter described Andrew Broaddus as a "polished speaker" who would occasionally "glide into the 'holy tone' with thrilling effect."[90] Jeremiah Vardeman had a "musical" voice that could be heard by an acre or more of people at one time. "His forte was exhortation, and he could emphasize in the most pathetic manner the interjection, Oh! and could paint in living colors the happiness of the redeemed and the torments of the damned. He weighed three hundred pounds and was well proportioned."[91]

The story of Southern Baptist pastors and evangelists is the story of men, but women have also been a vital part of the missionary movement. In addition to their supporting roles as wives and prayer warriors, they actively engaged in the formation of missionary societies. Leon McBeth discussed some of the work begun by women between 1800 and 1845.[92] Mary Webb helped form the Boston Female Society in 1800. Hepzibeth Jenkins Townsend teamed with Richard Furman to found the Wadmalow and Edisto Female Mite Society between 1807 and 1812. Other missionary support groups women formed were the Hyro Female Cent Society in North Carolina, about 1810; the Female Missionary Society in Richmond in 1813; and the Female Missionary Society of Baltimore about 1813. A mite society was also established in Rhode Island by 1809.[93] No number of detractors could stop the surge of missionary enterprises.

SUMMARY

The years from 1800 until 1845 were years of turmoil and serenity, of outreach and opposition, of union and division for the Baptist churches which eventually gave birth to the Southern Baptist Convention. On basic doctrines such as the Trinity and biblical inspiration, they remained unmoved. However, major changes began to be felt.

Calvinism peaked and began to retreat as two of its major tenets came under fire. The doctrine of the atonement took on Arminian overtones in favor of belief in Christ's death as being sufficient for all but efficient only in believers. Second, the doctrine of total depravity suffered assaults at the hands of those who believed that the lost could repent and believe prior to being born again.

The doctrine of the church also began taking a form conducive to the language adopted by the Landmarkers at the middle of the century. Belief that people with Baptist sentiments have existed from the time of Christ gained wide acceptance. Closed, or strict communion, was argued on the premise that only scripturally baptized believers (those immersed upon profession of faith by a qualified administrator) could partake of the Supper.

All three views of the millennium had advocates, but belief in the imminence of the coming age of peace had a salutary effect on evangelistic zeal. There was widespread belief that Christ was coming soon even though that conviction had seriously receded by the middle of the century.

Campbellism and anti-missionary preachers wreaked havoc across the South. Disagreement over slavery eventually caused Baptists North and South to divide. In spite of these developments, the missionary spirit took root and grew among Baptists.

NOTES

1. William L. Lumpkin, *Baptist Confessions of Faith*, (Philadelphia: The Judson Press, 1959), p. 358.
2. Ibid., pp. 365-366.
3. Ibid., pp. 360-361.
4. Joseph Biggs, *A Concise History of Kehukee Baptist Association, from Its Original Rise to the Present Time*, (Tarborough, North Carolina: Printed and published by George Howard, 1834), pp. 140-141.
5. Wood Furman, *A History of the Charleston Association of Baptist Churches in the State of South Carolina; with an Appendix Containing the Principal Circular Letters*, (Charleston, South Carolina: J. Hoff, 1811), pp. 25-26.
6. Material in this paragraph is based on a report in the *Analytical Repository* 1 (July-August 1802):51-59.
7. "Christian Union," *Christian Watchman* 4 (June 7, 1823):101.
8. "The Importance of Studying the Scriptures," *The American Baptist Magazine and Missionary Intelligencer* 2 (September 20, 1820):391.
9. "Introduction," *Christian Review* 1 (March 1836):9.
10. Robert G. Torbet, *A History of the Baptists*, 3rd ed., rev. (Philadelphia: The Judson Press, 1963), pp. 18-21; H. Leon McBeth, *The Baptist Heritage: Four Centuries of Baptist Witness* (Nashville: Broadman Press, 1987), pp. 49-60.
11. Lumpkin, *Baptist Confessions*, pp. 285-286.
12. Campbell, "Historical Sketch," *Millennial Harbinger* 1 (May 5, 1830):214.
13. Jesse Mercer, *History of the Georgia Baptist Association, compiled at the Request of that Body, by Jesse Mercer*, (Washington, Georgia: n.p., 1838; Reprinted by the Georgia Baptist Association, 1980), p. 196.
14. Ibid., pp. 196-198.
15. Ibid., p. 200.
16. Ibid.
17. Robert B. C. Howell, "Letter V," *The Baptist Banner* 3 (April 18, 1837):97.
18. Hosea Holcombe, *A History of the Rise and Progress of the Baptists in Alabama: with a Miniature History of the Denomination from the Apostolic Age Down to the Present Time, Interspersed with Anecdotes Original and Selected and Concluded with an Address to the Baptists of Alabama*, (Philadelphia: King and Baird Printers, 1840), pp. 14-15.
19. Ibid., p. 15.
20. Ibid.
21. J. B. Jeter, *The Sermons and Other Writings of the Rev. Andrew Broaddus, with a Memoir of His Life*, ed. A. Broaddus (New York: Lewis Colby, 1852), pp. 392-393.
22. W. C. Crane, "The Name 'Baptist,'" *Baptist Banner, and Western Pioneer* 6 (April 15, 1841):3.
23. "Origin of the Baptist Denomination," *Baptist Banner, and Western Pioneer* 6 (April 29, 1841):3.
24. Torbet, *A History*, p. 18. In this view, Baptists are said to have originated with John the Baptist and his ministry along the Jordan River.
25. G. H. Orchard, "A Brief Sketch of the Early History of the Baptists, in Different Counties," *Baptist Banner, and Western Pioneer* 9 (September 9, 1842):7.
26. Orchard, "XV. A Brief Sketch of History of the Baptists in Britain," *Baptist Banner, and Western Pioneer* 9 (September 29, 1842):6.
27. J. J. Burnett, *Sketches of Tennessee's Pioneer Baptist Preachers, Being, Incidentally, a History of Baptist Beginnings in the Several Associations in the State Containing, Particularly, Character and Life Sketches of the Standard-Bearers and Leaders of Our People*, (Nashville: Marshall and Bruce Company, 1913), p. 186.
28. Furman, *A History*, pp. 32-33.
29. *Minutes of the Mississippi Babtist [sic] Association, Convened at Zion-Hill, Amite County, Mississippi, on the 14th, 15th, 16th, & 17th Oct. 1820* (St. Francisville, Louisiana: Printed by Fielding Bradford, 1820), p. 5.
30. S. J. Conkwright, *History of the Churches of Boone's Creek Baptist Association* (Winchester, Kentucky: n.p., 1923), p. 181.
31. Ibid., p. 46.
32. *Minutes of the Antioch Baptist Church, Lafayette, Alabama, 1835*, Article 13 of the Bylaws.
33. Furman, *A History*, p. 43.
34. Robert A. Baker, *A Baptist Source Book with Particular Reference to Southern Baptists* (Nashville: Broadman Press, 1966), p. 50.
35. *Minutes of the Red River Baptist Association, Holden at Halfpone Meeting-house, in Robertson County, on Saturday Preceding Second Lord's Day in August, 1817* (Russellville, Kentucky: n.p., 1817), p. 7.
36. Ibid.
37. For example, see the article submitted by Lewis Leonard, moderator, entitled "The Hudson River Baptist Association, to the Several Independent Churches of which she is Constituted, sendeth Christian salutation," *The Columbian Star* 3 (September 4, 1824):2.

38. Simplicitas, "Address to the Baptists On Communion," *American Baptist Magazine and Missionary Intelligencer* 3 (July 1821):131-133.
39. William E. Hatcher, *Life of J. B. Jeter, D.D.* (Baltimore: Wharton and Company, 1887), p. 130.
40. "Communications," *The Columbian Star* 3 (October 9, 1824):461.
41. Jeter, *The Sermons and Other Writings*, p. 435.
42. A. C. Dayton, "Review of Elder R. Fuller's Views of the Immersion of Pedobaptists," *Southern Baptist Review* 3 (January 1857):127.
43. *Minutes of the Broad-River Baptist Association* (Columbia, South Carolina: Printed by D. and J. J. Foust, 1806), p. 2.
44. *Copy of the Old Waterlick Church Minute Book, Shenandoah County, Virginia, organized April 15th, 1787* (August 25, 1810), p. 51.
45. David Benedict, *Fifty Years Among the Baptists*, (Glen Rose, Texas: Newman and Collings, [1913]), p. 62.
46. Daniel Merrill, "Letter from Rev. D. Merrill to the Rev. E. W.," *Massachusetts Baptist Missionary Magazine* (May 1805), pp. 123-124.
47. Peter Philanthropos Roots, "Extracts," *Massachusetts Baptist Missionary Magazine* 1 (September 1805):155-157.
48. Clark Kendrick, "Letters," *Massachusetts Baptist Missionary Magazine* 1 (September 1804):83-86.
49. "The Testimony of Medicine, that to Baptize is to Plunge," *Massachusetts Baptist Missionary Magazine* 4 (December 1814):108.
50. "Introduction," *Christian Review* 1 (March 1836):11.
51. W. T. Brantly, "The Covenant of Circumcision, No Just Plea for Infant Baptism," *Tracts of Baptist's General Tract Society*, vol. 7 (Philadelphia: The Baptist General Tract Society, n.d.): 203.
52. Richard Fuller, *Baptism, and the Terms of Communion; an Argument, by Richard Fuller* (Baltimore: Cushing and Brother, 1850), p. 137.
53. George W. Purefoy, *A History of the Sandy Creek Baptist Association, from its organization in A.D. 1758, to A.D. 1858, by Elder George W. Purefoy, Being an Enlargement of the Centenary Sermon Delivered by Him at Its One Hundredth Annual Session, at Love's Creek Meeting-House, Chatham County, N.C., On The 3rd Day of October, 1858* (New York: Sheldon and Company, 1859), p. 79.
54. Ibid.
55. R. D. Owen, "Washing Feet," *Baptist Banner, and Western Pioneer* 9 (July 14, 1842):3.
56. Holcombe, *A History of the Rise and Progress*, p. 59.
57. Encyclopedia of Southern Baptists, s.v., "Analytical Repository, The" by John J. Hurt, Jr.
58. "Analysis of Prophecy," *Analytical Repository* 1 (January-February 1803):263.
59. Ibid, p. 264.
60. Ibid.
61. "The Savannah Baptist Society for Foreign Missions, to the Inhabitants of Georgia, and the Adjacent Parts of South-Carolina," *Massachusetts Baptist Missionary Magazine* 4 (March 1814):7.
62. *Minutes of the Mississippi Baptist Association Convened at Sarepta Church, Jefferson County, Mississippi Territory, October 14, 1815*, p. 7.
63. "Address of the Baptist Board of Foreign Missions for the United States," *American Baptist Magazine and Missionary Intelligencer* 2 (September 1819):165.
64. *Minutes of the Mississippi Baptist Association, Convened at the Meeting-House of Mars' Hill Church, State of Mississippi, Amite County, on the 18th, 19th and 20th October, 1823* (St. Francisville: Printed at the Experiment Office, 1823), p. 11.
65. "The Importance of Studying the Scriptures," *American Baptist Magazine and Missionary Intelligencer* 2 (September 1820):391.
66. "Approach to the Millennium," *Christian Watchman* 7 (April 28, 1826):81.
67. Ibid.
68. Alexander Campbell, "The Millennium—No. 1," *Millennial Harbinger* 5 (September 1834):454-459.
69. Uriel B. Chambers, ed., *The Baptist Chronicle, and Georgetown Literary Register* 1 (August 1830):125.
70. Torbet, *A History*, p. 279.
71. Ibid., p. 280.
72. "View of the Millennium," *Christian Watchman* 4 (September 13, 1823):160.
73. "Prophetic Times," *Christian Watchman* 23 (August 12, 1842):125.
74. Jeter, *The Sermons*, p. 475.
75. Lumpkin, *Baptist Confessions*, p. 358.
76. Ibid., p. 367.
77. Baker, *The Southern Baptist Convention*, p. 144.
78. Benedict, *Fifty Years*, p. 131.

79. Walter B. Shurden, *Not a Silent People: Controversies that Have Helped Shape Southern Baptists* (Nashville: Broadman Press, 1972), pp. 44-45.

80. Burnett, *Sketches*, p. 15.

81. Alvah Hovey, *A Memoir of the Life and Times of the Rev. Isaac Backus, A.M.* (Boston: Gould and Lincoln, 1859), p. 221.

82. Purefoy, *A History*, p. 66.

83. John Taylor, *A History of Ten Baptist Churches, of which the Author has been Alternately a Member: in Which Will be seen something of a Journal of the Author's Life, for more than Fifty Years* (Frankfort, Kentucky: Printed by J.H. Holeman, 1823), p. 160.

84. Burnett, *Sketches*, p. 425.

85. Conkwright, *History of the Churches*, p. 71.

86. Hatcher, *Life of J.B. Jeter*, p. 30.

87. Ibid., p. 27.

88. G. W. Purefoy, *A History of the Sandy Creek Association*, p. 86.

89. Ibid., p. 37.

90. Ibid., p. 83.

91. Hatcher, *Life of J. B. Jeter*, p. 30.

92. Purefoy, *A History of the Sandy Creek Association*, pp. 195-204.

93. Boyce, *Abstract*, pp. 50-54.

CHAPTER 5

OF HIGHER CRITICS AND CALVINISTS

When Baptists in the South separated from their northern brethren in 1845 and formed their own missionary organization, the Southern Baptist Convention, the division mirrored the profound sentiments plaguing the nation as a whole. The problem of slavery alone did not cause Baptists to separate, but it supplied the occasion seized by Southerners to go their own organizational way. Profound changes brought on by the ravages of the Civil War placed the convention in grave economic peril as it fought for its survival. At the same time that the leaders tried to forge a denominational consensus, Landmarkism and German rationalism in the form of higher criticism set the direction of their theological debates for the next century.

The strength of Calvinism continued to decline between 1845 and 1900. It is true that James P. Boyce, John L. Dagg, and other leaders professed and taught Calvinism, but its formal hold became more tenuous as its doctrines of limited atonement, total depravity, and irresistible grace underwent modification or outright rejection.

Furthermore, theological developments originating across the Atlantic Ocean began to touch Southern Baptists. The publication of Charles Darwin's *The Origin of Species* in 1859 exploded on the theological world with such force that its reverberations even today are intensifying in fervor. For those in the world's scientific community who accepted the concept of a universe closed to outside interference, i.e., a God who works miraculously, biological evolution provided an alternative to the Christian doctrine of creation by divine fiat.

Developments in the field of psychology paralleled many of those of the other sciences. David Hume (1711-1776), of Scotland, had already attacked the Christian view that man is composed of both body and soul. His treatise entitled

An Enquiry Concerning the Human Understanding marks the beginning of a new era in the doctrine of human nature. The work by Sigmund Freud (1856-1939), Carl Gustav Jung (1875-1961), Friedrich Wilhelm Nietzsche (1844-1900), and Karl Marx (1818-1883) suggested new directions for understanding the meaning of body and soul.

However, higher criticism took its first toll among Southern Baptists in the person of Crawford H. Toy (1836-1919). With the Toy controversy, Southern Baptist attention focused on the question of the authority of the Bible.

THE FIRST BATTLE FOR THE BIBLE

The higher critical school of biblical criticism in Germany added new devotees in the second half of the nineteenth century. Ferdinand C. Baur (1762-1860), a leader of the Tübingen School of radical criticism, had questioned the Pauline authorship of several books traditionally attributed to Paul, seeing Paul as the author only of Romans, Galatians, and 1 and 2 Corinthians.[1] David Friedrich Strauss (1808-1874), a student of Baur, "achieved instant notoriety" with his *Life of Jesus, Critically Examined*, a work published initially in 1835-36 in which he searched for the historical Jesus among what he believed to be many myths and traditions in the gospel accounts.[2] These epochal works were followed by *The Life of Jesus* in 1863 by Joseph Ernest Renan (1823-1892). Renan saw Jesus as a wandering teacher rather than as the Son of God.[3] Three other writers also played crucial roles in the development of historical criticism. K. H. Graf and the Dutch theologian Abraham Kuenen (1828-1891) wrote that a document, P, the priestly code, was the latest form of the Pentateuch.[4] Julius Wellhausen's *History of Israel* in 1878 supplied the other main ingredients of the Documentary Theory of the Pentateuch, popularly known as Graf-Wellhausen, the Documentary Hypothesis, or JEPD, explained below.[5]

Assuming that the more complex logically evolves from the simpler, the critics sought out the sources of the various biblical strands that were ultimately woven into a unit. Its main features were described by J. McKee Adams as follows.[6] The Pentateuch was put together through the centuries by redactors who, pursuing their own interests, gave it its present form. Moses had little or nothing to do with the actual articulation of the contents. A document existed in the Southern Kingdom, Judah, with its exaltation of the divine name Yahweh, or Jehovah. This is known as the J tradition. The Northern Kingdom, Israel, knew its deity as Elohim, hence, the E document. At some point, probably between 700-600 B.C., an unknown writer(s) combined the two documents into one story. About this same time, another writer, or writers, took the J, E, and JE documents and adapted them into a new synthesis thematically tied to the sanctuary in Jerusalem, forming the Deuteronomist, or D, document. Still later scribes further refined and amplified these narratives and, using their own document (P) as a framework, and completed the formation of the Pentateuch around 500-400 B.C. The theory is known today as the Documentary Hypothesis, or more simply as JEPD. The methodology is germane to historical criticism.

Higher, or historical, criticism approaches the text on a basis of such subjective judgments as the supposed cultural and theological developments of a given era, syntactical construction within the text, and other grammatical considerations. Upon these kinds of criteria, the critic proposes to decide the reliability of the text. By contrast, in lower, or textual, criticism one studies ancient manuscripts trying to get back as close to the biblical text as possible in view of the fact that all of the original manuscripts are lost.

The critics, of course, denied that Moses wrote the Pentateuch. When the implications of Darwin's biological evolution were added, the historicity of Genesis suffered a fatal blow in the system of the critics. All that was left was the spiritual message of Genesis as myth or saga. The first Baptist inroads by the critics came at The Southern Baptist Theological Seminary.

The founding of The Southern Baptist Theological Seminary in 1859 represented the culmination of a desire to provide a convention-wide institution for training Southern Baptist ministers, even though the school originally functioned independently of convention control. Its first four faculty members were President James P. Boyce (1827-1888), John A. Broadus (1827-1895), William Williams (1821-1877), and Basil Manly, Jr. (1825-1892).

The founders of the seminary adopted an *Abstract of Principles* to which each faculty member must subscribe, a policy which is still in effect. Article I is entitled "The Scriptures." It says, "The Scriptures of the Old and New Testaments were given by inspiration of God, and are the only sufficient, certain and authoritative rule of all saving knowledge, faith and obedience."[7] The definition did not specifically include statements about science and cosmology.

Boyce and Broadus were even more explicit in their individual teaching about the reliability of the Bible. In the preface of his work on systematic theology Boyce wrote, "The author has aimed to make the discussions in this volume especially scriptural. He believes in the perfect inspiration and absolute authority of the divine revelation, and is convinced that the best proof of any truth is that it is there taught."[8] Broadus was equally firm:

> But hold! The founder of Christianity and his inspired Apostles have spoken about them [i.e., Old Testament teachings], and whether you understand everything in the Old Testament or not, they have declared that the Scripture cannot be broken; that all Scripture is given by inspiration of God, and is profitable; that the holy Scriptures (the Old Testament) are "able to make wise unto salvation through faith which is in Christ Jesus."[9]

The actions of Boyce and Broadus offer further insight into their fears about the critical approaches of Graf-Kuenen-Wellhausen. Crawford H. Toy (1836-

1919) had been elected as Professor of Old Testament at the seminary in 1869. In the words of William A. Mueller:

> Some of Dr. Toy's teachings were both novel and disturbing. It became known even during his first session as a teacher in the Seminary that Dr. Toy had accepted Charles Darwin's theory of evolution. He had also become convinced of the plausibility of the Kuenen-Wellhausen theory of Pentateuchal criticism.[10]

When Toy sought to reconcile evolutionary theory with the Genesis account of creation, he found himself in conflict with Boyce and Broadus. Both believed in the historicity of Genesis.

Dissension followed. For his part, "Dr. Toy was fully convinced that the views he had adopted were correct, and would, by removing many intellectual difficulties, greatly promote faith in the Scriptures."[11] Boyce and Broadus were equally convinced he was wrong. Broadus gave his own views on the matter:

> If the Darwinian theory of the origin of man has been accepted, then it becomes easy to conclude that the first chapter of Genesis is by no means true history. From this starting-point, and pressed by a desire to reconstruct the history on evolutionary principles, one might easily persuade himself that in numerous other cases of apparent conflict between Old Testament statements and the accredited results of various sciences the conflict is real, and the Old Testament account is incorrect. This persuasion would seem to the critic to justify his removing various books and portions of books into other periods of the history of Israel, so as to make that history a regular evolution from simpler to more complex.[12]

Efforts at reconciliation were made in the hope that Toy would "break away from the dominion of destructive theories,"[13] but to no avail. In a letter to Broadus in 1876, Boyce wrote, "In a postscript to a letter to Toy I broke into a gentle remonstrance and earnest entreaty on inspiration."[14] Toy's resignation was accepted in 1879. Broadus wrote in a letter to Mrs. Broadus, "Alas! the mournful deed is done. Toy's resignation is accepted. He is no longer professor in the Seminary. I learn that the Board were all in tears as they voted, but no one voted against it."[15]

The worst fears of Broadus and Boyce for Toy were soon realized. Within eight years, Toy became a Unitarian.[16] This dramatic and unhappy affair set in bold relief the attitude of Boyce and Broadus toward evolutionary presuppositions as they related to biblical authority. Boyce and Broadus would tolerate no teaching which implied a low view of inspiration. The problem of evolution had now been forcefully injected into Southern Baptist thinking. Stopped for the moment, the issue would come up again.

TWO APPROACHES TO INFALLIBILITY

The Southern Baptist defense of the complete trustworthiness of the Bible began to assume definite form. Two years after Toy left the seminary, Jeremiah B. Jeter (1802-1880) of Virginia, widely known as an editor, writer, and pastor, contributed to a symposium edited by Charles A. Jenkins. Jeter reasserted the doctrine of plenary, or full, inspiration. He wrote: "That God can inspire men to reveal his truth infallibly to the world, it is atheistic to deny. That plenary inspiration seems necessary to secure the end of the avowed purpose of the scriptures—that men may believe in Christ, and believing secure everlasting life—can hardly be questioned."[17]

On the subject of supposed errors, Jeter pointed to the inevitability of seeming discrepancies. He observed that, because the original texts were written in remote ages by different authors, and because languages and cultures differed widely, interpretation of such documents is difficult.[18] He further observed that many "obstacles in the interpretation of the Scriptures have vanished before patient investigation and increasing knowledge. . . . The error . . . may be subjective and not objective."[19]

Nearly a decade later, Basil Manly, Jr., one of the four original faculty members at Southern Seminary, published a work defending inspiration. According to one biographer, it was "an apologetic treatise following the Toy controversy."[20] Manly discussed and rejected the following concepts of inspiration: (1) Mechanical Inspiration, or the Dictation Theory, because it left no room for human authorship;[21] (2) Partial Inspiration, the view that the Bible only *contains* the Word of God, because one depends on human consciousness to distinguish between the Bible and the "inner Bible";[22] (3) Different Degrees of Inspiration, because of the implication that there is error in Scripture;[23] (4) Natural Inspiration, because it degrades the whole idea of inspiration in ascribing inspiration to non-biblical writers;[24] and (5) Universal Christian Inspiration, because it implies that all Christians have the same kind of inspiration as the biblical writers.[25] He concluded, "The doctrine which we hold is that commonly styled PLENARY INSPIRATION, or Full Inspiration. It is that the Bible as a whole is the Word of God, so that in every part of Scripture there is both infallible truth and divine authority."[26]

The total process he described under four categories of thought. *Revelation* "is that direct divine influence that imparts truth to the mind. *Inspiration* . . . secures the accurate transference of truth into human language by a speaker or writer, so as to be communicated to other men."[27] *Preservation* refers to "a providential guardianship over the Word, by which it has been preserved remarkably incorrupt, and singularly attested as being substantially the same that proceeded from the original writers."[28] Finally, *Illumination* is "that influence of the Holy Spirit under which all the children of God receive, discern, and feed upon the truth communicated to them."[29]

The preservation of the text posed a problem to Manly in that the original texts have been lost. He admitted that inspiration applied only to the original texts and that textual uncertainties in copying have occurred. Does this not imply a fallible text? Manly believed not. "But when all these known errors are corrected, and all those doubtful readings are set aside, it is evident that there is no change as to any leading doctrine or fact of the Gospel."[30] To him, textual "uncertainties" did not affect the textual "certainties."

Manly dealt with apparent inaccuracies in various ways.[31] Some, he thought, arise from misinterpretation, some from misapprehension of the facts of history, others from present-day ignorance of historical events, and still others from error in transcription of the text. He explained many conflicts between Testaments on the basis of progressive revelation, a principle also invoked by Boyce.[32] From this perspective he concluded, "The idea of progressive, advancing revelation implies a relative imperfection in the earlier parts, and that this imperfection of incompleteness is perfectly consistent with truth, and with the divine origin of both earlier and latter. . . . Imperfect? Partial? Yes, but *not erroneous!*"[33] Finally, Manly pointed out that the purpose of the Bible is religious, not scientific, and its statements about science are meager. The biblical writers adopted unscientific terminology at times just as one does today when the sun is described as "rising and setting."[34] This concept is usually described as *accommodation*, although Manly did not use the term.

W. O. Carver would later, somewhat condescendingly, characterize Manly's thought as a "rather skillful summarizing of the traditional positions and of the arguments in their support in behalf of a rather rigid and literal theory of verbal inspiration. He labors a distinction between revelation and inspiration which a later generation has come to regard as at best superficial."[35] Carver further stated that, for thoughtful students, the work was "not very comprehensive nor very profound."[36] Perhaps not, but Carver misread the mood of the Southern Baptist Convention if he believed Manly's views were obsolete, as is witnessed by the dissension over biblical inspiration that has engulfed the convention since 1979.

Other members of the faculty at the seminary equivocated on the extent of biblical infallibility. F. H. Kerfoot (1847-1901), one of his colleagues, described the Southern Baptist belief in the Bible as an infallible guide as a distinguishing characteristic of theirs when he asserted:

> Baptists . . . are sure that the Word of God is the only infallible and all-sufficient rule of faith and practice, and that nothing should be taught for doctrine which is not contained therein; and that all that is taught therein must be believed; and that all that is commanded therein ought to be obeyed *as commanded*. This is their first and most fundamental principle as individuals and as a denomination. If this principle is not their distinctive and differentiating principle, the *emphasis* they place upon it *is*.[37]

Edwin C. Dargan (1852-1930), who came to the seminary in 1892, approached the subject in much the same way. He noted that one must make allowances for the intent of the Bible toward spiritual rather than scientific teaching as well as for the different times and characters of the human authors. He concluded, "Making just allowance for such things as these, we may say with all confidence that, passing by a few minor difficulties which may yet be explained, the Bible is free from error, as the absolute authority and guide in matters of religion."[38] Both men placed a restriction on the extent of infallibility. Kerfoot called it an "infallible and all-sufficient role of faith and practice." Similarly, Dargan saw the Bible as "the absolute authority in matters of religion." They did not necessarily apply infallibility to cosmological and scientific descriptions in the Bible.

THE BENEFITS OF TEXTUAL CRITICISM

Prior to the outbreak of the Civil War, some of the problems raised by the textual critics appeared in Southern Baptist publications. In an essay in *The Southern Baptist Review*, the writer discussed some of the issues thus raised. Surveying various weaknesses of the Authorized Version, he noted that it was based on the so-called Received Text which "was formed from a very small number of manuscripts, and those of modern date."[39] Earlier manuscripts differ from the Received Text, he said. "These differences, or *Various Readings* as they are technically termed, are stated, in round numbers, and amounting to the enormous sum of three hundred thousand."[40] Rather than seeing these differences as proving the unreliability of the Bible, the author saw the opposite. Admitting that confidence in the Bible is shaken when texts are proved by criticism to be spurious, the author could see benefit even then. Criticism would ultimately help, not hurt. He boasted:

> But give us a text which like gold tried in the fire has stood the surest tests of criticism, and no room will be left for these painful apprehensions. The removal of the things that can be shaken will add new strength and glory to those, which because they cannot be shaken abide, claiming the trust and obedience of man as the absolute revealed truth of God.[41]

John Leadly Dagg (1794-1884), a professor at Mercer University, also admitted that differences exist among the ancient manuscripts. Nevertheless, he believed that a continuous miracle of protection kept errors from creeping into the texts. Arguing for the doctrine of plenary inspiration on the basis that the Holy Ghost so moved upon the writers that they "were the instruments that God used to speak and write,"[42] he concluded that "the Bible must be either from heaven or from men. So pure a stream cannot proceed from a corrupt fountain."[43]

RESTATING TRINITARIAN THEOLOGY

Speculations about the nature of God emanating from European Rationalism found no place to lodge among Southern Baptists of the nineteenth century. George Wilhelm Friedrich Hegel (1770-1831), a German philosopher and theologian, mesmerized his students with his dialectical interpretation of Absolute Spirit objectively embodying itself in history, but his pantheism was too foreign to Southern Baptist practicality for them to give it serious consideration. The same could be said for the pessimistic pantheism of Arthur Schopenhauer (1788-1860) whose thesis is embodied in the title of his work of acclaim, *The World as Will and Idea*. As German rationalism promoted the inexorable shift in philosophy from theism to deism to pantheism to atheism, Southern Baptists stood firmly on the traditional Christian theology of God. During an era when the doctrine of the church split their fellowship, the doctrine of God was left untouched.

Theology began coming of age as Southern Baptist writers assumed the arduous task of systematizing doctrine. Calvinistic language as it relates to God's decree continued to prevail. John L. Dagg, a respected leader and an avowed Calvinist, published his book *Manual of Theology: First Part, a Treatise on Christian Doctrine*, the first systematic theology book to come from the hand of a Southern Baptist. Of his basic doctrines, Robert S. Gardner wrote:

> He mirrored the Southern Baptist mind at many points: general and specific revelation, the plenary inspiration of Scripture, the Ussherite chronology of creation, Augustino-federal doctrine of original sin, the vicarious atonement of the God-man, special providence, election, and particular redemption. His views of baptism, the local church, and closed communion received wide approval.[44]

James P. Boyce published his *Abstract of Systematic Theology* in 1887. Boyce thoroughly imbibed the Old School Calvinism of Charles Hodge at Princeton, under whom he studied.

The doctrine of the Trinity continued to be a favorite topic. Boyce warned against any kind of modalistic interpretation by saying:

> We have here, therefore, not the one God, manifesting himself sometimes as Father, and sometimes as Son; but a distinction of persons in the Godhead, in which we are taught that in that Godhead there exists a personal relation of Father to Son, and Son to Father, with a distinct individuality and personality of each.[45]

Further, "It will be seen by the foregoing statements that the Scriptures distinctly teach the existence of God in the personal relations of Father to Son, and that each of them is God."⁴⁶ E. C. Dargan called the deity of Christ "the greatest truth in human history and thought."⁴⁷ He summarized the doctrine of the Trinity in that "God exists and reveals himself in the three characters, or person, of the Father, the Son, and the Holy Spirit. This is not tri-theism, but tri-unity."⁴⁸ The doctrine of the Trinity can be resolved into the statement that God is one in nature, essence, and being, and three in office, person, and function.

Many of these men also saw a necessary connection between the divine nature of Christ and his ability to be a substitute for sinners. To accomplish this, the Word became flesh. In the incarnate Christ, two natures—divine and human—were united into one Person. J. M. Pendleton (1811-1891), for example, reasoned that Christ must be both divine and human because an incarnate Christ with a human body but no soul would not have been truly man. Conversely, the union of a human body with his divine nature would not make him a man. He concluded, "There must be the union of a human body and a human soul to constitute Jesus a man, and then there must be the union of the humanity with his divinity to constitute him the Christ. Nor are we for a moment to suppose that he has two personalities. He has two natures, but one person."⁴⁹

Southern Baptist soteriology has been Christ-centered, revolving principally around his work as a substitute for sinners. A discussion found in the 1816 *Minutes of the Cumberland Baptist Association* bears a strong resemblance to Anselm's view of the cross as a satisfaction for sin. The minutes said, "The sum of all we have said is this; man can suffer, but cannot satisfy; God can satisfy, but cannot suffer. But the second divine person, who was both God and man in one person, could both suffer and satisfy, and reconcile us to God, by his cross."⁵⁰

Substitutionary categories of thought have also continued to be influential. Note the words of J. M. Pendleton:

> Creatureship and substitution are not consistent with each other. . . . If Jesus was merely a created being, he must, like other creatures, act for himself alone. It is plain, therefore, that if Christ is not divine, he could not have taken the place of sinners, so as to die for them and make atonement for their sins.⁵¹

A dead Christ cannot atone for sin; he must be alive.

The literal resurrection of Christ was not a point of contention among Regular Baptists nor their forerunners. Consequently, analyses of that subject are scarce prior to the middle of the nineteenth century. Even the New Hampshire Confession, first adopted in 1833, has only a minimal statement about the resurrection of Christ, that he has risen from the dead and is now enthroned in heaven.⁵² Surprisingly, James Boyce, in his monumental work on systematic theology, did not include a separate section on the resurrection of Christ, although Boyce obviously believed that the body of Christ was raised and that it becomes a type of the Christian's resurrected body.⁵³ John A. Broadus was more specific.

After rejecting various positions which denied the actual resurrection of Jesus, he asserted, "The great fact stands."[54] He saw the resurrection as establishing the divine origin of Christ's mission as well as sanctioning his claims to be one with God.[55]

That Christ must be both God and Man continued to be a conviction among Baptists in the South. W. T. Brantly had raised the question, "Now what is it that gives to the blood of Christ its atoning efficacy?" and concluded that the blood must have an "intrinsic virtue," something which in its nature "was adapted to answer the demand of *absolute justice*."[56] Only by the union of the divine and human could God effect propitiation. Therefore, "the ineffable and incomprehensible *union* of divinity and humanity, was indispensable, in order that the act of either might be affirmed of his whole person."[57]

A few years after the work of Brantly, Boyce wrote on the same subject. He followed a more circuitous route but arrived at the same point. He reasoned that the doctrine of the Triune God was necessary for the work of the incarnation itself. Boyce believed that from a strictly monistic approach, God could become incarnate, but he could not empty himself of his rule and authority in an incarnation and maintain them at the same time. "Especially could he not make atonement to himself, and pour out his wrath upon his own head at the same time that he endures it."[58]

Regular Baptists believed that the Third Person of the Trinity, the Holy Spirit, is God. A. H. Strong, whose *Systematic Theology* has had a wide following among Southern Baptists, discusses five evidences for the deity of the Holy Spirit: (1) he is spoken of as God, (2) divine attributes are ascribed to him, (3) he does the works of God, (4) he receives the honor due only to God, and (5) he is treated as being equal with God both in the baptism formulas and in the apostolic benedictions.[59]

Strong gave several reasons for believing that the Holy Spirit is a Person.[60] The masculine pronoun, for example, is used when referring to the Holy Spirit. Further, his name is used in connection with people so as to imply personality. He also performs acts which are proper to personality, and he is affected by the acts of other persons.

In all of these sources of the Southern Baptist doctrine of God, one notes that redemption is personal, not social. God demands personal righteousness of man and makes it available to man through the incarnation-death-resurrection of Jesus Christ.

SEARCHING FOR A DOCTRINE OF THE ATONEMENT

Andrew Fuller of England led in the assault on the Calvinistic view of limited atonement. The appeal of limited atonement arose from two main presuppositions. The first was the belief that Christ's sufferings on the cross were quantifiable to the extent that what he suffered was applicable to a specific amount or number of sins. What he suffered exactly canceled the sins of those whom he came to save. The second presupposition was that God could not "collect" twice for the payment of sin. If Christ actually atoned for sin on the cross and if someone for whom Christ died should suffer in hell, the sins in effect were being paid for twice. That would be unethical. Conversely, if someone for whom Christ atoned went to hell, God would be charged with injustice on the grounds that the person's sins were canceled on the cross. Inferences from these propositions can lead in two directions. First, if Christ *actually*, and not *potentially*, paid the sins of the whole world, the whole world eventually would be saved. Conversely, however, since universal salvation does not seem to be the thrust of scriptural teaching, the limitation must be something intrinsic to Christ's sufferings, i.e., he atoned only for the elect. Andrew Fuller's evasion of this dilemma by locating the nexus of salvation in God's decree rather than in the death of Christ per se has been discussed previously.

Regular Baptists in the South widely accepted Fuller's modifications. They then set about giving meaning to the concept of satisfaction. J. M. Pendleton saw the work of Christ as an "expiation of sin by the satisfaction rendered to the law and justice of God through the obedience and death of Christ."[61] Likewise, Richard Fuller interpreted the death of Christ as a satisfaction to "Eternal Justice."[62] Alvah Hovey explained it in terms of judicial righteousness,[63] and E. C. Dargan saw it as a satisfaction before God's judgment seat.[64]

At the core of the issue lies the concept of the propitiation of sin. C. H. Dodd, in the next century, redirected the thinking of neoorthodox theologians on that issue, as is shown later, but Regular Baptists in the nineteenth century concluded that the work of Christ was two-dimensional: God-ward and man-ward. A representative sentiment can be found in the writings of Jesse Mercer who averred, "Strictly speaking, God was never unpropitious. But sin was not only *an offense* to him, but had thrown obstructions in the way of his mercy. The atonement, therefore, must be *that* in its nature which will honor him in the view of all rational intelligences."[65] Pendleton voiced almost exactly the same sentiments: "It is incorrect, therefore, to say that the atonement rendered God propitious to man; but it is strictly true to say that it rendered him propitious *according to law and justice*."[66] Since the work of Christ was seen in its two-dimensional effect, propitiation and expiation were used almost as synonymous terms. Indeed, Richard Fuller so used them.[67]

Along with satisfaction and propitiation, substitution was a dominant theme. That Christ suffered for sinners was often stated in explicit terms. Richard Fuller's comment on the words of Jesus on the cross, "Why hast thou forsaken me?" are typical of the day:

> That cup was charged with ingredients which only Eternal Justice could have collected, and no mere mortal could sip one drop of its wormwood and

live. The afflicting thunders of divine wrath were now to be quenched in his blood. He was placed before the very jaws of the pit, with hell vomiting its sulphurous smoke, and dashing its red lightnings in his face. Into a few hours were to be condensed miseries which should equal the everlasting damnation due to our sins. And amidst these torments he was to be forsaken by his Father, suffering a suspension of that ineffable communion which from eternity had been to him the source and essence of celestial beatitude.[68]

Fuller never saw this event as automatically effecting the salvation of sinners. A personal response in faith was necessary because "we can devise no benefit unless that atonement be cordially accepted by us."[69]

The substitutionary work of Christ was a favorite theme among nineteenth-century Southern Baptists, as can be seen by even a casual reading of sermons of the day. E. C. Dargan left one of the finest summaries of substitutionary atonement giving what he thought to be the "scriptural view":

This is that Christ voluntarily took the nature of man and with it the place of man as a sinner before God, though without personal sin; that so in man's stead he suffered the penalty of sin in his cruel death on the cross; that being God he could by becoming man offer himself as a sufficient and suitable substitute for man; and being man his death was a real human death, a penalty for sin; and further, being God-Man, the dignity and value of his person makes his penalty sufficient for all the race, though actually efficient only in the case of those who by faith accept him as their substitute.[70]

This stress upon the substitutionary aspects of Christ's death has continued to have its advocates. It is reflected in Sunday School Board materials produced for general use by the churches as well as in more scholarly journals. One example of the former is a statement going back to 1864. *The Sunday School Primer* states quaintly, "Jesus had nev-er [sic] done wrong. He was ho-ly [sic], and knew no sin. He bore the pain for you and for me, to save our souls from hell. He loved us, and died to take a-way [sic] our sins."[71] Calvinism's clearly defined doctrine of limited atonement, rejected by the majority of Southern Baptists, did not find a strong theological competitor.

TRYING TO UNDERSTAND DEPRAVITY

Regular Baptists in the South had questioned the Calvinistic doctrine of depravity as far back as Alexander Campbell. The second half of the century witnessed its almost total rejection. One of the exceptions can be found in James P.

Boyce, the first president of the Southern Baptist Theological Seminary. Charles Hodge's Old-School Presbyterianism comes through in Boyce's understanding of the salvation experience. He defined faith as the instrumental cause, but not the meritorious or procuring cause, of vital union with Christ.[72] Yet, faith must be preceded by regeneration. Boyce gave three reasons for making this assertion.[73] First, because the heart is the soil in which the seed is sown, and the seed can only bring forth fruit in good soil, the heart must be made good by regeneration. Second, since, as in the case of infants, regeneration exists apart from faith and repentance, "regeneration precedes." Third, the "enabling act of God must, in a creature, precede the act of the creature thus enabled." Boyce concluded, "There is not only antecedence, but in some cases an appreciable interval" between regeneration by God and faith by the believer.[74] He even asked plaintively, "Why, in another case, does he [God] allow a life of long continued sin in one for whom Christ has died, and who shall eventually be brought to Jesus? Why is he not regenerated from his birth, as we have reason to think some are?"[75] He gave no answer.

By the end of the nineteenth century, the situation in regard to depravity was almost exactly reversed. A few prominent leaders remained who held to the theology of Boyce, but their number was dwindling. E. C. Dargan, a former student of Boyce, used his position at The Southern Baptist Theological Seminary to advocate many of the very doctrines which Boyce had opposed. His doctrine of total depravity was closer to Brantly's than Boyce's. By depravity, Dargan meant that the whole sum of human life and being is perverted. He wrote, "All the faculties of man are more or less twisted out of shape by sin."[76] Depravity, therefore, does not rule out one's capacity to respond in faith. Rather, Dargan saw repentance and faith as necessary prerequisites. In words that formerly would have evoked the charge of Arminianism, he said, "It does not put the matter too strongly to say that man's part is necessary. If man is saved he must have a hand in the work."[77]

THE ORIGIN OF THE SOUL

James Boyce was one of the first Southern Baptists to discuss in detail the origin of the soul. He described and rejected the idea of the soul's pre-existence.[78] Pre-existence may take three forms. One theory supposes that all souls were created by God at the same time Adam was created. Souls are subsequently united with the appropriate body as each body comes into being. A second theory sees souls as fallen angels who take human form as a kind of probationary stage to a better life in realms to come. Another theory describes pre-existence as unfallen angels who voluntarily assume union with a body to gain higher relationships with God through the redemption wrought in Christ. As far as their writings reveal, no Southern Baptists have ever held to any doctrine of the pre-existence of the soul in the senses just enumerated. The traducian explanation of both body and soul existing seminally in Adam, the closest Baptists ever come to a belief in the soul's pre-existence, has not been universally accepted. Following the thought of Charles Hodge, Boyce rejected it, although he admitted that the theory has a certain plausibility in that it helps account for the transmission of the sinful nature and the inherited mental characteristics.[79] However, Boyce did not see how traducianism could explain that Christ was born without a sinful nature if he inherited both body and soul from Mary.[80] Further, the soul must be material in some sense if it is other than the body but capable of being transmitted. This Boyce considered to be almost the "only objection to this theory of any weight."[81] Therefore, he adopted the creationist theory that God creates each soul at the time of conception of the fetus in the womb of the mother.[82]

SUMMARY

Southern Baptists in the second half of the nineteenth century remained nominal Calvinists in their orientation of thought. James P. Boyce, the president of their only seminary at that time, served as a corrective balance to a precipitous slide into Arminianism. Even his presence, however, could not reverse what had begun with Andrew Fuller and others. The high esteem for the Bible so characteristic of Calvinism showed itself across the spectrum of Southern Baptist theology. However, in spite of Basil Manly's contribution to the explication of inspiration, both Dargan and Kerfoot injected a note of uncertainty into the discussion when they limited infallibility to the religious themes of the Bible.

On the subjects of God, human nature, sin, and the atonement, little developed beyond the concepts initiated earlier in the century. Those professing belief in limited atonement were out of step with the Arminian drift dominating Southern Baptist thought at the end of the century.

NOTES

1. *New International Dictionary*, s.v. "Baur, Ferdinand Christian (1762-1860)."
2. Ibid., "Strauss, David Friedrich (1808-1874)."
3. Ibid., "Renan, Joseph Ernest (1823-1892)."
4. Ibid., "Kuenen, Abraham (1828-1891)."
5. Ibid., "Wellhausen, Julius (1844-1918)."
6. J. McKee Adams, *Ancient Records and the Bible* (Nashville: Broadman Press, 1946), pp. 136-137.
7. The entire "Abstract" is printed in William A. Mueller, *A History of Southern Baptist Theological Seminary* (Nashville: Broadman Press, 1959), pp. 238-241.
8. James Petigru Boyce, *Abstract of Systematic Theology*, (Philadelphia: American Baptist Publication Society, 1887), p. vii.
9. John A. Broadus, *Sermons and Addresses* (Nashville: The Sunday School Board of the Southern Baptist Convention, 1896), p. 158.

10. William A. Mueller, *A History of Southern Baptist Theological Seminary* (Nashville: Broadman Press, 1959), p. 256.
11. John A. Broadus, *Memoir of James Petigru Boyce, D.D., LL.D.* (New York: A. C. Armstrong and Son, 1893), p. 262.
12. Ibid., pp. 260-261.
13. Ibid., p. 262.
14. Archibald Thomas Robertson, *Life and Letters of John Albert Broadus* (Philadelphia: American Baptist Publication Society, 1910), p. 301.
15. Ibid., p. 313. Baker says there were two dissenting votes. Robert A Baker, *A Baptist Source Book with Particular Reference to Southern Baptists* (Nashville: Broadman Press, 1966), p. 168.
16. Mueller, *A History*, p. 142.
17. Jeremiah B. Jeter, "The Inspiration of the Scriptures," in *Baptist Doctrines; Being an Exposition, in a Series of Essays by Representative Baptist Ministers, of the Distinctive Points of Baptist Faith and Practice*, ed. Charles A. Jenkins (St. Louis: Chancy R. Barns, 1818), pp. 49-50.
18. Ibid., p. 61.
19. Ibid., p. 62.
20. *Encyclopedia of Southern Baptists*, s.v. "Manly, Basil, Jr.," by Joseph Powhaten Cox.
21. Basil Manly, *The Bible Doctrine of Inspiration Explained and Vindicated* (New York: A. C. Armstrong and Son, 1891), p. 44.
22. Ibid., p. 50.
23. Ibid., p. 52.
24. Ibid., p. 54.
25. Ibid., p. 56.
26. Ibid., p. 59.
27. Ibid., p. 37.
28. Ibid., p. 82.
29. Ibid., p. 40.
30. Ibid., p. 83.
31. Ibid., 195-204.
32. Boyce, *Abstract*, pp. 50-54.
33. Manly, *The Bible Doctrine of Inspiration*, p. 120.
34. Ibid., p. 241.
35. W. O. Carver, cited by Mueller, *A History*, p. 98.
36. Ibid.
37. F. H. Kerfoot, "Why the Baptist Doctrine," *Baptist: Why and Why Not*, ed. J. M. Frost (Nashville: Sunday School Board, 1900), pp. 23-24.
38. Edwin Charles Dargan, *The Doctrines of Our Faith* (Nashville: Sunday School Board, 1905), p. 22.
39. "Errors of the Received Greek Text," *The Southern Baptist Review* 1 (September 1860):258.
40. Ibid.
41. Ibid., p. 360.
42. John L. Dagg, *Manual of Theology: First Part, A Treatise on Christian Doctrine* (Charleston, South Carolina: Southern Baptist Publication Society, 1859), p. 23.
43. Ibid., p. 27.
44. Robert S. Gardner, "John Leadley Dagg, National Leader" *Quarterly Review* 31 (October-November-December 1973):52.
45. Boyce, *Abstract*, p. 130.
46. Ibid., p. 129.
47. Dargan, *The Doctrines of Our Faith*, p. 71.
48. Ibid., p. 64.
49. James Madison Pendleton, *Christian Doctrines: A Compendium of Theology* (Philadelphia: The Judson Press, 1878), p. 203.
50. *Minutes of the Cumberland Baptist Association*, 1816, p. 13.
51. Pendleton, *Christian Doctrines*, p. 74.
52. William L. Lumpkin, *Baptist Confessions of Faith* (Philadelphia: The Judson Press, 1959), p. 363.
53. Boyce, *Abstract*, p. 456.
54. John A. Broadus, "Matthew," vol. 1 in *An American Commentary of the New Testament*, ed. Alvah Hovey (Philadelphia: The American Baptist Publication Society, 1886), p. 588.
55.. Ibid., p. 589.
56. Brantly, "The Troubled Conscience," p. 258.
57. Ibid., p. 259.

58. Boyce, "The Doctrine of the Suffering Christ," *The Baptist Quarterly* 4 (October 1870):387.
59. Augustus Hopkins Strong, *Systematic Theology: A Compendium and Commonplace-Book Designed for the use of Theological Students* (New York: A. C. Armstrong and Son, 1902), p. 150.
60. Ibid., pp. 155-157.
61. Pendleton, *Christian Doctrines*, p. 223.
62. Richard Fuller, *Sermons by Richard Fuller, Preached During His Ministry with the Seventh and Eutaw Place Baptist Churches, Baltimore 1747-1876* (New York: Sheldon and Company, 1877), p. 148.
63. Alvah Hovey, *Manual of Systematic Theology and Christian Ethics* (Boston: Henry A. Young and Company, 1877), p. 212.
64. E. C. Dargan, *The Changeless Christ, and Other Sermons* (New York: Fleming H. Revell Co., 1918), p. 40.
65. C. D. Mallary, *Memoirs of Elder Jesse Mercer* (New York: Lewis Colby, 1844), p. 288.
66. Pendleton, "The Atonement of Christ," *Southern Baptist Review and Eclectic* 2 (January-February 1856):47.
67. Fuller, *Sermons*, pp. 25, 136 and *passim*.
68. Ibid., p. 157.
69. Ibid., p. 325.
70. Dargan, *The Doctrines of Our Faith*, p. 139.
71. *The Sunday School Primer* (Greenville, South Carolina: Sunday School Board of the Southern Baptist Convention, 1864), p. 23.
72. Boyce, *Abstract*, p. 392.
73. Ibid., pp. 380-381.
74. Ibid., p. 381.
75. James P. Boyce, *Life and Death, the Christian's Portion* (New York: Sheldon and Co., 1869), pp. 6-7. In the light of this discussion, one resolution of the convention in 1931 represents more sentiment than historical awareness. J. W. Porter of Kentucky offered a resolution to correct a misunderstanding of "our historic and scriptural position concerning the plan of salvation." The resolution, which was adopted, reads, "*Be it Resolved*, That we reaffirm our belief, that salvation is secured through repentance toward God and faith in the Lord Jesus Christ, and that in the plan of salvation repentance, philosophically and scripturally, uniformly precedes faith," *Southern Baptist Convention Annual*, 1931, p. 61.
76. Dargan, *The Doctrines of Our Faith*, p. 101.
77. Ibid., p. 147.
78. Boyce, *Abstract*, p. 201.
79. Ibid., pp. 203-204.
80. Ibid., p. 205.
81. Ibid.
82. Ibid., p. 207.

CHAPTER 6

LANDMARKISM ON THE RISE

At the same time that the Southern Baptist Convention was formed, James Robinson Graves (1820-1893) began preaching a brand of Baptist successionism now known as Landmarkism. For half a century it became so entwined within the convention that its effects on the doctrine of the church were still felt, though seriously muted, some eighty years after the Landmarkers formally left the convention in 1905 to form their own organization, the American Baptist Association.

Southern Baptist theology and attitudes can hardly be understood without a firm grasp of Landmarkism and the pervasive effect it has exerted on Southern Baptists. Truly, it is one of the issues that have shaped them, to borrow the language of Walter B. Shurden.[1]

ADOPTING A NAME

J. R. Graves (1820-1893) is usually considered the father of Landmarkism, but the name comes from J. M. Pendleton's work entitled *An Old Landmark Re-Set*. From that book, the Landmark movement was given a rallying cry that would capture the imagination and zeal of Southern Baptists. Graves was a proclaimer more than an innovator. Historian W. Morgan Patterson evaluated Graves's impact in this way:

> J. R. Graves has often been depicted as the originator of Baptist succession by those unsympathetic with his ecclesiastical pronouncements. . . . Yet, his relation to the view may be more accurately designated as that of popular-

izer and promoter. . . . Probably to him more than to any other individual was due the wide acceptance of Baptist succession as orthodoxy among Southern Baptists.[2]

R. B. C. Howell, the editor of *The Baptist*, unwittingly influenced the life of Southern Baptists for the next century and more when he added Graves to the staff of the paper in 1846. According to J. J. Burnett, when Graves "took charge" of *The Baptist* (the name was changed to *The Tennessee Baptist* the next year), the circulation was about 1,000; at the beginning of the Civil War the paper had attained the largest circulation of any Baptist paper in the world.[3] There, as editor of *The Tennessee Baptist*, Graves gained a forum. At the age of twenty-seven, he was able to begin exerting an influence that would affect Southern Baptists for more than a century. The Southern Baptist Convention was only two years old in 1847. Graves came on the scene at a strategic time.

Graves's doctrine of the church was interwoven with his view of history. For the latter he was indebted to G. H. Orchard of England. Orchard sought to prove that Baptist beliefs had been held by various groups from the time of Christ until Orchard's time. Graves, picking up Orchard's thought, saw history as a battlefield in which "Hierarchism" and "Rationalism" were the culprits. In a long discourse before the Mississippi Baptist Education Society, he proclaimed:

> Now, there are two most powerful agencies operating with *tremendous*, though imperceptible *power* upon the masses of this country, working silently the overthrow of our republican government and our free institutions, and they are operating for its destruction in the most effective manner, through *religion*. These agents are *Papal and Protestant* HIERARCHISM and RATIONALISM.[4]

He believed that Papal Rome was the "Babylon" of Revelation 18.[5] Therefore, "every sect that has come out of Rome, is in scripture called her '*daughter*', i.e., child."[6] The "mark of the beast" Graves identified as "the changing of the immersion of the whole body, the badge of the discipleship to Jesus Christ, to sprinkling or pouring a little water upon the forehead—or as now, putting a moistened hand on the forehead!"[7]

Against the threat of Roman domination, Graves believed God had established the "two witnesses" as prophesied in Revelation. These were the Bible and the Baptists because "Baptists are silenced and the pure Word interdicted throughout the dominions of Papal Rome."[8] He had begun to appeal to Southern regionalism and fears. The Jesuits were said to rule "every cabinet and throne in Europe, directing every political and religious movement."[9] He asked, "Has not Rome devised a plan for the subversion of this government, and has she not been carrying it into execution, aided by all the crowned heads of Jesuits of Europe for years past, and with a success that has astonished even herself?"[10] Immigrants from Ireland and "Catholic and infidel Germany"[11] were implied to be antagonistic to religious freedom. Quoting the Executive Committee of the American Home Missionary Society as his source, Graves saw the Western States as a battleground to decide whether the land was to be occupied for Christ or whether it would be the stronghold of the papacy.[12] Protestant denominations could not be counted on to oppose Roman Catholicism because "each and every one of them is a hierarchy."[13] In the mighty ecclesiastical revolution which was developing, Graves saw but two options, either to align with the Catholics on one side, or the Baptists on the other.[14]

THE COTTON GROVE RESOLUTIONS

With this background of Graves' thinking, the actions in 1851 by him and some of his followers, in what is now known as the Cotton Grove Resolutions, can be appreciated. Robert G. Torbet lists the five resolutions which were debated and approved at Cotton Grove:

1. Can Baptists, consistently with their principles of the Scriptures, recognize those societies not organized according to the pattern of the Jerusalem Church, but possessing different *governments*, different *officers*, a different class of *members*, different *ordinances*, *doctrines*, and *practices*, as churches of Christ?

2. Ought they to be called gospel churches, or churches in a religious sense?

3. Can we consistently recognize the ministers of such irregular and unscriptural bodies as gospel ministers?

4. Is it not virtually recognizing them as official ministers to invite them into our pulpits, or by any other act that would or could be construed into such recognition?

5. Can we consistently address as *brethern* [sic] those professing Christianity, who not only have not the doctrine of Christ and walk not according to his commandments, but are arrayed in direct and bitter opposition to these?[15]

The issues were thereby defined and the battle lines drawn. When J. M. Pendleton published *An Old Landmark Re-Set* in 1854 at Graves's insistence, a rallying cry, Landmarker, was born. The controversies precipitated by Graves were somewhat abated by the Civil War, but his ideas have continued to be influential. Why, then, did he have such an impact on Southern Baptists?

First, he arrived on the historical scene at the right time. The Southern Baptist Convention had been in existence for only one year when Graves joined *The Baptist*. He helped mold attitudes when the convention was in its formative period.

Second, persecution by the established churches was not far in the past. Massachusetts was not completely freed from an established church until 1833. John Leland, (renown for his contributions to religious freedom), lived until 1841,[16] well into Graves's era.

Third, Graves knew how to capitalize on regional pride. How strong that regionalism was felt can be seen in a statement from *The Confederate Baptist* during the Civil War. An editorial said:

> While the Yankees are vainglorious and confident; boast of successes never achieved, and defy all creation; the people of the South are modest, calm and resolved. Adequate to every crisis to which they have been summoned, they have never made themselves ridiculous by vaunting promises or undue exaltation.
>
> . . . .
>
> Let us cultivate our peculiar national spirit, and develop more fully our national character. Let us watch with a jealous eye, all these influences coming from Yankeedom, which would debase our understandings or our hearts. We must be a peculiar people, and the best means of attaining this end, consists in abjuring everything that smacks of the despicable race, from whom we have effected our separation.[17]

Fourth, Graves was able to capitalize on the fears generated by movements of new peoples as immigrants from Europe settled throughout the Mississippi Valley. As Graves saw history, this movement was part of a devious plot by Rome, "the Mother of Harlots," to subvert the "Great West."[18] He warned, "Let no one think for a moment that Popery has changed its spirit or lost its intolerance through age. It would, had it but the power, re-enact the bloody scenes of Piedmont in this valley, and throughout this land."[19] Further, he saw "Papal and Ecclesiastical hierarchies" as a threat to the American form of government.[20] He feared the designs of Roman Catholicism in infiltrating the public school system in northern cities and voiced his sentiments in scathing language. He warned, "The Catholics of those cities and states are determined to overthrow the common school system, and get a large portion of the public money for their own purposes—to pay their unmarried *fathers* and their sisters to teach the children of the West Catholicism."[21]

Fifth, Graves presented a simplistic sequence of thought about the Kingdom of God that appealed to a constituency that frequently lacked formal training. Later in his life, Graves propounded these "facts" concerning the earthly ministry of Jesus and the implications for Baptists: that Christ established a visible kingdom of which each local church is a constituent part and that Christ established only one kingdom with parts antagonistic with each other.[22] Since Graves believed with most Baptists of his day that baptism was necessary for church membership and immersion was the only valid New Testament mode, only Baptist churches were New Testament churches. Without baptism there could be no visible church.[23]

THE LOCAL CHURCH OF LANDMARKISM

The spirit of Landmarkism was soon felt throughout the convention. Leaders openly declared to be in sympathy with its tenets. Its methodology began to appear in various publications. One such example is found in an article entitled "Who Are the Old Baptists?" that appeared in *The Commission* in 1859. The article was written to combat the twin evils of antimissionism and Campbellism. The former was refuted by showing that missionary Baptists existed long before their opponents; therefore, missionary Baptists are the Old Baptists. The claims of the Campbellites to be the true church were attacked on the grounds that such groups as the "ancient Waldenses and Abbigenses [sic] were Baptists in faith and practice."[24]

The same style of argument was used nearly two decades later in *Kind Words*, a publication intended for use in Baptist Sunday Schools. The author asked why some people thought that Baptist churches have existed among the true witnesses of Christ and on what basis Christians, who are called by different names at different times, were designated Baptists. The answer came that if their *principles* were the same as those of the Baptists, then they could be classified as *Baptists*. Some of the principles discussed were reverence for the Bible as the sole guide in religious matters, regeneration before church membership, immersion of believers only, and separation of church and state. The article concluded, "So we can see many strong points of resemblance, which is enough to make us call those Christians *Baptists*, though they had other names."[25]

D. B. Ray's book on Baptist church succession, written in 1870, summarizes well the spirit of Landmarkism. Those who disagreed with its basic tenets were knowledgeable. In one passage he alleged:

> All well-informed Baptists are agreed in the belief that we, as a people, have continued from the time of Christ until the present.... They believe that the Baptist succession exists; that there has been no period of time since the death of Christ when Baptists have not existed. But Baptists do not claim *"apostolic succession,"* because they admit that the apostolic office expired with the death of John the beloved.... Neither do we claim *Popish succession*, for this is only the succession of Antichrist.[26]

Denominational pride was often exuded by convention leadership. J. B. Gambrell traced non-Baptist denominations to Rome, "the scarlet-robed persecutor of Christ's Church.... If Rome be not the real church, then are not these denominations branches of the true church."[27] Nevertheless, Gambrell was less rigid on the question of direct church succession while preserving the essence of it. Historian J. J. Burnett quoted him as saying:

> "I do not place much stress," he says, "on historical succession—but the New Testament reads as though things were started to go on. Let me illustrate my idea of succession: A man lost a gray horse. He finds some horse tracks step by step for a hundred miles. The he comes upon the horse—but it is a black horse. That is historical succession. Tracks are not worth a cent. If, on the other hand, you find the gray horse, it does not make any difference if you do not find any tracks. The whole business lies in the identity; we have the horse hunted for. So, the man who takes the New Testament and finds a church in his neighborhood or elsewhere like the one in the Book, has succession."[28]

Gambrell's failure to attach much importance to demonstrable direct succession contrasted with Landmarkism at that point.

How pervasive did the idea of the local church eventually become? It touched every facet of the convention, as will be shown. The Southern Baptist Theological Seminary was founded in 1859, a time when Landmarkism was at its zenith. The *Abstract of Principles*, adopted as the theological guide, generally reflects the mood and temperament of the era. It describes Christ as "the Head of the church, which is composed of all His true disciples, and in Him is invested supremely all power for its government."[29] The same article continues:

> According to his commandment, Christians are to associate themselves into particular societies or churches; and to each of these churches he hath given needful authority for administering that order, discipline and worship which he hath appointed. The regular officers of a Church are Bishops or Elders, and Deacons.[30]

That article may be taken as the classic Southern Baptist emphasis for the next several generations. That is, the universal church was usually defined in such an abstract way that it had no real meaning for the particular church. They were two separate ideas.

The hermeneutical principle followed by Edward T. Hiscox in *The New Directory for Baptist Churches*, a work read widely in the convention, is illustrative of the commonly followed procedure. Hiscox discussed the Greek word (*ekklesia*), translated *church* in the New Testament. Of the one hundred ten times it is so translated, he noted that more than ninety references are applied to a visible, local congregation.[31] Any other meaning of the word is "purely topical and secondary."[32] He formally defined the local church as he believed Baptists understood the term, stating, "They hold that a Church is a company of disciples, baptized on a profession of their faith in Christ, united in a covenant to maintain the ordinances of the Gospel, and the public worship of God; to live godly lives, and to spread abroad the knowledge of Christ as the Saviour of men."[33]

Admittedly, the definition of the church in its broad sense can be found in many Baptist writings. A. H. Strong called it "the whole company of regenerate persons in all times and ages, in heaven and on earth"; it was "invisible," and "universal."[34] E. C. Dargan described the universal church as the collective number of professing Christians, as the sum total of all believers everywhere. However, the church universal was an abstraction with little practical significance for him.[35]

The Landmark view of the church caused friction in the denominational structure when the Foreign Mission Board tried to establish the qualifications of missionaries it appoints. Ben Bogard, a former missionary to China, believed that the local church, not the denomination, possessed that authority.[36] At the end of the century, the furor surrounding the Whitsitt Controversy revealed both the strengths and weaknesses of Landmark sentiments. William H. Whitsitt had published anonymously in 1886 an article in *Johnson's Universal Encyclopedia* alleging that immersion of believers had not been recovered until 1641. Upon his election as president of the Southern Baptist Theological Seminary in 1895, his name was linked to the article. There was an outcry almost immediately. The Concord Association in Kentucky adopted a resolution affirming "that our beloved brother, Dr. William H. Whitsitt, has signally failed in his efforts to prove that no adults upon a profession of faith were immersed by English Baptists in England between the years 1500 and 1641."[37] Whitsitt was called upon to produce evidence proving his views or else resign as a teacher. This action was but one of many. W. W. Barnes indicated the extent of the argument: "The controversy raged in Baptist papers, in associations, in state conventions, in the Southern Convention—wherever and whenever Baptists assembled."[38] Whitsitt resigned the presidency of the seminary in 1899.

That personal as well as theological issues were equally involved in the controversy can be seen in retrospect. In the first place, Whitsitt's successor in the field of church history, W. J. McGlothlin, taught the same view as Whitsitt had taught. Further, many Landmarkers formally withdrew from the convention in 1905 and formed the General Association of Landmark Baptists, later (in 1924) re-named American Baptist Association.[39] As W. W. Barnes aptly observed, the Landmarkers "won the battle, but lost the war."[40]

Baptist successionism as a spirit continued to live, though muted, within the convention. John T. Christian of the Baptist Bible Institute in New Orleans (now the New Orleans Baptist Theological Seminary) wrote a two-volume work *A History of the Baptists*. J. M. Carroll, brother of B. H. Carroll, the founder of the

Southwestern Baptist Theological Seminary, composed a tract still read called *The Trail of Blood*. Both authors sought to prove the succession of Baptists through various dissenting historical groups.

LANDMARK IMPACT ON THE ORDINANCES

There has always been a strong sentiment among many Baptists that the Lord's Supper is for baptized believers only and that only those who have been immersed by a proper administrator are scripturally baptized. Backus argued as much in the eighteenth century. However, some Baptists from 1800-1845 interpreted baptism to be a gospel rather than a church ordinance. William B. Johnson, the only man to serve as president of both the General Missionary Convention and the Southern Baptist Convention, believed that any believer was entitled to baptism and any evangelist was entitled to perform the rite. He wrote:

> Baptism is committed to ministerial hands—the Lord's Supper is not. Baptism is a personal, individual ordinance; the supper is a social church ordinance. The one is the ordinance of the kingdom of Christ; the other, of the churches of Christ. The evangelist is an officer of the kingdom, not a church of Christ.[41]

Later, after the founding of The Southern Baptist Theological Seminary, two of its faculty members, William Williams[42] and F. H. Kerfoot, argued in favor of accepting alien immersion by Baptist churches. A. T. Robertson added that Kerfoot modified "his views to an intermediate position between the two extremes on the alien immersion question" after further study at the seminary.[43] Nevertheless, sentiment was against alien immersion. A mediating position was impossible in an environment where the devil was credited with originating infant baptism[44] and in which those who sprinkle are not authorized to baptize under the authority of Christ's commission.[45]

The decisive factor in the change in the Southern Baptist attitude toward alien immersion came from the strong personalities who led the Landmark movement. They helped foster in Southern Baptists a disdain for other theologies that preempted cooperation with other cultural institutions, including other denominations. The Landmarkers quickly realized that if baptism is a gospel ordinance rather than a church ordinance, they would have to modify their doctrine of the church. In a lengthy article in 1855, a contributor to the *Southern Baptist Review and Eclectic*, edited by Graves and Dayton, conceded that many Baptists thought of baptism as a gospel ordinance. He objected to that interpretation on the grounds that baptism is a prerequisite to church membership which "introduces those who are baptized into the local, visible church whose fellowship bids them welcome." As a gospel ordinance the church would actually have no control over baptism, one of its requirements for membership.[46] Disciplinary control of the ordinance must remain within the local church.

A. C. Dayton assailed Richard Fuller's argument that baptismal succession could not be demonstrated. He contended that it was specious at best. A supposed break in the chain "in the long gone past" was no real ground for a church to sanction a baptism "which she *knows* to be illegal and unscriptural, concerning which there is not even a *pretense* that the administrators were qualified."[47] Church order must be observed.

As the attack on alien immersion intensified, its opponents linked baptism and the Supper into one dogma with two sides. *Kind Words*, a Sunday School periodical published for a time by the Home Mission Board, often featured doctrinally apologetic articles. One of these appeared in 1875. The author noted that only those who had faith to discern the broken body and shed blood of Jesus were allowed by the apostles to commune because the apostles knew who had such faith by observing who had submitted to baptism. He concluded the article with an appeal to denominational pride:

> Let our young readers learn carefully from this now, why Baptists do not permit other denominations to commune with them: it is because they have not been baptized in the only and correct way, according to the belief of Baptists. It is not because Baptists are bigoted, or think themselves better than others, but because they think *baptized believers* only are authorized by the Bible to partake of the communion. Do you think you can defend the Baptists now, when you hear them called narrow-minded and bigoted?[48]

Southern Baptist denominational leaders defended the Baptist position as they understood it. J. M. Frost, founder of the Sunday School Board, attacked infant baptism in a book entitled *Pedobaptism: Is It from Heaven or of Men?*[49] In a symposium edited by Frost, R. M. Dudley put restricted communion as a "Baptist distinctive."[50] E. C. Dargan, who taught at The Southern Baptist Theological Seminary, believed that each church must satisfy itself that a "real Christian baptism has been received before admitting any applicant to its membership," although he concluded that differences of opinion existed as to what constitutes valid baptism in some cases.[51] He held that only a properly baptized person acting under the authority of a church should baptize.[52] A. H. Strong, whose work on systematic theology has been widely used among Southern Baptists, warned that open communion leads to open membership, and open membership results in "virtually an identification of the church with the world."[53] Paradoxically, Strong was willing to accept Campbellite immersion "wherever it appears that there was intent to profess an already existing faith and regeneration."[54] Neither was baptism again to be administered to one who later decided he was mistaken in his earlier profession as long as the intention had been to express faith in Christ.⁵⁵ The Charleston Association had come to that conclusion in 1810 in answer to the question, "Whether it is warrantable to baptize a second time, a person who at first was baptized in an unconverted state?"⁵⁶ It answered in the negative.

However, J. R. Graves, the great popularizer of Landmarkism, identified a practice which was already undermining the tenets of Landmarkism. The Supper was becoming a denominational rather than a church ordinance, "thus immeasurably weakening the whole line of defense, and, in fact, abandoning" the "chief bulwark to the enemy," and, by that practice, "perverting the sacred symbolism of the Supper."⁵⁷ He realized that communion based on "like faith and order" could be but a step from open communion. He died in 1893, twelve years before many Landmarkers would withdraw from the convention in 1905 to form their own association.

THE ASCENDANCY OF AMILLENNIALISM

Millennialism has a way of being put to rest by one generation only to be rejuvenated with vigor by another. Premillennialism especially has suffered at the hands of its adherents who permitted eschatological fervor to trample common sense. The chiliasts of the radical reformation in Europe alienated large segments of the population by their excessive zeal from 1525 until about 1540. The Fifth Monarchy men in England under Cromwell did little to enhance the public image of millennialists. When one adds Alexander Campbell and J. R. Graves to the premillennial list, the image becomes well-nigh irretrievable.

Graves made premillennialism a prominent feature of Landmarkism. Like Isaac Backus before him, he saw the Revelation of John as a continuous history of the Christian church. The *Southern Baptist Review and Eclectic*, edited at various times by Graves, J. M. Pendleton, and N. M. Crawford, president of Mercer University, published extensive excerpts from G. H. Orchard's work on Baptist history to which Graves wrote an introduction.⁵⁸ Premillennialism was ardently supported.

A statement in the *Southern Baptist Review and Eclectic* in 1855 is striking. It said, "All christians [sic] are millennialists, but they are divided into two classes—*Post*-millennialists, or, *Pre*-millennialists."⁵⁹ That the assessment had a degree of validity can be verified from other sources. John A. Broadus testified in a letter to E. Y. Mullins, "The popular view, which I was accustomed in youth to hold in a vague way, [was] that, before the coming of our Lord, there will be a thousand years of universal and perfect Christian piety."⁶⁰ Other Baptist writers of the period vouched to the preponderance of the two views. In a personal letter to Broadus, A. J. Gordon of Boston, whom one biographer called "a precursor of fundamentalism, especially concerning inspiration, soul-winning, and premillennialism,"⁶¹ stated, "All in this part of the country are strongly and avowedly post-millennial, and the other view is for the most part looked upon with great disfavor."[62]

Boyce had strong opinions about the Calvinistic doctrines of grace. On the millennial question, he hesitated to commit himself to a definite system. His language shows an almost casual use of the word, Kingdom. Boyce, just twenty-one years old, wrote in 1848, "Let our efforts at least be exerted for the furtherance of Christ's Kingdom upon earth."[63] Boyce incorporated a modified postmillennial theory into his book of theology which he taught at the Southern Baptist Theological Seminary. He believed in a personal return of Christ and a general resurrection.[64] However, the thousand year reign was an uncertain period. Boyce said:

> The thousand years of the binding of Satan is a period of time, of unknown, perhaps of indefinite length, possibly from the time of Christ's conquest of Satan, in his death, resurrection, and ascension, or possibly from some other period, even perhaps of a later epoch in the history of Christianity, during which Satan is restrained from the exercise of the power he might otherwise put forth against man; the thousand years terminating at some time prior to the day of Christ's second coming; at which time Satan shall be loosed to consummate his evil deeds by such assaults upon the saints as shall bring down the final vengeance of God at the appearing of Christ in glory.[65]

When F. H. Kerfoot revised Boyce's book, he added a footnote to Boyce's postmillennialism. Kerfoot's note began, "There are very grave difficulties in the way of accepting either the pre-millennial or the post-millennial theory."[66] He believed that Christ would triumph over Satan and sin, and stated, "Whether he will first achieve this triumph and then reign a thousand years, or whether the thousand years is some period that will close with his coming, it is impossible to say. Neither is it very important for us to know. Our hope is in his coming. Our theology should somehow lead us to expect it."[67] Kerfoot, who had succeeded Boyce as professor of systematic theology, was thus exhibiting the trend toward amillennialism in Southern Baptist theology.

John A. Broadus arrived at a de facto amillennialism. As early as 1875, he admitted in private conversation with J. B. Gambrell that he did not know which millennial view was correct.[68] Nearly twenty years later, Broadus expressed his uncertainty in a letter to E. Y. Mullins, saying, "I am neither a Pre-millenniarian nor a Post-millenniarian, in the usual sense of those terms."[69] Broadus saw grave difficulties in both views. He contented himself with a belief in the personal return of Christ. Later, Mullins came to hold "substantially the same view as that indicated in the letter of Doctor Broadus."[70]

Prominent Baptists joined the chorus. B. F. Corley published material in 1856 favoring a modified postmillennialism.[71] The periodical which carried it was the *Southern Baptist Review and Eclectic*, co-edited by J. R. Graves and J. M.

Pendleton. Although Graves was a vocal premillennialist, Pendleton was a postmillennialist. His hand can probably be seen in the Corley article. Pendleton himself believed in a time when truth and righteousness would be prevalent throughout the world. He wrote, "My belief that the millennium will precede the personal coming of Christ has been sufficiently indicated."[72]

Postmillennialism persisted for several decades among Southern Baptists and then gradually died out. A. H. Strong, whose work on systematic theology was used extensively among Southern Baptists, espoused postmillennialism.[73] That E. C. Dargan seemed to lean in that direction may be inferred from his words, "Perhaps the larger number of Bible students and theologians consider that the second coming will be at the close of the Millennium period."[74]

As amillennialism grew in influence, premillennialism came under intense criticism from certain quarters. Part of the criticism was an outgrowth of the identification of the kingdom of God with the visible church which led almost inevitably to a conception of the kingdom as "here and now." A theological oddity came about. On the one hand, Landmarkism made the kingdom synonymous with the local church. A. C. Dayton used the concepts interchangeably in the following quotation:

> He who has professed his faith in Christ and has been baptized, is regarded by the churches as *initiated*; and it is on this ground alone that he is regarded by the churches as eligible to membership in any church. But it is evident that [for] this ceremony of *initiation* to be a valid one, [it] must be performed according to the law of the kingdom, and by those properly authorized to administer that law. Now if baptism be the door of entrance, it is certain that the unbaptized have not come in. They being out of the kingdom can have no authority in it.[75]

On the other hand, amillennialism itself came to identify the kingdom with the church in its broad sense. Those who see the kingdom of God as the rule of God in the hearts of believers often describe the universal church as composed of all the believers of all the ages. Premillennialists are more inclined to make a radical break between the church and the kingdom of God.

THE NECESSITY OF THE RESURRECTION

Nearly all millennialists hold to a physical resurrection of the body. Until late in the twentieth century, nearly all Southern Baptists affirmed with the *Philadelphia Confession* that at death the body returns to dust to await the resurrection. In the theology of the confession, the souls of the righteous go directly to paradise to be in the presence of Christ, whereas the souls of the wicked proceed directly to hell and remain in torment until the judgment.[76] Both soul-sleep and annihilationism were rejected in the affirmation that departed souls neither die nor sleep. Purgatory was not even considered a possibility because the Scriptures acknowledge only two places of abode for departed souls.

Until the middle of the twentieth century, Southern Baptist theologians did not take serious issue with the theology of death described in the confession. Boyce wrote, "The Scriptures teach that the soul and body that have been separated in death, will be reunited at the Judgment Day."[77] At the beginning of the twentieth century, E. C. Dargan saw the implications of a theology in which resurrection and judgment are spiritual and figurative, occurring for each individual at death. Said Dargan:

> According to this fanciful notion, for the believer death and the resurrection are simultaneous, if not identical. He rises as soon as he dies; this corruptible puts on incorruption by escaping forever from the old body and taking on just then a totally distinct spiritual body! This view not only crosses the plain meaning of scripture concerning the resurrection, as we shall see in unfolding that meaning, but also requires a corresponding change of view in regard to the Second Coming of Christ and the Judgment. This view virtually denies the reality of all these events as future occurrences and makes them only continuous processes, or events only to each individual at his death.[78]

Not until implications drawn from the view of the psychosomatic entity view of man's nature have any Southern Baptists differed publicly from Dargan's appraisal. Those variations will be pointed out below.

ORGANIZING FOR THE CAUSE OF MISSIONS

The Southern Baptist genius for organization found its ultimate expression in the structure of the Southern Baptist Convention in which it subsumed foreign and home missions, Sunday School work, and other functions under one general organization. To highlight how that structure differs from previous Baptist missionary organizations, one may go back to the beginning of the modern missionary movement with William Carey in England in 1792. Carey and Andrew Fuller were the guiding spirits of the fourteen men who met in a widow's house October 2, 1792, in Kettering, England, to form the first Baptist missionary society, The Particular Baptist Society for the Propagation of the Gospel Among the Heathen. The society was not controlled by any group of churches. Baptists in America adopted a similar organizational structure in 1814 with the establishment of the General Missionary Convention and in 1832 with the Home Mission Society, to the extent that each organization was responsible for one type of work. They instituted a societal, rather than, associational structure.

Baptists in the South were ready to launch out in a new direction in 1845 when they formed the Southern Baptist Convention in Augusta, Georgia. Baptists North and South divided as a result of the slavery question. Because the Home Mission Society had difficulty enlisting missionaries willing to serve in the South, Baptists in the South felt that their region was being neglected. When the HMS refused to appoint slave-holders as missionaries, Baptists in the South interpreted the refusal as a violation of the constitution adopted by the HMS. Baptists in the North minimized the constitutional violation as they emphasized the violation of ethical and scriptural principles posed by the practice of slavery. Cultural factors also played a part. Lynn E. May, Jr., notes, "This denominational schism did not occur over-night. Nor can it be simply explained as a result of the slavery controversy, for the causes of the break were far more complex than this single issue. The milieu of the antebellum South contributed significantly to the birth of the Southern Baptist Convention."[79] Furthermore, geographical distances, poor roads, and poor means of communications all contributed to a fragmentation of ideals and loyalties.

Diverse national origins of the peoples were also a factor. English influence was stronger in the North than in the South. Spanish influence dominated Florida. Charleston was typical of the Carolinas, with its cosmopolitan flavor, as immigrants from France, Ireland, New England, and the West Indies settled there.[80] Frenchmen settled the Louisiana territory. Georgia was later settled under the sponsorship of an Englishman, John Oglethorpe, but the situation was unique. Oglethorpe, moved by a humanitarian desire, established a refuge for debtors who would otherwise be sent to prison. He began with a hundred settlers and founded Savannah, but other immigrants soon came from Scotland and Wales.[81] Slaves by the thousands brought new practices, new language patterns, and new responsibilities for their owners. They posed a spiritual burden and a spiritual opportunity. Therefore, Southerners were more than transplanted New Englanders. They were given the ingredients for a life-style of their own. This proclivity can be seen in Southern Baptist ecclesiastical structures.

To protect the autonomy and independence of the local churches, Southern Baptists follow the same format previously established in the relationships between the churches, associations, and state conventions. Churches and other entities send delegates (messengers) to the associations and state levels who in turn form the associations and state convention. Strictly speaking, no churches are members of the association or state convention. All three levels are hierarchically independent of each other. So it was with the Southern Baptist Convention. The churches send messengers to the Southern Baptist Convention but no actions of the convention are binding on the churches. The convention constitution and bylaws adopted in 1845 spelled out the specific goals of the fledgling organization, namely to unite Baptists for the purpose of propagating the Gospel.[82]

The propagation of the gospel being the sole purpose of the convention, its founders then set up a Board of Domestic Missions and a Foreign Mission Board, each given evangelistic responsibilities at home or abroad. Article V of the constitution stated the right of the convention to establish as many boards or agencies as it deemed necessary to fulfill its purposes. The Board of Domestic Missions (the Home Mission Board of today), now in Atlanta, was located originally in Marion, Alabama. The Foreign Mission Board was located in Richmond, Virginia, where it still remains.

The differences between the societal and the convention way of carrying out missionary endeavors sheds some light on the debate carried on in the 1980s. The societal method places the sponsorship of the work under an independent, usually self-perpetuating, board of directors in which the society is responsible for overseeing the work. Money is solicited wherever it can be found, but no group of churches controls the society. In the convention approach, several programs are placed under one organization. It, in turn, is controlled by the sponsoring churches. When pastors today are accused of being "independent fundamentalists," one implied accusation is that their churches do not participate in the method of central giving for missions. Instead, they carry out their missionary enterprises only through the local church.

Before closing this section, the role of women in missions deserves recognition. At its inception in 1845, the convention limited its membership to male messengers. As late as 1885, women attempted to gain seats at the convention on the premise that Article Three of the constitution mentioned members, not men. A committee was appointed and the constitution was amended to say *brethren* by a vote of 131 to 42.[83]

The women were down but not out. Charlotte "Lottie" Moon (1840-1912) had been appointed by the Foreign Mission Board to China in 1873. Her letters to women across the South pleading for missionary support developed into a Christmas love offering for missions in 1888. From this inauspicious beginning came the annual Lottie Moon Christmas offering for foreign missions. To promote missionary enterprises, Southern Baptist women founded the Woman's Missionary Union in 1888 as an auxiliary to the Southern Baptist Convention. Annie Walker Armstrong (1850-1938) served without pay as the corresponding secretary from 1888 until 1906. It is in her honor that convention churches inaugurated the Annie Armstrong offering for home missions. Women have deeply influenced the direction of Southern Baptist missions.

SUMMARY

The most pervasive theological issue consuming Southern Baptist attention from 1845-1900 was ecclesiology, particularly Landmarkism. J. R. Graves, whose name conjures up the Landmarker image for those familiar with Southern Baptist history, capitalized on a belief which Baptists had been proclaiming for half a century, Baptist church succession, and gave it new impetus.

Under Landmark preaching, the ordinances gradually became local church ordinances. No longer would Southern Baptists of the nineteenth century describe the rite of baptism as a gospel ordinance with the concomitant teaching that traveling evangelists had the right to baptize irrespective of local church authority. Neither would they further entertain the possibility of an observance of the Supper in any setting other than that of a local church.

Premillennialism suffered a loss in popularity among convention leaders until it was supplanted by amillennialism. Postmillennialism still claimed some adherents at the end of the century, but its days were numbered.

The cause of missions gained ground incalculably as a result of the formation of the Woman's Missionary Union in 1888. Lottie Moon and Annie Armstrong left their names to Baptist posterity in the form of annual offerings for foreign and home missions collected in their names across the convention.

NOTES

1. Walter B. Shurden, *Not a Silent People: Controversies That Have Helped Shape Southern Baptists* (Nashville: Broadman Press, 1972), pp. 21-32.
2. W. Morgan Patterson, *Baptist Successionism: A Critical View* (Valley Forge: Judson Press, 1969), p. 26.
3. J. J. Burnett, *Sketches of Tennessee's Pioneer Baptist Preachers, Being, Incidentally, a History of Baptist Beginnings in the Several Associations in the State Containing, Particularly, Character and Life Sketches of the Standard-Bearers and Leaders of Our People*, 2 vols. (Nashville: Marshall and Bruce Company, 1919) 1:186.
4. J. R. Graves, *The Watchman's Reply* (Nashville: Graves and Shankland, 1853), p. 20.
5. Ibid., p. 8, footnote.
6. Ibid., footnote 2.
7. Ibid., footnote 3.
8. Ibid., p. 12. Nearly three decades later, Graves had decided that the two witnesses were the Baptist ministry and Baptist churches. See the dedication page of his work *Intercommunion Inconsistent, Unscriptural, and Productive of Evil*, 2nd ed. (Memphis: J. R. Graves and Son, 1890), p. iii.
9. Graves, *The Watchman's Reply*, p. 12.
10. Ibid., p. 21.
11. Ibid., pp. 24-25.
12. Ibid., p. 25.
13. Ibid., p. 31.
14. Ibid., p. 59.
15. Robert G. Torbet, "Landmarkism," in *Baptist Concepts of the Church*, ed. Winthrop S. Hudson (Philadelphia: Judson Press, 1959), p. 175.
16. William A. Carleton, "Influence in Continental America," *Baptist Advance*, gen. ed. Davis C. Woolley (Nashville: Broadman Press, 1964), p. 391.
17. *The Confederate Baptist* 1 (April 29, 1863):2.
18. Graves, *The Watchman's Reply*, p. 25.
19. Ibid., p. 26. Graves was reflecting an attitude that was widely held in his day. Even Charles Hodge, stalwart of Old School Presbyterianism at Princeton, identified the papacy as the Antichrist. Charles Hodge, *Systematic Theology*, 3 vols. (New York: Scribner and Co., 1873) 3: 812-823.
20. Graves, *The Watchman's Reply*, p. 65.
21. Ibid., p. 27.
22. Graves, *Intercommunion Inconsistent*, pp. 17-20.
23. Ibid., p. 34.
24. "Who Are The Old Baptists?" *The Commission* 3 (February 1859):225-228.
25. "The Baptists," *Kind Words* 12 (May 15, 1877):3.

26. D. B. Ray, *Baptist Succession: A Hand-Book of Baptist History*, 18th ed. (St. Louis: National Baptist Publishing Co., 1870), pp. 15-16.

27. J. B. Gambrell, "The Multiplicity of Denominations [an] Evil," *Baptist Doctrines: Being an Exposition, in a Series of Essays by Representative Baptist Ministers, of the Distinctive Points of Baptist Faith and Practice*, ed. C. A. Jenkins (St. Louis: Chancey R. Barns, 1881), p. 296.

28. Burnett, *Sketches*, p. 194.

29. Article XV. The entire *Abstract of Principles* is printed in William A. Mueller, *A History of Southern Baptist Theological Seminary* (Nashville: Broadman Press, 1959), pp. 238-241.

30. Ibid.

31. Edward. T. Hiscox, *The New Directory for Baptist Churches* (Philadelphia: Judson Press, 1894), p. 24.

32. Ibid., p. 25.

33. Ibid., p. 15. This definition is slightly enlarged from one given in 1880. See Hiscox, *The Star Book of Baptist Church Polity* (New York: Ward and Company, 1880), p. 28.

34. A. H. Strong, *Systematic Theology: A Compendium and Commonplace-Book Designed for the Use of Theological Students*, (New York: A. C. Armstrong and Son, 1902), p. 494.

35. E. C. Dargan, *Ecclesiology: A Study of the Churches*, 2nd ed., rev. (Louisville, Kentucky: Charles T. Dearing, 1905), p. 51.

36. For a survey of the schisms in the convention precipitated by Landmarkism, see Robert A. Baker, *The Southern Baptist Convention and Its People, 1607-1972*, (Nashville: Broadman Press, 1972), pp. 277-284.

37. J. N. Waldrop, *History of the Concord Association Covering a Period from 1821 to 1906* (Owenton, Kentucky: News-Herald Print, 1907), p. 47.

38. W. W. Barnes, *The Southern Baptist Convention, 1845-1953* (Nashville: Broadman Press, 1954), p. 138.

39. *Encyclopedia of Southern Baptists*, s.v. "Landmarkism," by W. Morgan Patterson.

40. Barnes, *The Southern Baptist Convention*, p. 138.

41. Dayton, "A Review of Dr. W. B. Johnson's Article on 'Unbaptized Evangelists,'" *Southern Baptist Review* 4 (January 1858):3-4.

42. George Boardman Eager, "Rev. William Williams, D.D., LL.D.," *Review and Expositor* 6 (July 1909):417-418.

43. A. T. Robertson, *Life and Letters of John Albert Broadus*, (Philadelphia: American Baptist Publication Society, 1910), p. 301.

44. James Whitsitt, "Ordinances Administered by Pedobaptists," *Southern Baptist Review* 5 (September 1859):390.

45. Ibid., pp. 379-380.

46. "The Scriptural Meaning of the Term Church (Concluded)," *Southern Baptist Review and Eclectic* 1 (February-March 1855):67.

47. A. C. Dayton, "Review of Elder R. Fuller's Views of the Immersion of Pedobaptists," *Southern Baptist Review* 3 (January 1857):139-140.

48. "Our Defense," *Kind Words, For the Sunday School Children* 10 (January 12, 1875).

49. J. M. Frost, *Pedobaptism: Is It from Heaven or of Men?* (Philadelphia: American Baptist Publication Society, 1875).

50. R. M. Dudley, "The Distinctive Baptist Why," *Baptist: Why and Why Not*, ed. J. M. Frost (Nashville: Sunday School Board of the Southern Baptist Convention, 1900), p. 32.

51. Dargan, *Ecclesiology*, p. 279.

52. E. C. Dargan, *The Doctrines of Our Faith*, (Nashville: Sunday School Board of the Southern Baptist Convention, 1905), p. 176.

53. Strong, *Systematic Theology*, p. 552.

54. Ibid., p. 534.

55. Ibid.

56. Wood Furman, *A History of the Charleston Association of Baptist Churches in the State of South Carolina; with an Appendix Containing the Principal Circular Letters to the Churches*, (Charleston, South Carolina: J. Hoff, 1811), p. 37.

57. Graves, *Intercommunion*, p. 11.

58. Graves, "Introductory Essay," in G. H. Orchard, *A Concise History of Foreign Baptists: Taken from the New Testament, The First Fathers, Early Writers, and Historians of all Ages; Chronologically arranged: Exhibiting their Distinct Communities, with their orders in various Kingdoms, under several Discriminative Appellations from the Establishment of Christianity to the present age: with CORRELATIVE INFORMATION, SUPPORTING THE EARLY AND ONLY PRACTICE OF BELIEVERS' IMMERSION: ALSO OBSERVATIONS AND NOTES ON THE ABUSE OF THE ORDINANCE, AND THE RISE OF MINOR AND INFANT BAPTISM* 9th ed. (Nashville: Graves, Marks & Rutland, Agents of Tennessee Publication Society, [1855]).

59. "Chiliasm," *Southern Baptist Review and Eclectic* 1 (October-November-December 1855):636.

60. Robertson, *Life and Letters*, p. 417.

61. *Encyclopedia of Southern Baptists*, s.v. "Gordon, Adoniram Judson," by Hugh Wamble.

62. Robertson, *Life and Letters*, p. 310.
63. James P. Boyce, "Our Missionary Intelligence," *The Southern Baptist* 3 (November 29, 1848):531.
64. James P. Boyce, *Abstract of Systematic Theology*, (Philadelphia: American Baptist Publication Society, 1887), p. 452.
65. Ibid., p. 461.
66. James P. Boyce, *Abstract of Systematic Theology*, rev. by F. H. Kerfoot (Philadelphia: American Baptist Publication Society, 1899), p. 408, footnote 1.
67. Ibid., p. 409, footnote.
68. J. B. Gambrell, "My First Southern Baptist Convention," *Southwestern Journal of Theology* 5 (April 1921):44.
69. Robertson, *Life and Letters*, p. 417.
70. Ibid., p. 418, footnote 1. Also see Mullins, *The Christian Religion in Its Doctrinal Expression*, pp. 466-472.
71. B. F. Corley, "The Advancement of Christ's Kingdom through the Restoration and Conversion of the Jews," *Southern Baptist Review and Eclectic* 2 (March-April 1856):188-202.
72. J. M. Pendleton, *Christian Doctrines: A Compendium of Theology* (Philadelphia: The Judson Press, 1878), p. 383.
73. Strong, *Systematic Theology*, pp. 571-574.
74. Dargan, *The Doctrines of Our Faith* (Nashville: Sunday School Board of the Southern Baptist Convention, 1905), p. 204.
75. [A. C. Dayton] "Review of Elder R. Fuller's Views of the Immersion of Pedobaptists," *Southern Baptist Review* 3 (January 1857):133.
76. Lumpkin, *Baptist Confessions*, pp. 293-294.
77. Boyce, *Abstract*, p. 446.
78. Dargan, *The Doctrines of Our Faith*, p. 194.
79. Lynn E. May, Jr., "Factors Contributing to the Origin of the Southern Baptist Convention," *Quarterly Review* 31 (October-November-December 1970):53.
80. John D. Hicks, *The Federal Union*, 2nd ed. (Cambridge, Massachusetts: Houghton-Mifflin Co., 1952), p. 41.
81. Ibid., pp. 46-47.
82. Robert A. Baker, *A Baptist Source Book with Particular Reference to Southern Baptists* (Nashville: Broadman Press, 1966), p. 116.
83. *Southern Baptist Convention Annual, 1885*, p. 30.

PART III

EVANGELISTIC EVANGELICALISM, 1899-1960

Chapter 7. Committed to Evangelism
Chapter 8. Contending with the Critics
Chapter 9. E. Y. Mullins and Neoorthodoxy

OVERVIEW

Although Landmarkism did not die with the coming of the twentieth century, it had peaked as a doctrinal movement with the capacity to garner new masses of followers. Calvinism also continued its slide into theological oblivion. In their stead, Southern Baptists forged their own brand of evangelistic evangelicalism as they isolated themselves from the world of academic pluralism. In spite of this development, however, both fundamentalism and neoorthodoxy made inroads, albeit belatedly. Major theological changes were more than half a century away. After the debate about biblical inspiration temporarily was resolved in 1925, theological calm settled over the convention until the sixties. It was during this respite from strife, while Southern Baptists devised programs for surviving financially during the Great Depression, that they solidified the doctrinal basis for evangelism. They also forged a denominational structure for evangelism and hammered it into one of the greatest missionary implements since first century Christianity, increasing in membership from 1.66 million in 1900 to 9.7 million in 1960. The annual number of baptisms during the same period went from 80,465 to 386,469. It was a fruitful time.

The three chapters in this unit of study cover the period from the firing of W. H. Whitsitt in 1899 to the firing of Theodore R. Clark at the New Orleans Baptist Theological Seminary in 1960. Both firings are symptomatic of a change in the theological winds of Southern Baptists. Chapter 7 gives a survey of the impact of evangelism on Southern Baptist theology. Chapters 8 and 9 pick up the development of two schools of thought that eventually shook Southern Baptist denominational unity, fundamentalism and neoorthodoxy.

CHAPTER 7

COMMITTED TO EVANGELISM

The beginning of the twentieth century ushered in a new era as a more relaxed mood accompanied the excitement of the Gay Nineties. Orville and Wilbur Wright forever altered the course of history on the windswept dunes of Kill Devil Hill, near Kitty Hawk, North Carolina, when Orville flew his contraption 120 feet on December 17, 1903, for mankind's first powered flight. It would not be long before Henry Ford helped revolutionize social structures by making automobiles available to the average individual.

Christendom also felt the impact of the new mood. People of many theological persuasions speculated about the time of Christ's second coming to earth, about the fulfillment of prophecy. Postmillennialism gained in favor with its promise of a Golden Age on Earth. The mood was rudely shattered when Serbian nationalists assassinated Archduke Franz Ferdinand of Austria on June 28, 1914, and plunged the world into global warfare. The war also devastated carefully erected theological systems. For example, in the ravages of battle, Karl Barth laid aside his liberal theology in favor of a new orthodoxy. He sought a more secure base for his theology.

Southern Baptists were not untouched by the change of mood about 1900. Even theological curricula reflected the optimistic mood. Theology in some respects became less abrasive, less combative. In The Southern Baptist Theological Seminary report to the Southern Baptist Convention in 1914, attention was brought to the change in the mood of the school:

> In the older time the second year in Theology was given to Latin Theology. Little by little more attention was given to the study of some of the greater doctrines in addition to the Latin readings. . . . The school of Polemics has

been greatly changed. . . . The study of the ordinances has been transferred to Ecclesiology; the emphasis is now placed rather upon Apologetics than Polemics.[1]

The report accurately summarized the spirit of the day and, at the same time, pointed the direction of the Southern Baptist attitude of peaceful exposition of theology which would be coupled with fervid evangelistic zeal. Southern's scholars were studiously constructing a theological mood which would be devoid of the strident voice of fundamentalism.

The noncombative theological mood at The Southern Baptist Theological Seminary found its counterpoint in a tendency toward doctrinal inbreeding among Southern Baptists as they developed their own academic system. State conventions continued to work toward establishing their network of Baptist educational institutions, having chartered Furman in South Carolina (1827), Georgetown in Kentucky (1829), Mercer in Georgia (1833), Wake Forest in North Carolina (1834), Samford in Alabama in 1842, and Judson College in Alabama (organized as a school for women in 1839 and accepted by the state convention in 1843), and others as the century progressed.[2] Steady growth in the number of graduates from Baptist and secular colleges led to the formation of an additional seminary, Southwestern Baptist Theological Seminary, which the convention voted to accept in 1925, a school which grew out of Baylor University in 1908 under the leadership of B. H. Carroll.[3] Through their college-seminary system and the influence of literature published for the churches by the Baptist Sunday School Board, the powerful publication arm of the convention, Southern Baptists built and maintained a denomination dedicated to evangelistic outreach. Factors both human and divine could be cited to explain their phenomenal growth during this period, but theology surely was at the center.

Calvinism as a dominant force in the convention dissipated dramatically in the twentieth century until its voice was little more than a whisper. The combined strength of a Fullerite interpretation of the atonement and a Dargan-like understanding of the depravity of human nature reduced Calvinism to theoretical arguments about the sovereignty of God and tepid interpretations of election based on foreknowledge. Its surviving stalwarts fought defensive battles from the security of academic enclaves or an occasional pulpit, but the war was over.

Even Landmarkism had reached its zenith by the beginning of the twentieth century. It reached a plateau which lasted for about five decades, but its mood and dogmatism no longer found ready acceptance among Southern Baptists. Its aggressiveness was reduced to rearguard defensiveness among those who continue to profess it. Although its influence among Southern Baptists exceeds that of Calvinism, its capacity to excite theological debate and to precipitate widespread dissension has died away. Apart from the tensions brought about by the controversy over biological evolution and the trauma induced by indebtedness, evangelism and missions dominated Southern Baptist thought.

ELECTION BECOMES FOREKNOWLEDGE

Concerning the doctrine of the Trinity, Southern Baptists of the twentieth century kept the faith of those of the nineteenth but with a decisive difference in focus. In the nineteenth century they speculated endlessly about the sovereignty of God and his divine decrees. In the twentieth, they were more concerned with the Second Person of the Trinity, in making salvation available to all peoples. Nevertheless, they remained firmly committed to a thoroughgoing trinitarian theology.

At the center of trinitarian theology is the necessity of maintaining meaningful distinctions within the Godhead without sliding into tritheism. Tertullian (ca. 160/170-ca.215/220), the famous Latin theologian from Carthage, was one of the first to expound systematically the doctrine of the Trinity and to make use of term. Expositions can be found in *Against Praxeas*, written about 215. Other early Christians devoted years of argument and voluminous writings as they attempted to understand and explain the relations of the Trinity and the nature of Christ. For Southern Baptists in the early twentieth century, E. Y. Mullins phrased the contending positions well when he inquired whether the Trinity is immanent or merely economic.[4] Those who teach the latter, Modalists, believe that God revealed himself in successive stages as Father, Son, and Holy Spirit, but in himself, he was not Father at the same time he was Son. Therefore, there are no distinctions within the Godhead. Mullins specifically rejected such a concept, believing that the distinctions lie within the Godhead.[5]

Other Baptist thinkers espoused the doctrine of the Trinity. Harold W. Tribble expressed one definition acceptable to most Baptists. He wrote:

> In the New Testament the essence of the doctrine of the Trinity is given. God the Father is revealed in the Son, and God the Holy Spirit makes the revelation complete and effective. Yet God the Father, God the Son, and God the Holy Spirit are but the three personal manifestations of the one God. They are one. Thus it is not tritheism, three gods, but triunity, three persons in the one Godhead.[6]

Walter T. Conner (1877-1952) also explained God as trinity in unity.[7]

On other facets of their doctrine of God, Southern Baptists continued their inexorable redirection away from Calvinism. Thomas J. Nettles studied the contributions of two former seminary presidents whose writings and influence contributed to the Arminiazation of Southern Baptist theology, E. Y. Mullins and L. R. Scarborough (1870-1945). Nettles chronicled Scarborough's shift from strong Calvinistic sentiments toward a more anthropocentric theology. To illustrate the former, he quoted a Scarborough report to the Baptist General Convention of Texas in 1913, which embraced the doctrine of predestination and advocated a worldwide program of evangelism.[8] Nettles referred extensively to

Scarborough's many books on evangelism and soul-winning, citing instances to show how emphasis on man's choice "eats up the Sovereignty of God" and produces "an ever-diminishing acquaintance with the Doctrines of Grace."[9] With his analysis of the writings of Mullins and Scarborough, Nettles concluded his study of the impact of Calvinists who influenced the convention. The two men, committed to Calvinism's doctrines of grace, nevertheless represented "the two major influences producing the gradual theological shift of Southern Baptists from a thoroughgoing Calvinism to semi-Arminianism."[10] They were also pivotal in growing within the convention a theology of evangelistic outreach.

Walter T. Conner (1877-1952) also wrote during the period of time when Southern Baptist theology further divested itself of its Calvinistic cloak. Conner, as did so many of his colleagues, approached the doctrine of God under the felt obligation of giving an account of God's sovereignty and decrees as they impinge on belief in human freewill and accountability. In his book *Christian Doctrine*, popular with theological students a generation ago, Conner's language sounded thoroughly Calvinistic when he discussed God's purpose as it relates to the salvation of the individual. When a person is saved, Conner believed the salvation experience does not come to pass by chance. God saves because he intends to save.[11]

It is in Conner's explication of God's electing purpose that the erosion of Calvinism emerges. He could say that "all saving efficiency is of God,"[12] and he even spoke about an "efficacious call,"[13] but he never grounded election in the divine decree. At times, he described election as meaning that "God takes the initiative in our salvation."[14] He added, "The doctrine of election is simply the recognition of the fact that the good that comes into our lives comes as a result of God's purpose."[15] He also concluded that election is a process:

> Having purposed eternally to save us, he works out in time his purpose for us. His purpose is effected in and through the social and historical order to which we belong. His purpose concerning our salvation includes all the factors and relations of this social and historical order, just as a father plans the education of his son, but plans it in view of the social and educational influences and agencies that are available or can be made available. God instituted the social and historical order with a view to our salvation.[16]

How can one account for Conner's almost frenetic grasping for an understanding of predestination and election devoid of Calvinistic overtones? Although there is no simple explanation for complex realities, part of the answer derives from the historical happenstance of Conner's career among Southern Baptists. He lived and formulated his theology at a time when Southern Baptist theology was separating itself from the Calvinistic dogmas of God's sovereignty. With Andrew Fuller's writings in the middle of the nineteenth century, the doctrine of limited atonement suffered a mortal blow. During the remainder of the century, the doctrines of irresistible grace and total depravity were redefined in the direction of Arminianism. The thoughts of Mullins, Scarborough, and Conner typify the final stages of those who begin with God's sovereignty and try to reconcile free will with it. In contrast, Southern Baptists of the last quarter of the twentieth century are more inclined to begin with human free will and then adjust the concept of sovereignty to it. In a general sense the older theology was theocentric; that of today is anthropocentric.

The Southern Baptist theology of evangelism that was being developed was not merely attached to a Calvinistic framework that was being jettisoned. Outstanding leaders dedicated their ministries to the promotion of evangelism and missions. Scarborough's famous work on evangelism *With Christ After the Lost: A Search for Souls*, first published in 1919 and republished in 1952 after revision by E. D. Head, was a basic seminary textbook well into the sixties. He wrote *Endued to Win* in 1922 and *How Jesus Won Men* in 1926. Isaac Jacobus Van Ness (1860-1947) of the Sunday School Board deeply influenced church evangelism with his *Training in Church Membership* in 1908, revised in 1936. His *Training in the Baptist Spirit* of 1914 was revised by him in 1940. Roland Quinche Leavell (1891-1963), pastor, evangelist, teacher, and seminary president, left his imprint on evangelistic endeavors with such books as *Helping Others to Become Christians* (1939), *Saving America to Save the World* (1940), and *Winning Others to Christ* (1936). His magnum opus, *Evangelism, Christ's Imperative Commission* (1951) was revised and republished by his nephew Landrum P. Leavell. Directors of the Home Mission Board, Woman's Missionary Union, pastors, teachers, and lay people gave themselves in a combined effort to win people to Christ. Soul-winning bordered on becoming an obsession.

PSYCHOLOGY AND THE SOUL

Southern Baptists fought among themselves over teachings arising from the biological sciences. Could one reconcile belief in biological evolution with belief in the historicity of Genesis 1-11? How would acceptance of biological evolution impact on the doctrine of human nature? In an evolutionary framework, what is the soul? What is the spirit? What is the Image of God? How and when did the conscience arise? Not until the sixties and seventies would these and similar questions gain theological attention among Southern Baptist thinkers.

Biological evolutionists were not alone in questioning whether humans have a non-material aspect about them separable from the physical body, be it called soul or spirit. René Descartes (1596-1650), ostensibly a French mathematician, but a profound thinker in his own right, set for himself the task of questioning all knowledge until he could find indubitable data. His famous assertion "I think; therefore I am" came out of his meditation. His name now graces the view that a human being is composed of both body and soul, Cartesian dualism.

Descartes's dualism came under attack from David Hume (1711-1776), who searched for a personal soul, and found it not. He concluded that one has no soul; consciousness is a series of impressions and nothing more. When a person dies, all impressions cease.

Neither philosophers nor psychologists have been able to resolve the issues raised by Descartes and Hume. By the end of the nineteenth century, psychology began breaking away from philosophy to form its own field of research. Five major schools of thought developed.[17] William Wundt (1832-1920) founded Structuralism, which emphasized that one must focus on the elementary processes of conscious experience. By analytic introspection, one discerns the structures of the mental life. John Dewey (1859-1952), an American noted for his pragmatic approach, emphasized the uses of the mental life in the context of life. He helped found Functionalism. Behaviorism is associated with John B. Watson (1878-1958) and B. F. Skinner (1904-1990). They studied the mechanics of behavior, giving particular attention to the effects of stimuli on consciousness. Ivan Pavlov (1849-1936) performed his epoch-making experiments with dogs to see what insights the study of animal behavior might shed on that of humans. The Gestalt Psychology of Max Wertheimer (1880-1943) took a broader view. He believed that people perceive the world as unitary wholes. The totality of the person must be considered. Psychoanalysis, of course, can never be dissociated from the name of Sigmund Freud (1856-1943) who pioneered studies in abnormal behavior. He believed that traumatic experiences in childhood, repressed and unconsciously preserved in the subconscious, affected adult behavior. By psychoanalysis, repressed emotions could be brought to the surface.

Psychology has gone beyond the five basic schools of thought with varying degrees of recombinations and applications. Philosophies of the mind also have a bearing on understanding the mental processes. When speculation about biological evolution is injected, theology has a stake in the developments. In Southern Baptist theology prior to the middle of the century, Baptists cast their lot with some form of Cartesian dualism. For a people committed to soul-winning, the choice was inevitable.

CREATIONISM AND TRADUCIANISM

One question that Baptist writers addressed concerns the origin of the soul. Does God create a new soul for each body at the time of conception (creationism), or does one inherit both soul and body from one's parents (traducianism)? Creationism in the psychological sense apparently never gained much more than a foothold among Southern Baptists. Although the doctrine has never been a cause of theological divisiveness, those who have voiced their opinion have usually favored traducianism. A. H. Strong, a favorite of many Southern Baptists, endorsed it.[18] E. Y. Mullins asserted that it best satisfies the reason and explains the facts.[19] B. H. Carroll, founder of Southwestern Baptist Theological Seminary, believed that Eve, and therefore the human race, derived both soul and body from Adam.[20]

In the traducian interpretation, the question of the fate of infants who die poses a problem. Apart from those who believe in election to reprobation, and that number among Southern Baptists today is small, Southern Baptists cherish the notion that infants who die before reaching what Baptists refer to as the "age of accountability" will be in heaven. Three lines of argument are usually followed to show that those infants will go to heaven. The first group sees the infants as being regenerated before death by an act of God. As discussed previously, Boyce took that position. A. H. Strong slightly modified that approach. He held that there is no evidence to indicate that infants are regenerated prior to death. He thought it more likely that the work of regeneration is "performed by the Spirit in connection with the infant soul's first view of Christ in the other world."[21] The residue of natural depravity, therefore, is eradicated *at* death, not *by* death, "through the sight of Christ and union with him."[22] Strong cited no specific Biblical evidence to buttress his theory.

A second interpretation associates infant salvation with the atonement of Christ. Mullins believed that everyone is rendered corrupt, guilty, and condemned by hereditary and actual sin; infants dying in infancy before actual sin has been committed "somehow" share in the blessings of the atonement of Christ because he atoned for all the race.[23] Likewise, A. T. Robertson taught, "The sinful nature which they inherit is met by Christ's atoning death and grace. No longer do men speak of 'elect infants.'"[24] C. W. Koller wrote that the redemptive work of Christ left infants in a position comparable to that of unfallen Adam.[25] Because depravity was forensically canceled by the atonement, infants are born in a "safe" position. They become sinners at the time of actual sin in later life.

The third approach holds that the guilt of sin is not hereditary. W. T. Conner observed that no theory is needed to explain how one is guilty of Adam's sin "for the simple reason that we have no such guilt. Guilt is a personal matter and is not possible apart from a personal agent who is morally responsible."[26] In this context, how infants can be saved is a moot question. They are safe because they have no guilt.

The third position above also allows room to explain the sinless nature of Jesus. While all Southern Baptists believe in the incarnation of Christ, they do not believe he was born with a depraved nature. Doubtless, there are those who ascribe Jesus' sinless nature to his lack of a human father. They generally hold to the theory that depravity is propagated through the father, not the mother, and since Jesus had no earthly father, he was born without a depraved nature. Such subtleties are lost upon many Baptists, however, and they would agree with the sentiment expressed by Harper Shannon, "The most important thing in the miraculous conception is not the absence of a man, but the presence of the Holy Spirit in the man's absence!"[27]

BODY, SOUL, AND SPIRIT

There is yet another school of thought. In it, the entire discussion of the soul's depravity is academic because a person is said *to be* a soul, not *to have* a soul. This view suggests the larger problem of the relation of the body and soul. A brief overview will help clarify more sharply the theological implications.

Southern Baptists are not always careful in their choice of theological terms. The resulting semantic barrier must be hurdled before a position can be established. This problem is especially acute when words like spirit, soul, and life are used interchangeably. Those who believe that a person is a trichotomy of body, soul, and spirit may be more numerous than specific writings indicate. Albert H. Newman (1852-1933) wrote in 1915 that theologians were about equally divided on the question of dichotomy or trichotomy.[28] Newman criticized A. H. Strong's rejection of trichotomy on the ground that it was "lacking in conclusiveness."[29] Newman himself seemed to lean toward trichotomy. Thus, the soul is propagated with its sinful nature and hereditary traits; it is the soul that one has in common with the brutes that perish. The spirit is a direct impartation from God and constitutes the person a "spiritual being, with self-consciousness, self-determination, capacity for religion, and (probably) immortality."[30]

William C. Boone, writer of a study course book published in 1936, also adopted the theory of a trichotomy. He described a person as a trinity of body, mind, and spirit. An equilateral triangle has three sides which form one triangle. In a similar manner the "trinity is there in every human being."[31]

However, other Southern Baptists lean toward the dichotomous understanding of human nature. Boyce gave careful attention to the biblical terms and usage. He alleged that Pauline thought borrows "Greek popular speech" when it sees a human being consisting of a rational spirit, animal soul, and body.[32] Boyce then quoted Charles Hodge to show that these concepts described popular notions of the human nature. Actually, the words for spirit and soul were used interchangeably by the biblical writers, said Boyce, and he concluded, "The constituent parts of man are simply body and soul."[33]

Others have followed the lead of Boyce. Strong found fault with trichotomy in that it endangered the unity of the higher nature by holding that it consists of three substances, or three component parts.[34] Mullins later espoused a dualistic view of human nature. On the one hand, he maintained the spiritual nature against materialists, who sought to demonstrate that mind is a product of matter.[35] On the other, he defined physical death as the "separation of soul and body."[36] Harold W. Tribble agreed with Mullins when he said of man that he "has a body" and "he has a soul"; by nature man is physical, spiritual, and immortal.[37]

Not all Southern Baptists have held either to trichotomy or dichotomy. In recent years, many have criticized the emphases of both of these as unscriptural and unscientific. As far back as the 1920s, J. M. Price, of Southwestern Baptist

Theological Seminary, complained that much soul-winning was based on an imperfect conception of the soul as "something apart from the living self, a kind of entity that may be deposited in the safety vault of heaven while all go on our way rejoicing—too often in worldliness."[38] Price categorized such attitudes as coinciding with neither the Bible nor psychology which identifies the soul with the self.

CHRIST'S SUBSTITUTIONARY DEATH

Southern Baptists also modified the doctrine of the atonement to meet their evangelistic mood. Almost all writers stood firmly for a substitutionary interpretation, but they no longer understood it in the Calvinistic sense. Note a typical example from the *Adult Bible Class Quarterly* in 1918. The author stated that "no better summing up could be made in brief than that which is found in Boyce's *Abstract of Systematic Theology*."[39] The author gave Boyce's summary of the benefits of the death of Christ, but Boyce's view of limited atonement was not mentioned. This omission is predictable when one remembers that Calvinism was declining in popularity among Southern Baptists. The enunciation of Christ's death as a real atonement, a substitute, penalty, and ample satisfaction were the chief concerns of the quarterly.

Subsequent Sunday School materials followed the substitutionary theme. God was described in 1928 as one who could not "be satisfied with mere repentance; nothing less than the death of his holy Son could satisfy the requirements of his holy love."[40] The *Adult Quarterly* for 1940 also voiced the opinion that the only redemption which could avail before God for lost souls was another life. The sacrifice of the Lamb of God, therefore, was a propitiation for the sins of the world.[41]

Several of the study course series writers declared openly for substitutionary atonement. This is true of Howard P. Colson[42] and J. Clyde Turner.[43] William C. Boone added the further thought that Christ's sacrifice "was ample to satisfy the claims of God's broken law."[44] Herschel H. Hobbs also emphatically stood for substitution, especially noting that the Greek word *huper*, translated "for" in John 11:50, means "instead of," "in place of," or "as a substitute for."[45]

Materials produced for the general use of the churches have not been alone in promoting atonement in its vicarious sense. Sally Neill Roach argued for such an interpretation in the *Review and Expositor* in 1929. Noting that the resurrection of Jesus is clothed with power that is judicial and declarative, she added:

> In the High Court of the universe, where God-the-loving-Father is judge, and where, under the awful majesty of Divine Law, no trace of sin may be permitted to pass unnoticed and no sinner may escape uncondemned, the Resurrection is not only the message of Infinite Power to the Adversary and

to man in his guilt, but, in the fullness of its Guarantees, it becomes to the penitent sinner his plea to Infinite Justice as well.[46]

However, one of the most eloquent and influential voices was raised by A. T. Robertson. Of satisfaction he wrote, "It is the justice of God that calls for punishment for sin and the gift of the Son on the Cross is the expression of the Father's love for the sinner and satisfaction for his own justice."[47] While alleging that "redemption" and "propitiation" are both metaphors, he warned that "they are not to be emptied of real meaning and value."[48] After an analysis of Galatians 3:10-13, he concluded, "There is no way to erase substitution from these words without violating every rule of grammatical exegesis."[49]

Robertson was equally adamant in defining the Greek word *hilaskomai* and its cognates. He saw the offering in Romans 3:25 as a "propitiatory gift."[50] He later averred again that the idea means to make propitiation: "There is no longer room for doubting its meaning in Romans 3:25."[51]

Another idea that occurred frequently in Robertson's thought centers around the word *ransom*. In commenting on Matthew 20:28, he claimed that papyri usage shows it "as the price paid for a slave who is then set free by the one who bought him. . . ."[52] He added, "There is the notion of exchange also in the use of *anti*."[53] In another context of thought he wrote, "He was born at all only to die for our sins. Else had he no message to teach that was other than ethical and ineffective."[54]

A listing of Southern Baptists who hold to substitutionary atonement is both impossible and impractical. Most of them would probably agree with the sentiment, if not the wording, as preached by R. G. Lee in 1951:

> We are blood-bought—bought with the precious blood of Christ, God's lamb without blemish and without spot (I Peter 1:19). With blood in the bowl, we must ever minister, though both blood and bowl be despised by the world of unbelief. By Christ's blood, Hell's gates are shut, Heaven's gates opened, God's claims and the Law's demands met, all barriers between God and Man taken away, and the vilest sinner's access and acceptance assured, his death sentence revoked, every charge brought against him by Satan nullified, his exemption from all future judgment made sure.[55]

Note that these writers saw salvation in personal, not social terms. It was a theology tailored to fit evangelistic preaching.

LAST VESTIGES OF SUCCESSIONISM

The firing of Whitsitt in 1899 as president of The Southern Baptist Theological Seminary brought an era to a close. The convention tired of the constant confusion precipitated by that unfortunate event, but, even though the Landmarkers officially withdrew in 1905, their view of the New Testament church as a local entity continued to surface in the convention. The Landmark belief in church successionism lasted for a while and then gradually died out. The attempt to see Baptist church polity in Christian groups prior to the seventeenth century is no longer a serious option for most Baptists. As W. W. Barnes pointed out, "In most instances these groups, however, held to doctrines and practices that would disqualify them for membership in the average 20th-century Baptist church or association."[56] Baptist successionism is practically dead. Only occasionally do phrases occur which hark back to the earlier sentiments.

Strong denominational stances have given way to an incipient mood of religious tolerance in much of American Christendom today. That trend has helped foster a lack of direction among Southern Baptists as it clashes with their strong denominational loyalties. Especially is it observable in their belief about the church and its purposes. The older, more dogmatic definition still had its advocates at the middle of the century. W. T. Conner, one of Southern Baptists most respected theologians, brushed aside general uses of the term church found in Ephesians 5:22-23. "The only ecclesiastical organization found in the New Testament," he proclaimed, "was that of a local church."[57] W. R. White expressed the same idea a decade later: "There is no actual, functioning universal church, whether invisible or visible, in existence today. Nowhere is such an idea taught in the New Testament."[58] J. Clyde Turner, in one study course book that was studied by churches associated with the convention, did not even discuss the universal church. He observed about the Greek word for *church* that "in the New Testament the word is never used to designate a building. Neither does it mean a national or worldwide organization."[59] He then described the local church as "a company of baptized believers, voluntarily associated in covenant relations, organized according to the New Testament pattern, and living in obedience to Christ, the great head of the church."[60] These citations are typical of that day.

Turner's work represents the culminations of an era of Southern Baptist thought in which the universal church was mentioned, defined, and largely forgotten. The characteristics of the local church then absorbed the attention. Usually, the definition included the necessity for a regenerate membership, baptism, worship, and correct observance of the ordinances. E. C. Dargan's definition is a good example. It states, "A church, then, in the Baptist view of the matter, is a local body or society of baptized believers in Christ, where the true worship of God is observed, the word of God is preached and the ordinances of the New Testament are properly administered."[61] Dargan also ascribed other characteristics to the local church such as a common place for meeting and mutual instruction for Christian service.[62] I. J. Van Ness adopted the less restrictive view of A. H. Strong, which has no specific reference to baptism in the definition.[63] H. E. Dana pointed to L. R. Scarborough's classic statement as expressing the fundamental character of the church. As Scarborough defined it, "The church is a group of baptized believers going with Christ after the lost."[64] The church universal found few advocates among Southern Baptists prior to the mid-century.

Landmarkism lost its formal hold on Southern Baptist thought, but the fallout from its belief in the primacy of the local church contributed to at least three convictions among Southern Baptists that directly affected their evangelism. First, they believed that Christ meant an organized, functioning body of believers when he promised to build a church that the gates of hell would not prevail against. Second, they believed that Baptist churches, if not traceable from the New Testament nucleus, were the closest to the New Testament pattern of all the denominations. Third, they believed that evangelism stood at the forefront of the church's commission. Armed with these three principles, they launched their denominational programs. The prevailing attitude toward the church ordinances—discussed below—reenforced their denominational commitment.

THE ORDINANCES: CHURCH RITES

Throughout the first half of the twentieth century, few Southern Baptists questioned that the Lord's Supper is a church ordinance and that baptism is a prerequisite. I. J. Van Ness's *Training in Church Membership*, published originally in 1908, revised in 1936, and reprinted in 1959, was studied throughout the convention. His argument followed what had become the traditional line of thought, that the ordinances of baptism and the Lord's Supper are church ordinances. The churches must see that they are properly observed. He recounted that in apostolic days there were no divisions into sects or denominations, and so there was no question about who should partake of the Supper. He expressed wonder that Baptists were charged with unchristian attitudes because they restricted the Lord's Supper to those who have been immersed upon profession of faith and are in good standing in Baptist churches.[65]

The experiential sequence of belief followed by baptism, church standing, and then participation in the Supper was reiterated or implied in publications for the next several decades. Note the following examples. Hight C. Moore argued for closed communion and then appealed to Baptists to stand firm because "we lose by laxity if we ought to be strict, even more than we lose by narrowness when we ought to be broad."[66] H. E. Dana said, "There is nowhere any record of anyone in the apostolic age except baptized believers partaking of the Supper."[67] Similar thoughts were written by Harold W. Tribble, William Cooke Boone, W. T. Conner, W. R. White, Edward A. McDowell, J. Clyde Turner, Wilbur C. Lamm, and Conrad R. Willard, to name a few whose writings have appeared among convention publications.[68] Most of these statements occurred in literature written for the churches and were thereby gained extensive exposure in the convention.

Footwashing gradually passed from the scene. A paragraph was devoted to foot-washing in a 1929 lesson in the *Adult Bible Class Quarterly*. The author explained that footwashing was not observed as an ordinance because it does not symbolize the atoning work of Christ. "It was a social courtesy rather than a church ordinance among the early Christians."[69] Today, Southern Baptists rarely give serious consideration to footwashing as a church ordinance. Few of them have participated in a footwashing service and even then only as it might occur in remote or isolated geographical areas. Instead, they try to implement the message of the rite, namely, that Christ in the original encounter exemplifies the goal of service to the church and community. Just as leaven works slowly and imperceptibly, Christians must live the Christian life in the world to permeate it with the teachings and spirit of Christ. They change the structures of society from within.

DE FACTO AMILLENNIALISM

Premillennialism and postmillennialism had strong followings in the nineteenth century, but by the second half of it, amillennialism gained in popularity. James P. Boyce and John A. Broadus, noted for their non-espousal of premillennialism, exemplified a host of people whose eschatological systems were not dominant features of their thought. Nevertheless, the basic elements of amillennialism were destined to become, prior to 1984, the sole position promoted in Southern Baptist literature produced for local church use. There were several reasons for this development.

First, the confessions of faith which Southern Baptists have adopted are amillennial. Chapter X of the Baptist Faith and Message (1963) advocates a visible return of Christ at the end of the age, a general judgement, and places of eternal bliss or punishment. The statement outlines elements common to all three millennial positions. Premillennialists add many more details, but most of them could agree with the broad features outlined thus.

Second, premillennialists perpetuated their reputation for divisiveness. Alexander Campbell, William Miller, and J. R. Graves left their marks. In the twentieth century, other premillennialists and the groups they formed shattered the peace of the convention. One group was begun by J. Frank Norris of Fort Worth, Texas. His agitation in the early twenties finally resulted in his exclusion by the Baptist General Convention of Texas in 1924. He organized the Premillennial Baptist Missionary Fellowship in 1934.[70] Other premillennial fellowships have followed. One, the Southern Baptist Premillennial Fellowship, was established, in 1946.[71] Another, the Southern Baptist Fellowship, was organized in Chattanooga, Tennessee, in 1956.[72]

There is a third reason for amillennialism's increased popularity, the neglect of the doctrine by writers of material intended for the churches. Writers of study course books generally avoided the millennial question. Harold W. Tribble in 1936 at least allowed for the possibility of a millennial reign of Christ. He foresaw a time when Christ will establish supremacy over Satan but could not locate this event in regard to a millennial framework.[73] Most writers, however, did not grant that much. William Cooke Boone in *What We Believe* had no chapter on eschatology. Neither did W. H. White in *Baptist Distinctives*, nor Robbie Trent in *The Faith We Share*.[74] Howard P. Colson, while not discussing millennialism as such, arrived at a kind of amillennialism in *Living in the Faith*.[75] J. Clyde Turner gave space to both pre- and postmillennialism but professed to believe that the average Christian was more concerned about working for the Lord than in debating when and how the Lord will return.[76] Only rarely did premillennial essays appear in Southern Baptist periodicals. One was published in 1929 in *The Southwestern Evangel*.[77] Further, the demise of postmillennialism contributed to the popularity of amillennialism. The postmillennialism of B. H. Carroll, founder of Southwestern Seminary, is too widely interspersed throughout his writings to need extensive documentation. One sample may suffice:

> There is not in the Bible one thought more clearly taught than this, viz.: The Jews must be converted before Messiah comes again. The salvation of the Jews in one day, as set forth in many prophecies, and many other events of the tribulation and the advent of our Lord, as is shown in his second great prophecy—Revelation.[78]

L. L. Gwaltney, editor of the Alabama Baptist, was a quiescent postmillennialist,[79] and Walter T. Conner moved from postmillennialism to amillennialism.[80] The words are still true, however, which were penned by W. O. Carver in 1940, "Since Dr. B. H. Carroll, Southern Baptists have no recognized 'postmillennialist teacher.'"[81] Postmillennialism died out among Southern Baptists.

SUMMARY

The first sixty years of the twentieth century witnessed gradual but profound changes at work in the Southern Baptist Convention as it extended its boundaries geographically and added to its membership numerically. Calvinism experienced further widespread rejection on the lay and professional levels. By the sixth decade, only the doctrine of the perseverance of the saints continued in popularity.

Landmarkism held on through the middle of the century, but it, like Calvinism, began falling by the wayside as Baptist church successionism withered away. Commitment to closed communion remained strong as did belief in immersion as the only mode of baptism.

In regard to eschatology, Southern Baptist literature published for the churches remained in the amillennial tradition. Few articles even admitted the strong following enjoyed by premillennialism in the convention at large.

NOTES

1. *Southern Baptist Convention Annual*, 1914, pp. 14-15.
2. Robert A. Baker, *The Southern Baptist Convention and Its People, 1607-1972* (Nashville: Broadman Press, 1974), p. 146.
3. Ibid., pp. 303-304, 437-438.
4. E. Y. Mullins, *The Christian Religion in Its Doctrinal Expression* (Philadelphia: The Judson Press, 1917), p. 206.
5. Ibid., p. 207.
6. Harold W. Tribble, *Our Doctrines* (Nashville: Convention Press, 1936), pp. 25-26.
7. W. T. Conner, *Christian Doctrine* (Nashville: Broadman Press, 1937), pp. 121-122.
8. L. R. Scarborough, "Distinctive Baptist Doctrines," *Baptist Courier* 49(November 7, 1918): 1, cited by Thomas J. Nettles, *By His Grace and for His Glory: A Historical, Theological, and Practical Study of the Doctrines of Grace in Baptist Life* (Grand Rapids: Baker Book House, 1986), p. 259.
9. Thomas J. Nettles, *By His Grace and for His Glory*, p. 263.
10. Ibid., p. 264.
11. Conner, *Christian Doctrine*, p. 155.
12. Ibid., p. 156.
13. Ibid., p. 157.
14. Ibid.
15. Ibid., p. 158.
16. Ibid.
17. The material in this paragraph is based on a discussion in Henry L. Roediger, III, and others, *Psychology* (Boston: Little, Brown and Co., 1984), pp. 7-12.
18. Augustus Hopkins Strong, *Systematic Theology: A Compendium and Commonplace-Book Designed for the Use of Theological Students* (New York: A. C. Armstrong and Son, 1902), p. 252.
19. Edgar Young Mullins, *The Christian Religion in Its Doctrinal Expression*, (Philadelphia: The Judson Press, 1917), p. 263.
20. B. H. Carroll, "The Fall of Man," *Southwestern Journal of Theology* 5 (October 1921):41.
21. Strong, *Systematic Theology*, p. 357.
22. Ibid.
23. Mullins, *Baptist Beliefs* (Louisville: Baptist World Publishing Co., 1912), p. 25.
24. A. T. Robertson, *Word Pictures in the New Testament*, vol. 4 in *The Epistles of Paul* (Nashville: Broadman Press, 1931), p. 358.
25. C. W. Koller, "The Salvation of Infants," *The Southwestern Journal of Theology* 10 (January 1926):291.
26. Conner, *The Faith of the New Testament* (Nashville: Broadman Press, 1940), p. 291.
27. Harper Shannon, *Beliefs That Are Basic* (Grand Rapids: Zondervan Publishing House, 1969), p. 14.
28. Albert H. Newman, "Strong's Systematic Theology," *Baptist Review and Exposition* 2 (January 1905):53.
29. Ibid.
30. Ibid., p. 55.
31. William Cooke Boone, *What We Believe* (Nashville: Convention Press, 1936), p. 32.
32. James Petigru Boyce, *Abstract of Systematic Theology* (Philadelphia: American Baptist Publication Society, 1887), p. 198.
33. Ibid., p. 200.
34. Strong, *Systematic Theology*, p. 245.
35. Mullins, *The Christian Religion*, pp. 87, 458.
36. Ibid., p. 458.
37. Tribble, *Our Doctrines*, p. 20.
38. J. M. Price, "Soul Winning: Psychologically Considered," *Southwestern Journal of Theology* 4 (October 1920):63.
39. *Adult Bible Class Quarterly* (June 16. 1918), p. 29.
40. "The Meaning of the Cross," *Adult Bible Class Quarterly* 27 (June 17, 1928):45.
41. "The Cost of Our Redemption," *Adult Quarterly* 39(First Quarter, 1940): 39.
42. Howard P. Colson, *Living in the Faith* (Nashville: Broadman Press, 1954), pp. 39-40.
43. J. Clyde Turner, *These Things We Believe* (Nashville: Convention Press, 1956), pp. 66-67.
44. Boone, *What We Believe*, p. 56.
45. Herschel H. Hobbs, *Fundamentals of Our Faith* (Nashville: Broadman Press, 1960), p. 48.
46. Sally Neill Roach, "The Power of His Resurrection," *Review and Expositor* 24(July 1927):297-298.
47. A. T. Robertson, "Expositions," *Review and Expositor* 30(October 1933): 431.

48. Ibid.
49. Ibid., p. 432.
50. Ibid.
51. Robertson, *Word Pictures*, vol. 4 *Studies* p. 348.
52. Robertson, *Word Pictures in the New Testament*, vol. 1, *The Gospel According to Matthew: The Gospel According to Mark* (Nashville: Broadman Press, 1930), p. 163.
53. Ibid.
54. Robertson, *Key Words in the Teaching of Jesus* (Philadelphia: American Baptist Publication Society, 1906), p. 39.
55. Robert G. Lee, "President's Address," *SBC Annual, 1951*, p. 63.
56. *Encyclopedia of Southern Baptists*, s.v. "Baptists," by W. W. Barnes.
57. Conner, *Christian Doctrine*, p. 259.
58. W. R. White, *Baptist Distinctives* (Nashville: Sunday School Board, 1946), p. 53.
59. Turner, *These Things*, p. 105.
60. Ibid.
61. E. C. Dargan, *Ecclesiology: A Study of the Churches*, 2nd ed., rev. (Louisville: Charles T. Dearing, 1905), p. 22.
62. Dargan, *The Doctrines of Our Faith* (Nashville: Sunday School Board of the Southern Baptist Convention, 1905), p. 165.
63. I. J. Van Ness, *Training in Church Membership* (Nashville: Convention Press, rev., 1936: reprint, 1959), p. 1.
64. H. E. Dana, *A Manual of Ecclesiology* (Kansas City: Central Seminary Press, 1941), p. 53.
65. Van Ness, *Training*, pp. 5, 38.
66. Hight C. Moore, "'Open' or 'Close' Communion—Which?" *Kind Words* 52 (May 11, 1919):4.
67. Dana, "The Lord's Supper," *Southwestern Journal of Theology* 4 (April 1920):64.
68. Harold W. Tribble, *Our Doctrines* (Nashville: Sunday School Board, 1929), p. 145 (p. 117 of the 1936 revision); William Cooke Boone, *What We Believe* (Nashville: Convention Press, 1939), p. 81; W. T. Conner, *Christian Doctrine* (Nashville: Broadman Press, 1937), p. 289; W. R. White, *Baptist Distinctives* (Nashville: Sunday School Board, 1946), p. 29; Edward A. McDowell, "The Church and Its Ordinances," *Sunday School Adults* 55(February 20, 1955): 31-33; J. Clyde Turner, *These Things We Believe* (Nashville: Convention Press, 1956), p. 115; Wilbur C. Lamm, "The Church Observes the Ordinances," *Sunday School Adults* 58 (March 30, 1958):48.
69. "The Place of Baptism and the Lord's Supper in the Christian Life," *Adult Bible Class Quarterly* 28 (March 19, 1929):35.
70. *Encyclopedia of Southern Baptists*, s.v. "Norris, John Franklin," by Wilburn S. Taylor.
71. *Encyclopedia of Southern Baptists*, s.v. "Premillenial Baptist Groups," by Robert A. Baker.
72. Ibid.
73. Tribble, *Our Doctrines*, p. 111.
74. Robbie Trent, *The Faith We Share* (Nashville: Convention Press, 1947).
75. Colson, *Living*, p. 129.
76. Turner, *These Things*, p. 126.
77. Charles T. Alexander, "Is the Millennium Taught in the Old Testament?" *The Southwestern Evangel* 14 (October 1929):21-24.
78. B. H. Carroll, *An Interpretation of the English Bible*, Part II, *The Four Gospels*, ed. J. B. Cranfill (Nashville: Broadman Press, 1913), p. 268.
79. Hal D. Bennett, "An Inquiry into the Life and Works of Editor Leslie L. Gwaltney of Alabama," (Th.D. dissertation, New Orleans Baptist Theological Seminary, 1956), pp. 134-135.
80. *Encyclopedia of Southern Baptists*, s.v. "Conner, Walter Thomas," by J. L. Garrett.
81. W. O. Carver, "Life Factor and Tendencies," *Review and Expositor* 37 (April 1940):195.

CHAPTER 8

CONTENDING WITH THE CRITICS

The optimistic mood of the early part of the twentieth century was not without its omens of the theological forces already gathering strength for battles yet to come. Researchers in the nineteenth century began to apply the techniques of historical criticism to the biblical text. Their conclusions about authorship, date of writing, and reliability of the accounts raised a storm of protest from evangelicals.

Opposition to higher criticism and the liberalism it spawned took two forms. On the evangelical side, it gave birth to a phenomenon now known as fundamentalism. On the liberal side, it gave birth to a mediating position between fundamentalism and liberalism known as neoorthodoxy. An understanding of the development of those three schools of thought and the reactions of Southern Baptists to them is crucial to comprehending tensions in the convention in the eighties.

THE DEVELOPMENT OF FORM CRITICISM

About 1900 higher criticism gradually assumed a new approach, form criticism. Source criticism, the predecessor of form criticism, had posited for the Synoptic Gospels a tradition from which Mark first and then Matthew and Luke derived much of their materials. The underlying assumption was that the gospels contained genuine accounts of the man called Jesus based upon an oral tradition and/or a common source called *Q* by the critics.

The birth of form criticism roughly coincided with the advent of the twentieth century. One of its founders was Hermann Gunkel (1862-1932). Schooled in the thought of Wellhausen, he published in 1901 his commentary on Genesis in which he tried to go back to the life situation (*Sitz im Leben*) in which the spoken tradition arose prior to its being written down. Gunkel believed this could be discerned by studying songs, comments, sermons, and liturgies of the times.[1]

About the same time that Gunkel arrived at his position, Wilhelm Wrede (1859-1906) broke drastically with the critical schools in favor of form criticism. He argued that source materials gradually had been narrowed from the whole New Testament in the Synoptics to Mark to *Q*. Whereas the critics believed they could somehow eliminate the traditions to reveal the historical Jesus, Wrede wrote that the entire book of Mark was a fabrication by the early church following the death of Christ.[2] The early church, he believed, proclaimed the gospel (i.e., the *Kerygma*), in a series of sermons or pericopes (*forms*) which it later embodied in the gospel accounts.

By the 1920s, form criticism gained other adherents such as Martin Dibelius (1883-1947) and Rudolph Bultmann (1884-1976). The latter pushed it to the limits by rejecting *all* of the historical accounts of the life of Jesus except the cross itself, which alone is both historical and mythological.[3] He thought the liberal theologians of the last century worked in the wrong direction in trying to eliminate the mythological; rather it should be interpreted. He wrote, "Perhaps we may put it schematically like this: whereas the older liberals used criticism to *eliminate* the mythology of the New Testament, our task today is to use criticism to *interpret* it."[4]

The form critics paid a costly theological price. The liberals at least believed that somewhere within the traditions lurked a historical Figure; the form critics jettisoned the Figure in favor of the myth and its message. To be sure, Bultmann defined myth in a specific way, namely, the use of imagery to express abstract truths. For example, space speaks of divine transcendence.[5] Form criticism with its mythical Christ, however, could not long survive in that state. Hugh Anderson correctly notes that one must assume certain truths about the traditions or else one succumbs to a Christology that is purely mythological.[6]

The method of higher criticism meshed smoothly with the developing liberal Protestant theology with which it coincided. Virgilius Ferm gives four affirmatives employed by liberal Protestants in coming to grips with the modern world: (1) the scientific spirit, (2) the authority and universality of religious experience, (3) the importance of continuity between God and man, and (4) confidence in human nature to overcome stresses in the social order and establish God's reign on earth.[7] In theology, it leaned toward pantheism; in soteriology, it stressed human nurture; and in eschatology, it identified God's Kingdom with social betterment on earth.

Walter Rauschenbusch (1861-1918), Baptist professor and minister, exemplified the liberal spirit. For many years a professor of church history at Rochester Theological Seminary, he began working among the derelicts of New York City. His work resulted in what has come to be known disparagingly as the social gospel. Rauschenbusch's attempt to reform society by changing its social structures contrasted sharply with the revivalistic approach of changing society by changing individuals. William R. Estep, Jr., notes, "To him the social gospel and doctrine of the kingdom were practically synonymous."[8] The social gospel, steeped in the liberal tradition, eventually became anathema among its opponents who saw in it a substitute for conversionist theology.

FUNDAMENTALIST REACTIONS AGAINST LIBERALISM

Roman Catholics and fundamentalists alike saw the devastating impact that liberal theology could have. In Roman Catholicism, Pope Pius IX took measures to stem the tide of "modernism," as he called it. Fundamentalism among the evangelicals and neoorthodoxy within liberalism sprang up in opposition to it.

Prior to the end of the nineteenth century, evangelicals from various persuasions began meeting to formulate their defense against the rising tide of liberalism. They held a series of conferences at Niagara, Winona, and Rocky Mountain.[9] At the Niagara Conference in 1895, they composed and published a statement which encompassed what came to be known as the five basic points, or fundamentals, of the faith: the inerrancy of the Bible, the virgin birth of Jesus, his substitutionary death for sinners, his bodily resurrection, and his visible return at the end of the age, usually interpreted premillennially.

Fundamentalism gained a stronghold in the twentieth century by two developments. The first was the publication of about sixty essays in twelve volumes between 1910 and 1912 entitled *The Fundamentals: A Testimony to the Truth*, underwritten by two California laymen. Three of the articles were written by Southern Baptists. E. Y. Mullins wrote "The Testimony of Christian Experience," J. J. Reeve of Southwestern wrote "My Personal Experience with the Higher Criticism," and Charles B. Williams of Southwestern wrote "Paul's Testimony to the Doctrine of Sin." Southern Baptists experienced a formal touch with fundamentalism.

The second factor in the growth and popularity of fundamentalism—and one that Southern Baptists avoided—was the formation of The World's Christian Fundamentals Association in 1919, a transdenominational fellowship. In addition to the organization, powerful papers like *The Watchman Examiner* exhorted believers to stand firm for the fundamentals. Through sermons, conferences, pamphlets, radio, and the establishment of Bible schools, fundamentalism spread its influence. The doctrines found a receptive spirit among Southern Baptists, and many of the issues appeared from time to time at annual meetings of the convention as well as in the pronouncements of men like J. Frank Norris.

It is important to note at this point that the use of the word fundamentalism denoting a doctrinal stance in the first half of this century has a different connotation in the 1980s. As used by its Southern Baptist detractors today, fundamentalists are those who not only hold to the five points of fundamentalism, but also, when referring to pastors in the convention, those who are strong-willed individuals tending toward isolationism from the convention structure, who may not be ardent supporters of the Cooperative Program, who get directly involved in secular politics, and who may be critical of the literature produced by the Sunday School Board. Fundamentalism to some Southern Baptists is no longer just a *theological* term. The words of Leon McBeth, penned before the present controversy, sum up the low esteem fundamentalism holds in Southern Baptist academic circles when he declared:

> Perhaps more than a doctrine, or sociology, or psychology, or organization, fundamentalism is primarily a spirit and temperament. Fundamentalism is a fighting faith. It is angry, militant, and narrow. Generosity, tolerance, or simple kindness have too often been foreign to fundamentalism and its major spokesmen. The result is that church people and non-church people alike often identify fundamentalism more with meanness of spirit than purity of faith.[10]

However, Southern Baptists harbored no such reservations about the movement as it gained adherents about 1910.

SOUTHERN BAPTISTS AND THE FUNDAMENTALS

James P. Boyce and John A. Broadus at The Southern Baptist Theological Seminary endorsed the firing of C. H. Toy by the trustees when his advocacy of higher criticism became known. Leaders at Southern and Southwestern also took firm stands against the critics in the early part of the twentieth century. As already recounted, three Southern Baptist professors contributed articles to the fundamentalist statement of faith entitled *The Fundamentals: A Testimony to the Truth*. Attention is now turned to that series of essays.

Charles B. Williams of Southwestern contributed an essay entitled "Paul's Testimony to the Doctrine of Sin." He began with a study of ten Greek words Paul used to describe sin in the Book of Romans.[11] Trying to show that Paul's understanding of sin and its origin in the human race went beyond the Jewish teaching of the day, Williams interpreted Paul's affirmation in Romans 5:19 ("by one man's disobedience many were made sinners") to mean "doubtless, that all the race was seminally in Adam as its progenitor, and that Adam by the process of heredity handed down to his descendants a depraved nature."[12] Accepting the historicity of the Genesis account about the creation of Adam and Eve, Williams disavowed the evolutionist theory that emphasized "the upward tendency of all things"[13] in favor of the fall of man into sin as a result of the Adamic transgression.[14] Furthermore, the enormity of sin is revealed by the fact that "the loving and gracious God, in whom Paul believes, . . . hates and punishes it."[15] Williams gave no statement about believing in substitutionary atonement but contented himself with the innocuous statement that Christ "meekly submitted to the sufferings of human sin, in which submission He showed Himself above sin."[16] Williams hinted at the doctrine of the Virgin Birth. Christ, although "born of a sinful woman," was conceived "without sin."[17]

In his essay entitled "The Testimony of Christian Experience," E. Y. Mullins looked at extra-biblical proofs for the deity of Christ. He contended that "Christian experience, the experience of redemption and conversion, of moral transformation through Christian agencies, has evidential value in several directions."[18] Christian experience, he believed, "is the supplemental link to complete philosophy" because it is "the effect of God reaching down to man."[19] Christian experience, in the regenerated and morally transformed person, also proves the deity of Christ and "proves His presence in religious experience," Mullins believed, "because no man has moral resources to transform himself."[20] In a humorous vein he wrote, "The Indian myth that the Creator first laid the world egg and then hatched himself out of it will scarcely supply an explanation of the regenerated life."[21] The influence upon Mullins of B. P. Bowne's personalistic philosophy can be seen in his attempt to use Christian experience to prove Christ's deity.

The article by J. J. Reeve from Southwestern hit higher criticism directly. Entitled "My Personal Experience with the Higher Criticism," it was based on his knowledge of the movement as one who formerly believed it. Having drunk from the wells of Reuss, Graf, Vatke, Kuenen, and Wellhausen,[22] he gradually rejected a system so enticing in its prospects for biblical studies, in spite of his belief, that great gains have come from the investigations launched by the critics, particularly in regard to Old Testament studies. He wrote, "In spite, however, of the serious faults of the Higher Criticism, it has given rise to what is known as the Scientific and Historical methods in the study of the Old Testament."[23]

He granted that one's confidence in the reliability of the biblical texts is not compromised by holding "that certain documents existed and were ultimately combined to make up the five books of Moses,"[24] but if so, upon what was Reeve's criticism of the critics based? He saw two controlling presuppositions. First, the whole movement was based on the "result of the adoption of the hypothesis of evolution."[25] He saw a "grain of truth" in evolution if one is careful to define what is meant by evolution. He named several varieties:

There is the Idealism of Hegel, and the Materialism of Haeckel: a theistic evolution and an antitheistic; the view that it is God's only method, and the view that it is only one of God's methods; the theory that includes a Creator, and the theory that excludes Him; the deistic evolution, which starts the world with God, who then withdraws and leaves it a closed system of cause and effect, antecedent and consequent, which admits of no break or change in the natural process. . . . On examining the evolution of the leaders of the Critical School, I found that it was of a naturalistic or practically deistic kind.[26]

Regardless of his evolutionary views, Reeve believed in the historicity of Genesis 1-11, the stories of creation and the fall of man.[27]

Reeve became disillusioned with a second presupposition of the critics, the belief that "all nature and history are a product of forces within and in process of development."[28] The acceptance of a universe closed to outside interference by God allowed no room for the supernatural and miraculous. The Bible to the critics is no revelation at all. Reeve came to the conclusion that the traditional evangelical view is irreconcilable with the critical position. He believed it possible earlier in his studies to "accept the results of Higher Criticism without accepting its presuppositions," but later concluded, "This is saying that one can accept as valid and true the results of a process and at the same time deny the validity of the process itself."[29]

Reeve found fault with the presuppositions of the critics; neither did he condone their methods. Claiming to be scientific in their analysis, they instead leaned heavily on subjective data. He illustrated their method thus:

> The use of the Redactor is a case in point. This purely imaginary being, unhistorical and unscientific, is brought into requisition at almost every difficulty. It is acknowledged that at times he acts in a manner wholly inexplicable. To assume such a person interpolating names of God, changing names and making explanations to suit the purposes of their hypothesis and imagination is the very negation of science, notwithstanding their boast of a scientific method.[30]

Reeve's analysis included his defense of many texts in the Old Testament which had been questioned by the critics. The thrust of his argument against them revolved around their leaning heavily on subjective interpretations derived from their presuppositions.

Neither did Reeve like the spirit of the critics. For them, religious faith bows before reason. They deny fundamental doctrines such as "divine revelation, the miraculous birth, the life and resurrection of Jesus Christ, the God-man"; they have no room for "the fact of a supernatural power in regeneration."[31] He continued, "Rarely, if ever, can a thoroughgoing critic be an evangelist, or even evangelistic; he is educational."[32] In his final criticism of the spirit of the critics, he accused them of being less than honest: "Adherents of this movement accept the spiritual oversight of churches which hold fast to the Biblical view of the Bible, while they know that their own views will undermine many of the most cherished beliefs of the churches. Many try to be critics and conservative at the same time."[33] The spirit of his observation would be reiterated in the convention three quarters of a century later.

FURTHER ATTACKS AGAINST THE CRITICS

Many other Southern Baptist teachers and leaders were quick to realize the threat to traditional Southern Baptist thinking posed by higher criticism. A. T. Robertson, the eminent Greek scholar who was open toward some facets of biblical criticism, was one of the most influential Southern Baptists to raise his voice against the "radical critics," as he called them. He challenged:

> Let us call the critics to the judgment seat of Christ's own personality. There can be no compromise between the radical criticism and the Bible. They do not present the same Christ. It is not a mere reorganization of a creed that these critics suggest. It is not a mere revolution in theology that is attempted. It is nothing less than a new Bible that is presented with a new Christ, in fact, with no Savior at all but with simply a noble example, merely the climax of a religious development of the race. . . . Dr. W. Robertson Nicoll is justified in calling this a crisis in the very existence of Christianity.[34]

I. J. Van Ness, corresponding secretary of the Sunday School Board (1917-1935), also attacked the higher critics. He thought their belief in the uniqueness of the Bible was nullified by their attack on its authority. Further, Van Ness raised the issue that Broadus and Reeve had already pointed out, the subjectivism of the critics. He said, "These men would see so much of both truth and error in the Scriptures that the Scriptures no longer have for them final authority, for they claim the right, arbitrarily, to decide what is and what is not true in the Bible."[35]

B. H. Carroll, founder of Southwestern Baptist Theological Seminary, expressed ideas almost identical with those of Van Ness. Carroll questioned how anyone could ever doubt the verbal inspiration of the Bible. The Bible had to be written in words, Carroll said, because "words are signs of ideas, and if the words are not inspired, then there is no way of getting at anything in connection with inspiration."[36] Therefore: "If I am free to pick up the Bible and read something and say, 'That is inspired,' then read something else and say, 'That is not inspired,' and some one else does not agree with me as to which is and which is not inspired, it leaves the whole thing unsettled as to whether any of it is inspired."[37] Carroll admitted that his view of inspiration applied only to the original manuscripts (the autographs), not to the copies, but to him the copies have been marvelously protected by God's providence. If those "infinitesimal parts" which may depend upon scholarship for authenticity were blotted out, the Holy Scriptures would in no sense be destroyed.[38]

An excerpt from the report of the Committee on Evangelism, as given to the Southern Baptist Convention in 1906, sums up much of the feeling of the day:

> If there comes along a man with a blue pencil and scissors attempting to destroy our Bible, or any part of it, whether much or little, he is at once made

to feel that there are "no vacancies," and that he might as well move on to other quarters. Southern Baptists believe the Bible from Genesis to Revelation.[39]

MULLINS ON THE BENEFITS OF HIGHER CRITICISM

Nevertheless, theological change was in the air. The rigidity of thought which characterized the latter part of the nineteenth century was bending before the flexibility of the twentieth. One precursor of change was the election of Mullins as president of The Southern Baptist Theological Seminary in 1899. W. Boyd Hunt says that with Mullins a "decided forward step was taken away from the older Calvinism and toward the development of a theology truer to the distinctive genius of Southern Baptists."[40] As Hunt notes, Mullins contended for the accuracy and trustworthiness of the Scriptures while making no claim for verbal inerrancy.

Mullins himself traced the origin of the crisis in authority to the work of Friedrich Schleiermacher. The latter had placed Christian consciousness against "the Scripture, natural reason, and the Church." Mullins concluded prophetically, "Henceforth, the question of authority in religion shall occupy a more important place in man's thinking than ever before."[41]

Mullins agreed with some aspects of higher criticism. Although "its radically destructive tendencies" had been shattered "against life itself" and had become "in large measure a spent force," he thought much good had been accomplished.[42] The revised theories as to authorship and date of certain books were incomplete, but "the composite nature of some books seems to be clearly made out; that is, the view that the writers employed previously existing documents in composing them. Inspiration did not create what was unnecessary."[43] He thereby conceded an important point to the critics, that acceptance of some aspects of the documentary theory does not necessarily entail a low view of inspiration.

UPROAR OVER BIOLOGICAL EVOLUTION

The charitable attitude of Mullins, Reeve, and Robertson toward some benefits derived from the higher critics did not prevent an uproar in the convention over biological evolution. The Scopes trial in Tennessee highlighted the fears of many Christians that belief in biological evolution was incompatible with belief in the Genesis account of creation. Men like J. Frank Norris of Texas attacked suspected evolutionists who taught in Baptist schools, particularly Baylor University.[44] Recurring complaints at the annual meeting of the convention eventually led to an attempt to assuage the problem by the adoption of a statement of beliefs. This is now known as the 1925 Confession of Faith. Tensions persisted until George W. McDaniel concluded his presidential address to the convention in 1926 with these words: "This Convention accepts Genesis as teaching that man was the special creation of God, and rejects every theory, evolution or other, which teaches that man originated in, or came by way of, a lower animal ancestry."[45] M. E. Dodd of Louisiana, in a mood of exasperation, moved that the convention adopt McDaniel's statement, that no further consideration be given to the matter, and that the convention be about the business it was established to do. The motion carried unanimously.

Rumblings about evolution after 1926 gradually died out as more pressing matters absorbed the attention of Southern Baptists. J. Frank Morris alienated himself from, and was alienated by, the power structure in the convention to the point that he no longer had a discernible influence. The first stages of the Great Depression began among the farmers, and the Southern Baptist Convention, an agrarian denomination, suffered loss in income. Further, the Cooperative Program had developed out of the Seventy-five Million Campaign of the twenties, but unwise expenditures based on an unduly optimistic anticipation of the amount of money to be pledged plunged the convention into debt. Scandal in the Home Mission Board also rocked the convention at the revelation that Clinton S. Carnes, the Home Mission Board treasurer, had embezzled $909,461. Only one-third of the money was recoverable from his bonding and assets. The convention set upon the arduous task of paying the debt beginning in 1928.

Hard times left little opportunity or inclination for the luxury of theological bickering. Occasionally, the word *infallibility* occurred in print, as when H. E. Dana described the work of the Holy Spirit in supervising the record "to insure its infallibility."[46] William Cooke Boone even used the word *plenary*,[47] but the definition he gave fits what others have called the *dynamic* theory, that is, that the Holy Spirit guided the writers without the loss of their own styles, personalities, and experiences.

SUMMARY

The first battle involving the Bible receded into the background of the Great Depression and World War II. Convention leaders on all levels—church, academic, and administrative—saw the tenets of higher criticism as a destructive force which would undermine biblical credibility as well as belief in the person and authority of Jesus. In word and by convention vote, they let their opinions be heard.

The controversy over the Bible climaxed in votes by the convention affirming its commitment to the Genesis account of creation. Two other theological movements, fundamentalism and neoorthodoxy, were destined to imprint denominations and alter their courses. Ironically, E. Y. Mullins championed the causes of fundamentalism against the critics, but his doctrine of the cross was more compatible with the nascent neoorthodoxy of his day than with his professed fundamentalism. In that respect, he was the forerunner of neoorthodoxy in the convention. The origin of the new school of thought goes back to the beginning of the century. Attention is now turned to that development.

NOTES

1. Hugh Anderson, *Jesus and Christian Origins* (New York: Oxford University Press, 1964), p. 30: Heinz Zahrnt, *The Historical Jesus* trans. J. S. Bowden (New York: Harper and Rowe, Publishers, 1963), p. 113.
2. Harvey K. McArthur, *The Quest Through the Centuries: The Search for the Historical Jesus* (Philadelphia: Fortress Press, 1966), p. 113.
3. Rudolph Bultmann, *et al* ed. Hans Werner Bartsch, *Kerygma and Myth* (New York: Harper and Rowe, Publishers; Harper Torchbooks, 1961), p. 36.
4. Ibid., p. 12.
5. Ibid., p. 10.
6. Anderson, *Jesus*, p. 33.
7. Deane William Ferm, *Contemporary American Theologies: A Critical Survey* (New York: The Seabury Press, 1981), pp. 4-7.
8. William R. Estep, Jr., *Church Union and Southern Baptists* (Fort Worth: Baptist Book Store, 1955), p. 55.
9. Williston Walker, *A History of the Christian Church*, rev. by Cyril C. Richardson *et al* (New York: Charles Scribner's Sons, 1959), p. 517.
10. Leon McBeth, "Baptist Fundamentalism: A Cultural Interpretation" *Baptist History and Heritage* 13 (July 1978):17.
11. Charles B. Williams, "Paul's Testimony to the Doctrine of Sin," 12 vols. *The Fundamentals: A Testimony to the Truth* (Chicago: Testimony Publishing Company, [1910-1912])8:49-54.
12. Ibid., p. 54.
13. Ibid.
14. Ibid.
15. Ibid., p. 56.
16. Ibid., p. 63.
17. Ibid.
18. E. Y. Mullins, "The Testimony of Christian Experience," 12 vols. *The Fundamentals: A Testimony to the Truth* (Chicago: Testimony Publishing Company, [1910-1912])3:17.
19. Ibid.
20. Ibid., p. 81.
21. Ibid.
22. J. J. Reeve, "My Personal Experience with the Higher Criticism," 12 vols. *The Fundamentals: A Testimony to the Truth* (Chicago: Testimony Publishing Company, [1910-1912])3:100.
23. Ibid., p. 102.
24. Ibid., p. 108.
25. Ibid., p. 99.
26. Ibid., pp. 99-100.
27. Ibid., p. 105.
28. Ibid., p. 100.
29. Ibid., p. 101.
30. Ibid., pp. 104-105.
31. Ibid., p. 110.
32. Ibid., p. 111.
33. Ibid., p. 112.
34. A. T. Robertson, "The Biblical Picture of Jesus," *Baptist Review and Expositor* 2 (January 1905):20-21.
35. I. J. Van Ness, *Training in Church Membership* (Nashville: Convention Press, 1908), p. 28.
36. B. H. Carroll, "Our Articles of Faith," *Southwestern Journal of Theology* 5 (April 1921):7. A note at the beginning of the article states that this essay was a portion of Carroll's lecture in 1907-1908.
37. Ibid.

38. Ibid., p. 12.
39. *SBC Annual, 1906*, p. 41.
40. W. Boyd Hunt, "Southern Baptists and Systematic Theology," *Southwester Journal of Theology* 1 (April 1959):46.
41. E. Y. Mullins, "The Theological Trend," *The Baptist Review and Expositor* 2 (October 1905):508.
42. Mullins, *Freedom and Authority in Religion* (Philadelphia: The Griffith and Rowland Press, 1913), p. 360.
43. Ibid., p. 358.
44. This account can be found in several sources. A good one is Walter B. Shurden, *Not a Silent People: Controversies That Have Shaped Southern Baptists* (Nashville: Broadman Press, 1971), pp. 89-101.
45. *SBC Annual, 1926*, p. 18.
46. H. E. Dana, "The Bearing of Luke's Preface Upon the Doctrine of Inspiration," *Southwestern Evangel* 11 (February 1927):195.
47. William Cooke Boone, *What We Believe* (Nashville: Convention Press, 1936), p. 19.

CHAPTER 9

E. Y. MULLINS AND NEOORTHODOXY

The controversy in the convention about evolution climaxed with ostensible victory by the opponents of higher criticism. The convention voted its approval of the Genesis account of creation and affirmed its loyalty to the Bible. Its confession of faith adopted in 1925 had the ring of enough finality and authority to preserve the peace, but only for a generation. At the time Southern Baptists battled over evolution, a new theological school of thought was evolving, neoorthodoxy. It would have a more lasting effect on convention theology than liberalism. Unlike the liberal frontal attack on orthodox theology, neoorthodoxy, which began as a reaction against liberalism, eventually more deeply influenced the convention by working from within.

THE NEW ORTHODOXY

The impetus for neoorthodoxy goes back to the existentialism of the Danish philosopher Søren Kierkegaard (1813-1855), but Karl Barth (1886-1968) gave direction to its development in the twentieth century. Admitting the vacuity of his liberal theology in the horrors of World War I while serving as a German military chaplain, he sought for a more biblically based theology. The publication in 1918 of his commentary on Romans signaled the beginning of a "new orthodoxy," neoorthodoxy, a movement also associated with Rudolph Bultmann (1884-1976), Dietrich Bonhoeffer (1906-1945), Emil Brunner (1889-1966), and a host of others.

What distinguished neoorthodoxy from liberalism and fundamentalism? The lines of cleavage tend to blur, depending on which writer one studies. Paul K. Jewett, writing in *Baker's Dictionary of Theology*, aptly noted, "Some of the leading exponents of this new theology . . . are more 'neo' (Tillich, Niebuhr), others are more 'orthodox' (Barth, Brunner); but none is consistently liberal and none is consistently orthodox."[1] Neoorthodox theologians seek the middle ground in expanding and proclaiming the biblical kerygma without lapsing into the anti-scientific spirit of the fundamentalists and the anti-supernatural biases of the liberals. Barth's doctrine of the Word of God is a case in point.

Barth devoted two volumes in his *Church Dogmatics* to an exposition of the Word of God. Reading through these volumes, one senses the great esteem Barth gives to the Bible; at times he speaks the language of fundamentalism. Of the formation of the biblical canon, he argued that the Bible imposes itself on the church as authoritative.[2] He hesitated not to call this Bible the Word of God, but he emended a significant qualification when he asserted that the Bible, too, is the Word of God.[3] With the insertion of the word *too* Barth in effect set himself apart from fundamentalism. To be sure, fundamentalists could agree to the distinction between Christ as the Living Word and the Bible as the Written Word, but Barth did not see the Bible as being The Word of God in the fundamentalist sense. To Barth, the Second Person of the Trinity is the Word to which the Bible bears witness or testimony. The Word of God can come to one through reading the Bible or through hearing the proclamation of the kerygma, but the Bible as such is not the Word of God. Barth's doctrine of the Word allowed him to avoid the knotty problems of defining and explaining the extent of biblical inspiration over which the fundamentalists disputed. If the Bible is a *record* of revelation and *not* the revelation itself, it could be subjected to the same scientific tests applied to any other ancient documents. The neoorthodox theologians, like the liberals, embraced historical criticism as a legitimate tool for research.

Barth had experienced in World War I enough of the horror of the inhumanity of war not to doubt human sinfulness and the need for forgiveness. He also came to the conclusion that God is totally other than the creation and that sinners cannot know God until God chooses to reveal himself. Mankind needs God's revelation. Barth puts the need for revelation in the place where evangelicals place the need for the substitutionary death of Christ for sinners.[4]   Barth's system has no vital place in it for one of the basic doctrines of fundamentalism, the substitutionary death of Christ.

Barth's theology, although close to orthodoxy in some respects, differed from it enough to merit the opposition of many fundamentalists. Bultmann's theology, even more radical than Barth's, pushed neoorthodoxy further in the direction of liberalism but with a major difference: whereas liberalism sought to cut away the accumulation of stories about the person of Christ in its search for the essentials about him, Bultmann attacked the premise that the myths could be separated from the person of Christ. Indeed, the only historical fact worthy of note about Jesus was the cross itself. He ridiculed Barth's attempt to find a non-mythological "ultimate history."[5] "Whatever else may be true," he wrote, "we cannot save the kerygma by selecting some of its features and subtracting others, and thus reduce the amount of mythology in it."⁶ Arguing that the biblical cosmology of a three-storied universe with heaven above, hell below, and earth between was no longer acceptable to modern man, he rejected it outright as being "the language of mythology," the origin of which "can be easily traced in the contemporary mythology of Jewish Apocalyptic and the redemption myths of Gnosticism."⁷ With his rejection of biblical cosmology and the stories about Jesus, Bultmann jettisoned the other doctrines crucial to fundamentalism. There is no visible coming of the Son of Man,⁸ a person is not a dichotomy of body and soul,⁹ and there is no atonement because guilt cannot be transferred from one person to another.¹⁰

Years would pass before the neoorthodoxy of the Barthian and Bultmannian brand crept into Southern Baptist theology. The impact of C. H. Dodd was more direct in weakening the doctrine of substitutionary atonement. Dodd published an article in 1931 questioning the translation of the Greek word *hilaskesthai* as *propitiation* in Romans 3:25 in the Authorized Version.¹¹ To Dodd an act of propitiation carries overtones of pagan priests placating angry and offended deities by offering sacrifices to avert divine judgment. A loving God, argued Dodd, needs no propitiation; sin needs a remedy. Dodd suggested that the word *expiation* better suits the ethical demands because sin creates a need on the part of the sinner but not on the part of God. The offering up of a blood sacrifice symbolizes a life given in sacrificial living rather than a death given in propitiation. Sin is expiated, but God is not propitiated.

The influence of Dodd's frontal attack on the doctrine of the substitutionary death of Christ can be discerned in at least two areas. First, translators of the New Testament and commentators on texts dealing with *hilaskesthai* widely accept his use of *expiation* rather than *propitiation* as the better word. Second, since Christ's death comes to signify a life offered up in sacrificial living rather than a death in the place of guilty sinners, those holding Dodd's interpretation emphasize Christian nurture rather than the necessity of the new birth. Christ's death "in the place of" sinners becomes Christ's living the Christian life "along side of" sinners. His death on the cross, objectively, in the first century gives way to His ministry, subjectively, along side of the believer in the present century. When the neoorthodox concept of the death of Christ joined forces with the evolutionary belief in the inevitable perfectibility of the human race, the grounds for an accommodation with fundamentalism—if one is desired—crumble away.

THE APPEAL TO EXPERIENCE

The editors of *The Fundamentals: A Testimony to the Truth* chose E. Y. Mullins to write the article on the deity of Christ. It was an astute decision on their part because Mullins's position as president of The Southern Baptist Theological Seminary lent credibility to the series of essays. Furthermore, the grounding of his proofs in the Christian experience of regeneration doubtless confirmed to them his commitment to divine intervention in human affairs while at the same time avoiding the "proof text" procedures germane to fundamentalism. His method gave the appearance of being sound, both philosophically and empirically, thus forestalling cavils by critics. At the same time, fundamentalists may have had misgivings about the Mullins essay because not once did he quote the Bible to buttress his argument for the deity of Christ and only rarely did he refer to the Bible at all. He appealed almost exclusively to Christian experience. In short, Mullins was the forerunner of neoorthodoxy among Southern Baptists.

In appealing to experience, however, Mullins was not attempting to mislead his fundamentalist compatriots as to his own basic beliefs. Mullins served as pastor of the Baptist church in Newton Center, Massachusetts, from 1895 until he was elected president of the seminary in 1899, succeeding William H. Whitsitt who had been forced to resign because of a heated argument in the convention over his views about the historical beginnings of the Baptists. Newton Center is near Boston, and there Mullins came under the influence of the philosophy of personalism as advocated by Borden Parker Bowne (1847-1910),[12] a professor of philosophy at Boston University. John H. Lavely saw personalism of the theistic variety as being built around three main themes; an idealism which is personal, a plurality which involves society, and a theistic view of God who is the creator and ground of all being.[13] Personalism begins with experience.

Bowne himself faulted the idealism of George Berkeley as well as the various expressions of materialism as beginning at wrong points in philosophical speculation. Philosophy, he contended, must begin with the world of experience where people live, love, fear, hope, and labor.[14] Bowne further explained that by experience he meant nothing metaphysical but, instead, the world insofar as it is capable of being experienced.[15] Bowne's theistic personalism began with the data of experience and not with propositional truth based on divine revelation. Assuming that the human mind favors basal monism rather than pluralism in describing reality, he concluded that the world-ground "must be one and not many."[16] He argued additionally that it is intelligent, personal, and ethical.[17]

Begin with human experience. That orientation of thought permeates what Mullins wrote, as is exemplified in his essay published in *The Fundamentals*. The fact that it influences his total theology also poses a difficult problem for interpreters of his thought. At times he sounds like an ardent fundamentalist, but almost invariably he tempers dogma with an appeal to human—and not always to Christian—experience.[18]

REVELATION AND THE BIBLE

Mullins's "receptivity to existentialist modes of thought"[19] can be discerned in his doctrine of revelation and the Bible. On the subject of divine revelation, his language was orthodox: biblical revelation is, among other aspects, historical, experiential, regenerative, genetic, gradual, and progressive.[20] Above all else, of course, God reveals himself through Jesus Christ, a revelation which is both historical and experiential.[21]

How did Mullins relate the authority of the Bible to the revelation in Christ? Its authority must provide the basis of study if one is to serve the interests of God's Kingdom on earth.[22] In another context, he calls the Bible "an inspired literature which interprets a life"[23] and "an authoritative literature which leads us to Christ."[24] He defended biblical authority but not biblical inerrancy.

ELECTION

In explicating the doctrine of election, especially as it relates to salvation, Mullins focused attention on the outcome in experience rather than upon arbitrary choices by God. Mullins asked, for example, whether God's omniscience and foreknowledge of an event predetermined or necessitated the occurrence of the event. He answered in the negative, for otherwise one's choices would not be free choices at all.[25] Neither did Mullins see election as an arbitrary decree; rather it flows from the wisdom, grace, and skill of God in reaching people.[26]

Election is a process by which God intends to reach out redemptively toward the world. It also centers in Christ and in the benefits residing in him for believers. In commenting on Paul's teaching about election in Ephesians 1:3-6, Mullins noted that God's sovereign grace works in Christ as the sphere of the divine purpose.[27] Mullins even used the expression "prevenient grace," Calvinistic language to be sure, but his understanding of it was decidedly uncalvinistic. God's prevenient grace always works in accordance with free will and never by compulsion.[28]

THE SIN-DEATH PRINCIPLE

His understanding of the human experience and the necessity of relating the atonement of Christ to it kept Mullins's understanding of the atonement from taking on the juridical overtones found in fundamentalism. At times, Mullins sounded much like the fundamentalists. In his book *Baptist Beliefs*, he stated that the "atonement was necessary for the pardon, justification, and redemption of sinners," that it terminated not on sinners only but also on God, and concluded that it "was God's own arrangement and provision to meet an infinite necessity of his holy and loving nature."[29] In his commentary on Ephesians he observed that, although the New Testament nowhere states that a ransom was paid to the devil, it "does present the idea of Christ's death as a ransom." Rather than pursuing the ransom theme further, he focused on the redemption theme, seeing the necessity of that act as being "rooted in God, in man, and in the circumstances of the incarnation."[30]

What defect precipitated the need for Christ's redemptive act? Mullins saw it as the inevitable connection between sin and death (Mullins called it the "sin-death principle") which holds the entire race in its awful power.[31] For a sinner to be freed from the sin-death principle, its power must be broken. It is at this point of greatest need that God enters in the form of Jesus Christ and destroys the sin-death principle by the obedience-life principle. Mullins summarizes the two principles this way:

> In other words, Christ's death was God's means of relating himself in a saving way to sinful men. Christ became organically one with men, even to the point of dying for them in order that his righteousness might become a saving power in the race. The law of the Spirit of life in him overcame thus the law of sin and death in them.[32]

The destruction of the sin-death principle by the death of Christ on the cross infuses a new principle which is extended by the Holy Spirit. In Mullins's words, "The gift of the Holy Spirit was necessary to complete the process of divine immanence through the atonement."[33]

To summarize, Mullins retained some of the traditional concepts about the atonement. He saw it as having an effect on both God and sinners. He also saw objective value in the death of Christ because the obedience-death principle somehow canceled the sin-death principle. His explication of how the first principle annulled the second led him into an existentialist-like emphasis. He seemed to see the death of Christ as being efficacious in what could be described as an incarnational healing injected into the human experience. Instead of picturing the sin of believers as being projected backward in time and nailed to the cross, Mullins saw the cross as a healing power being brought forward into the present as a contemporaneous experience. He flirted with the moral influence theory of Horace Bushnell and others. In so doing, he was the forerunner of neoorthodoxy in the convention.

SUMMARY

The twentieth century began in a spirit of optimism which Southern Baptists shared. The polemical spirit at Southern Seminary, characteristic of the convention in the post-Civil War era, changed to fit the new mood as the convention began recovering from the blight of finances and spirit inflicted by the ravages of war. A new kind of war soon gained the attention of convention leadership as German rationalism in the form of higher criticism threatened, as the leadership believed, an understanding of the person of Jesus and the integrity of the Bible. The leaders of the convention thought, when they voted in 1925, that they had met the critics and conquered.

Not quite. Mullins was numbered *with* the fundamentalists, but he was not *of* them. His personalistic philosophy did not fit their aggressive dogmatism. His doctrine of the cross, for example, varied enough from the substitutionary view of fundamentalism to cause a breach in spirit if either side had courted the other too intensely. Southern Baptists walked the middle road between fundamentalism and liberalism in a spirit of denominational exclusiveness which has vexed all groups seeking their affiliation. In missions, ecumenicism, and doctrinal controversy, they have followed their own paths.

NOTES

1. *Baker's Dictionary of Theology*, s.v. "Neo-Orthodoxy," by Paul K. Jewett.
2. Karl Barth, *Church Dogmatics*, Vol. 1, *The Doctrine of the Word of God*, Part I, tr. G. T. Thomson (Edinburgh: T & T Clark, 1936; reprint ed., 1960), p. 120.
3. Ibid., p. 122.
4. See Gustav Wingren, *Theology in Conflict: Nygren—Barth—Bultmann* (Philadelphia: Muhlenburg Press, 1958), pp. 28-29.
5. Rudolph Karl Bultmann, et al., ed. Hans Werner Bartsch, *Kerygma and Myth: A Theological Debate* (New York: Harper and Row, Publishers; Harper Torchbook, 1961), p. 9.
6. Ibid.
7. Ibid., p. 3.
8. Ibid., p. 4.
9. Ibid., p. 6.
10. Ibid., p. 7.
11. C. H. Dodd, ίλάσκεσΘαι, "Its cognate, Derivatives, and Synonyms, in the Septuagint," *Journal of Theological Studies*, 32 (July 1931):352-360. For an able response to Dodd, see Roger R. Nicole, "C. H. Dodd and the Doctrine of Propitiation," *The Westminster Theology Journal*, 17 (May 1955):117-157; Leon Morris, *The Apostolic Preaching of the Cross* (Grand Rapids; William B. Eerdmans Publishing Company, 1956); and Leon Morris, *The Atonement: Its Meaning and Significance* (Downers Grove, Illinois: Intervarsity Press, 1983), p. 151.
12. As a small bit of supporting evidence, Mullins refers to a saying of "Professor Bowne" in the second paragraph of his essay in "The Testimony of Christian Experience," 12 vols., *The Fundamentals: A Testimony to the Truth* (Chicago: Testimony Publishing Company, [1910-1912])3:76.
13. *The Encyclopedia of Philosophy*, s.v. "Personalism," by John H. Lavely.
14. Border Parker Bowne, *Personalism* (Norwood, Massachusetts: The Plimpton Press, 1908), p. 25.
15. Ibid., p. 27.
16. Bowne, *Philosophy of Theism* (New York: Harper and Brothers, 1887), p. 46.
17. Ibid., chapters 2, 3, and 6.
18. Edgar Young Mullins, *The Christian Religion in Its Doctrinal Expression* (Philadelphia: The Judson Press, 1917), pp. 2-3.
19. Thomas J. Nettles, *By His Grace and for His Glory: A Historical, Theological, and Practical Study of the Doctrines of Grace in Baptist Life* (Grand Rapids: Baker Book House, 1986), p. 253.
20. Mullins, *The Christian Religion*, p. 145ff.
21. Ibid., p. 47.
22. Mullins, *The Axioms of Religion: A New Interpretation of the Baptist Faith* (Philadelphia: American Baptist Publication Society, 1908), p. 26.
23. Mullins, *Freedom and Authority in Religion* (Philadelphia: The Griffith and Rowland Press, 1913), p. 393.
24. Ibid., p. 394.
25. Mullins, *The Christian Religion*, p. 227.
26. Mullins, *Axioms*, p. 85.

27. Mullins, *Studies in Ephesians* (Nashville: Convention Press, Sunday School Board of the Southern Baptist Convention, 1935), p. 31.
28. Mullins, *Axioms*, p. 84.
29. Mullins, *Baptist Beliefs* (Louisville: Baptist World Publishing Company, 1912), p. 32.
30. Mullins, *Studies*, p. 32.
31. Mullins, *The Christian Religion* p. 319.
32. Ibid.
33. Ibid., p. 321.

PART IV

INERRANTIST EVANGELICALISM VERSUS NEOORTHODOX EVANGELICALISM, 1960-1989

    Chapter 10. At War Over the Word
    Chapter 11. The Last Stages of Calvinism
    Chapter 12. The Church Alive
    Chapter 13. Whence and Whither

OVERVIEW

Controversy over the Bible has profoundly shaken the Southern Baptist Convention since the sixties but especially in the eighties. It intensified dramatically when Paul Pressler, a probate judge in Texas, and Paige M. Patterson, the president of the Criswell Center for Biblical Studies, launched a movement in 1979 to redirect the theological drift of the convention by controlling the constituency of the various boards and agencies.

By what names shall the opposing groups be known? In the initial stages of the movement, denominational leaders reacted to the charge of liberalism by denouncing the troublers as independent fundamentalists. To minimize the damage inflicted by name-calling, the contending factions are now known as fundamentalist conservatives and moderate conservatives. Although these appellations are a marked improvement over the original ones, they lack historical definition. Further, the word fundamentalist is used almost universally as a term of opprobrium in Southern Baptist academic circles.

The approach taken here is the assumption that the overwhelming majority of Southern Baptists fall theologically within the evangelical tradition. Neoorthodox evangelicals as used here describes those whose theology has shifted away from fundamentalism. Inerrantist evangelicals applies to those shifting toward fundamentalism. No attempt is made in the following chapters to locate a given theologian's position on the continuum from one extreme to the other. The terms themselves are intended only to set the outside limits of theological variation in the convention. A given writer may hold views sympathetic with the inerrantist evangelicals on one issue and with the neoorthodox evangelicals on another.

Designating those of the fundamentalist orientation as inerrantist evangelicals is not an ideal description because doctrines other than inerrancy separate the two camps. However, inerrancy has been the focal point of the controversy, and it promises to hold that position for years to come. Chapter 10 sets forth the pivotal issues involved in that battle. Chapter 11 picks up the broader theological themes, especially of sovereignty and free will. The church and ordinances are the subjects in chapter 12. The last chapter concludes with an overview of the developing themes in Southern Baptist thoughts and a projection of possible future directions.

CHAPTER 10

AT WAR OVER THE WORD

The firing of Theodore R. Clark by the trustees of the New Orleans Baptist Theological Seminary in 1960 signaled the beginning of a new round of theological battles in the Southern Baptist Convention. He had studied under Paul Tillich, absorbed much of the latter's theology, integrated it into his own Baptist framework, and then, to his undoing, wrote his views in a book entitled *Saved By His Life*.[1] With the evidence before them, the trustees of the seminary found enough variance from Baptist theology to terminate his services in the spring of 1960.

Other indications of the dissensions to come soon manifested themselves. Ralph H. Elliott of the Midwestern Baptist Theological Seminary had a book published by Broadman Press, *The Message of Genesis*, which raised the ire of many of its Southern Baptist readers. To assuage the tumult, the editors at Broadman reassigned the copyright to Elliott. When he refused to promise the trustees of the seminary that he would not seek another publisher, they fired him for insubordination in 1962.

The next year, 1963, the convention adopted a revised confession of faith, now known as *The Baptist Faith and Message*, but if the convention entertained the notion that the adoption of a confession would have the calming effect of the 1925 confession, the hope was vain. Repeated motions at annual sessions to add the word inerrant to the statement about the Scriptures in section one of the confession have been unsuccessful, and this failure probably accentuates the feeling that something is amiss theologically in the convention. Additionally, Broadman's publication of Volume I of the *Broadman Bible Commentary* in 1969 precipitated an outbreak over the way G. Henton Davis handled certain texts in Genesis. The convention forced Broadman Press to withdraw Volume I and to have the Genesis section rewritten from a more conservative perspective. Clyde T. Francisco authored the revised material.

Before one can understand the issues surrounding the present debate over the Bible, the debate must be removed from an atmosphere of acrimony and suspicion and placed in a theologically definable context. The following section makes that attempt. Then an effort is made to demonstrate the growing acceptance of higher critical methods as reflected in Southern Baptist writings, followed by a section highlighting crucial issues in the controversy over the Bible. The final section focuses on hindrances preventing the achievement of a definition of inspiration acceptable to all.

THE THEOLOGICAL PARAMETERS

A popularized description of the controversy as it unfolded in the convention can be found in two books by James C. Hefley.[2] To summarize briefly, Texas Appeals Court Judge Paul Pressler, from Houston, Texas, and Paige Patterson of the Criswell Center for Biblical Studies in Dallas, Texas, initiated the battles in the convention with the formulation of a strategy for placing the convention administration control in the hands of people amenable to their doctrinal stance. The source of the objectionable doctrines emanated from the universities and seminaries. Because only the six seminaries owned by the convention are subject to convention control—the convention owns no colleges and universities in the United States—they have born the brunt of the charges. If some of the professors were teaching doctrines at variance with those of Southern Baptists at large, what could be done to bring about a realignment?

The strategy chosen to implement change rested on Article Twenty-one of the convention bylaws. It gives to the president of the SBC the right to appoint, in consultation with the vice-presidents, the Committee on Committees. That committee then brings before the convention in annual session the nominations for the Committee on Committees. If presidents holding to biblical inerrancy could be elected over a period of years, inerrantists could be appointed to the Committee on Committees as members rotated off. When inerrantists obtained a majority on the Committee on Committees, people holding similar views could be nominated to the Committee on Nominations and Committee on Boards. The strategy could not work, of course, unless the convention elected most of the nominees placed before it.

The strategy proved to be successful. Adrian Rogers, pastor of the Bellview Baptist Church in Memphis, Tennessee, served in 1979. He refused to have his name placed in nomination for the customary second term of 1980. His successors were Bailey E. Smith, 1980-1981, pastor of the First Southern Baptist Church, Del City, Oklahoma; James T. Draper, Jr., 1982-1983, pastor of the First Baptist Church, Euless, Texas; Charles F. Stanley, 1984-1985, pastor of the First

Baptist Church, Atlanta, Georgia; Adrian Rogers, 1986-1987; and Jerry Vines, 1988-1989, co-pastor of the First Baptist Church, Jacksonville, Florida. Inerrantists have controlled the presidency since 1979.

As a group of new faces began appearing on committees and at other levels of the convention, cries of alarm soon went up. Regrettably, the fray rapidly declined to the level of name-calling. Poorly chosen words voiced from both sides caused tempers to flare. The controversy has its political side, but the root of it lies in theological diversity.

Carl F. H. Henry, formerly the editor of *Christianity Today*, was one of the first to voice concern over a perceived drift in the convention toward neoorthodoxy. In his eyes, the inroads of neoorthodoxy in the seminaries compromised the doctrine of biblical inerrancy.[3] Harold Lindsell, also formerly with the same magazine, cited examples in 1976 of those within the convention who no longer accepted biblical infallibility. He predicted dire results unless the orthodox majority could eradicate the disease eating at the vitals of the convention.[4]

Other doctrines play a part in the controversy, but the central point has been arguments over the nature of biblical inspiration. Is all of the Bible inerrant, infallible, trustworthy, and reliable, or do such terms apply only to the autographs, if at all? Or, are only parts of the Bible infallible? If so, which parts? Two broad schools of thought command the widest allegiance in the convention, the inerrantist evangelical and the neoorthodox evangelical definitions; what distinguishes one from the other?

DEFINING THE POSITIONS

The locus of the argument over inspiration can be seen in the question, Does God inspire *people* only, or does he also inspire *sacred writings*? The neoorthodox evangelicals accept the former unreservedly but the latter only with extensive reservations. Conversely, inerrantist evangelicals adamantly insist that the Bible itself is inspired. Taking their cues from verses like II Timothy 3:6 ("All scripture *is* given by inspiration of God"), Paul's statement in I Thessalonians 2:13 ("when ye received the word of God which ye heard of as ye received it not *as* the word of men, but as it is in truth, the word of God"), and the words of Jesus in John 10:35 ("and the scripture cannot be broken"), they have made the doctrine of biblical inspiration the cornerstone of their system of beliefs.

Inerrantist evangelicals generally agree with Basel Manly's definitions, as given previously, that *revelation* refers to the initial unveiling of a truth or event by God. It may have come in the form of a dream, vision, theophany, inner awareness, or in some other way. The second aspect described by Manly is *inspiration*, the process by which the Holy Spirit moved upon those who wrote down their experiences. *Preservation* describes the overseeing of the Bible through the centuries by the Holy Spirit. In *illumination*, a reader of the Bible or a hearer of the proclamation is brought by the Holy Spirit to understand and accept the truth of the revelation.

How does the process of inspiration work? Russell H. Dilday, Jr., summarizes eight different theories of the method of inspiration. He lists five which generally do not find wide acceptance among Southern Baptists: the dictation theory, the natural theory, the general Christian inspiration theory, the theory of partial inspiration, and the theory of levels of inspiration. Because of his statement that "most Southern Baptists hold one or more of the last three theories," they merit closer scrutiny, as follows:

> 6. *The plenary theory.* This is the viewpoint that every part of the Bible is inspired and is therefore authoritative truth. The Bible as a whole, not just various parts, is the Word of God.
> 7. *The verbal theory.* This term is used to indicate that not only are the ideas or truths of the biblical message inspired but also the words chosen to convey the message are inspired. . . .
> 8. *The dynamic theory.* Simply stated, this theory says the Holy Spirit's control over the process of writing was such that the freedom and personality of the human author was allowed to operate. The writer's vocabulary, style, and the personal peculiarities of his culture and time are evident in the Scriptures. But under the Holy Spirit's control, the result of his writing, in spite of his humanity, was precisely the message God wanted to convey.[5]

The three theories tend to intersperse. The definition Dilday gave for the dynamic theory often merges with the other two as given by other writers, but the word *plenary* is probably more popular among evangelicals of all denominational affiliations. Loraine Boettner in *Baker's Dictionary of Theology* says evangelicals hold to "the plenary inspiration of the Scriptures"; they also believe "the Scripture is the word of God written, and that it is therefore infallible in its original autographs."[6]

In contrast to the inerrantist evangelical preoccupation with theories of inspiration, those of the neoorthodoxy persuasion emphasize that God inspires men, not writings. Nevertheless, they see the Bible as encompassing a class of writings by itself. That it is esteemed as a unique witness to God's revelation and even witnesses infallibly to that unveiling is widely accepted. However, neoorthodox use of terms, while often being the same as those found among evangelicals in general, often has different meanings. Variations occur in at least four areas.

First, neoorthodox writers speak of the Bible as the Word of God, but it is so only in a restricted sense. The Bible is a witness to and a record of the Incarnate Word, God in Christ. The Bible is the Word of God only insofar as it bears witness to God and his saving acts, i.e., the religious motif. If the word *infallible* is to be applied to the Bible at all, it can only be used in reference to those verses (the *Kerygma* or proclamation) bearing witness to the Word. Writing in *Baker's Dictionary of Theology*, Paul K. Jewett points out a major difference between the neoorthodox and the orthodox understanding of Scripture when he says, "Yet, since this kerygma is a witness *to* the Word, it is a mistake on the part of the orthodox, with the most serious consequences, to identify the words of Scripture with the Word of God."[7]

Second, the neoorthodox adherents believe the Bible is uniquely inspired and is completely reliable in giving testimony to the God and his redemptive nature,[8] but it is also a human book. Therefore, it speaks in broken and imperfect forms.[9]

Third, the Bible in its humanness, although the record of revelation, shows evidence of a pre-scientific perception of the world. Consequently, the neoorthodox have little interest in formulating definitions of biblical inspiration. If the autographs were discovered by researchers, they would still need to be demythologized.

Fourth, neoorthodoxy follows the existential mood in disdaining propositional truths. If theological statements contain only symbolic truths, one must go beyond the symbol to grasp the reality. However, some neoorthodox theologians follow Tillich and others in a kind of sacramental approach. The sacrament participates in the reality it portrays. Note that propositions apparently do not participate in the realities to which they point. Nevertheless, the neoorthodox evangelicals in the convention are being forced into defining their belief about biblical inspiration. The widespread acceptance of higher critical techniques and belief in the multiple authorship of most books of the Bible (especially the Pentateuch, Isaiah, Daniel, and the four gospels) point to the chasm separating the neoorthodox evangelicals from the inerrantist evangelicals.

THE GROWING POPULARITY OF HIGHER CRITICISM

Profound changes in attitude toward the composition of the books of the Bible have come about in academic circles in the convention in the past thirty years. Some of the teachers at Southern Seminary apparently already had departed in the sixties from any inerrantist evangelical approach to the question of authorship in favor of that growing out of higher criticism. At this point, however, a summary of the development of the fields of biblical criticism can aid the reader.

First, of the two broad areas of criticism, textual (or lower) criticism and higher criticism, the former finds acceptance among evangelicals in general while being rejected outright by extreme fundamentalists who resent even the hint of a suggestion that scribal errors have crept into the text through the centuries. They sometimes tend to equate the King James Version with the original Greek text. Inerrantist evangelicals are inclined to accept the validity of textual criticism as a beneficial means of trying to arrive at an authentic manuscript by comparing ancient writings with each other.

Second, higher criticism has had a more turbulent history. Because it came out of the rationalism of the eighteenth and nineteenth centuries and quickly gained the image of a subjectively-based attack on the Bible, it became anathema among fundamentalist evangelicals. Yet, between the two polarities of extreme fundamentalists and the avowed liberals, there are broad areas of overlapping methodologies. Many biblical researchers prefer to use the expression historical criticism as more descriptive of their work. They accept some of the methods of source criticism as they try to sort out the origins of the biblical accounts. Luke, for example, wrote that he knew of other declarations of the life and work of Jesus (Luke 1:1-4). Historical critics also see benefits that can be derived from form criticism as they study the grammatical and stylistic forms of the different writers. Redaction criticism, i.e., the function of editors like the compiler of the materials found in I and II Kings, contributes to one's understanding of which accounts were accepted and why. Were these passages, for example, chosen to exhibit a moral or theological theme?

There are other nuances in the field of historical criticism, such as tradition criticism, but the question can now be posed, How much is historical criticism used as a tool among Southern Baptist researchers? The answer is, extensively. Page H. Kelly confirmed his commitment to it in 1985 when he said, "For the past 26 years I have made use of the findings of higher criticism in my Old Testament classes at Southern Seminary."[10] As a reading of Southern Baptist literature shows, the acceptance of the composite nature of many of the disputed books of the Bible has gained in popularity.

The *Broadman Bible Commentary* is illustrative. Many Southern Baptist pastors and other leaders felt the need for a Bible commentary written under the direction of the Baptist Sunday School Board. The *Broadman Bible Commentary* was the outcome. However, after the volume on Genesis was published, some Southern Baptists voiced opposition to it. The commentary on Genesis had been written by G. Henton Davies of England. The complaint was that the way Davies handled certain passages seemed to cast doubt upon the reliability of the biblical text. His interpretation of Genesis 22:2, which states that God commanded Abraham to offer up Isaac as a human sacrifice, was one of the disputed passages. Davies argued that no Christian or humane conscience could regard that kind of command as coming from God.[11] His commentary stirred the wrath of Southern Baptists. When the convention met in 1970 in Denver, Colorado, Gwin T. Turner of California moved that, because the sentiment voiced in parts of the Commentary on Genesis did not express the beliefs of the vast majority of Southern Baptists, the volume be withdrawn and rewritten from a conservative viewpoint. The motion carried, 5,394 to 2,170.[12] The Genesis section of volume one was revised by Clyde T. Francisco and was published in 1973. The rest of volume one remained as originally written. Dissension quieted for a time.

Although Genesis alone was singled out for criticism, an analysis of other books in the *Broadman Bible Commentary* indicates how deeply the higher critical approach to the Bible has become embedded in Southern Baptist scholarly circles. General Editor Clifton J. Allen set the tone when he embraced the main tenets of the documentary theory.[13] Other writers agreed.[14]

Many of the men who wrote the commentaries on the books of the Pentateuch, as well as related essays, indicated their allegiance to the documentary hypothesis. In his revision of Genesis, Clyde T. Francisco, although granting some mosaic influence, nevertheless saw evidences of two distinct collections of materials in Genesis.[15]

On the composition of Exodus, Roy L. Honeycutt, Jr., stated, "Thus, while one may legitimately ascribe materials both oral and written to Moses, the book of Exodus remains in the main anonymous."[16] Ronald L. Clements also rejected the Mosaic authorship of Leviticus. According to Clements, "This view was at one time widely accepted within the Christian church. With the rise of a more critical and precise historical scholarship, this view has been almost entirely abandoned. . . ."[17] J. D. W. Watts accepted the documentary theory in his comments on Deuteronomy.[18] Sentiments favoring it were expressed in articles by Francisco,[19] John I Durham,[20] and Eric C. Rust.[21]

Several books traditionally seen as coming from the pen of a single author are now viewed as composites coming from a later period. To illustrate, John Joseph Owens sees the book of Daniel as having been written in 336 B.C. or later.[22] The book of Isaiah comes under the same kind of scrutiny. Many interpreters see at least two authors (hence, Deutero-Isaiah), three authors (Trito-Isaiah) or even many more. Much of the book, according to those who hold to the multiple authorship theory, was written during the exile. Page H. Kelly alleges that Deutero-Isaiah is almost universally accepted.[23]

Other Old Testament books receive a similar evaluation. John T. Bunn, on Ezekiel,[24] and B. Elmo Scoggin, on Micah,[25] state that the multiple authorship of those books is widely accepted. Even though A. J. Glaze, Jr., believed the book of Jonah was based on the life of a real person, he considered the book as being probably "a consummate religious masterpiece presenting its moral along the lines of what we know today as a short story. Apparently the postexilic period produced at least three of these works: Jonah, Ruth, and Esther."[26]

Higher critical methods also were used by commentators on New Testament books, especially the gospels. Ray Summers described the historical critical method as "basic to all competent contemporary approaches in New Testament study," warning also against the danger of extreme subjectivism in "an otherwise helpful method of study."[27] Frank Stagg hesitated to ascribe authorship of the book of Matthew to the apostle by that name, but noted, "That the apostle stood in some relationship to it is probable. Most likely it was as the compiler of the *logia* (cf. Papias), used extensively in this Gospel."[28] According to William E. Hull, the book of John shows evidence of three different stages in the compilation of the materials which were joined by a final editor who added materials from three other minor sources.[29]

The *Broadman Bible Commentary* does not stand alone in showing evidence of those who employ historical criticism. Note the following selections from the *Bible Survey Series*, an overview of the Bible produced for laymen in 1969. L. D. Johnson, one of the authors, said that Moses had some connection with the first five books of the Bible. He may be thought of, said Johnson, as the human agent responsible for the precepts and principles given at Sinai. "It is an oversimplification, however, to think of Moses as sitting down and writing the first five books of the Old Testament as they appear in the Bible."[30] Johnson further asserted that "we are led to feel that these are not the products of a single hand."[31] Rather, several accounts were probably formed into a composite story. Page H. Kelly was more explicit in dealing with the authorship of the Pentateuch. He devoted one page to "Mosaic Authorship" and three pages to "Composite Authorship."[32] In the latter section, he detailed the essential features of the documentary view, although he did not personally commit himself there to that theory.

Writers who apparently hold to the multi-authorship of Isaiah can be found among authors of Sunday School lessons. Joe H. Music seems to lean in that direction. He wrote a study entitled "Anticipating a New Beginning" in an attempt "to bridge the gap between the end of the Old Testament and the beginning of the New Testament." Using Isaiah 40, he stressed that the setting for the chapter is immediately prior to the release of the Jews from exile; he treated Isaiah 40 as history, not as prophecy.[33] Both William L. Hales, *Sunday School Adults*,[34] and Robert W. Kicklighter, *The Adult Teacher*,[35] looked upon the setting of the second half of Isaiah as exilic. These references sufficiently indicate the extent to which historical criticism has become a part of Southern Baptist research techniques.

DISAGREEMENT OVER RELIABILITY

Disagreements over the composition of many books of the Bible are only one of the contemporary developments in Southern Baptist theological circles causing tensions between inerrantist evangelicals and neoorthodoxy evangelicals. A second relates to the scope of biblical reliability. In attempting to define biblical inerrancy, one hurdle is the fact that none of the original manuscripts, the autographs, are extant. The earliest papyrus fragment of any portion of the New Testament (P52, containing John 18:31-33, 37-38) goes back no further than about 135 A.D. Researchers, known as textual critics, study ancient records of all kinds trying to push back the accounts as close as possible to the original era. In the eyes of inerrantist evangelicals, a discovery of the autographs would add little new information. They believe that, for the most part, scholars have delved into the origins of the various texts of the New Testament and have produced documents essentially like the autographs.

Higher critics take a different approach. Leaving textual criticism, they sometimes study the texts and make judgments based on syntax, vocabulary, and style in accepting or rejecting texts. For example, the word *Elohim* for God appears in Genesis one; hence the E document. *Yahweh* (Jehovah in the KJV) occurs generally in Genesis two; hence the J document. These and other data suggest two different documents to many investigators.

Another method historical critics use to arrive at the most authentic text is to study the level of theological development as a criterion for passing judgment on textual authenticity; ethical considerations also play a prominent part. G. Henton Davies rejected on ethical grounds Genesis 22:2 when, as cited above, he asked, "Did God make, would God in fact have made, such a demand upon Abraham or anybody else, except himself?" He replied, "Our answer is no. Indeed what Christian or humane conscience would regard such a command as coming from God?"[36]

The discoveries and pronouncements of scientists in various fields also impinge directly on biblical interpretation. The battles between religion and science date back at least to the Roman Catholic Church's forced humiliation of Galileo over his teaching that the earth revolved around the sun. As an unfortunate aftermath, religious leaders—intimidated by scientists and their pronouncement—only reluctantly forage in scientific fields. If modern astronomy has rendered obsolete a cosmology in which heaven is above the earth and hell is beneath, if the human race evolved from lower forms of life, and if the earth does not have four corners, what other biblical imagery must be reevaluated? Nobody wants to give the appearance of being unscientific in a world dominated by science and technology. Further, many Southern Baptist pastors and teachers professed Christ in childhood, dedicated themselves to the ministry, and pursued an ecclesiastical career early in life. They have neither the background nor propensity for leaving their fields of expertise to make judgments in disciplines beyond their own. Too often, they acquiesce to science when science seems to contradict the Bible. A route easily taken and often pursued is to affirm that the Bible is a book about religion, not about science, and that its authority rests in the areas of the religious and moral. Reactions to biological evolution illustrate the point.

Charles Darwin's publication of his epoch-making book *The Origin of Species* in 1859 has been nothing less than revolutionary. No longer is his belief about biological evolution treated as a theory in most scientific journals. It is treated as a fact. Its impact upon biblical interpretation is incalculable. In the face of the constant hammering in biology textbooks, newspaper articles, and by detractors of all kinds, many Christians waver in their commitment to biblical accounts which seem to conflict with scientific dogma. To gain a perspective, note the manner Southern Baptists handle the Genesis account of creation.

Some believe in a literal interpretation. Robert E. Naylor commented on the phrase "after his kind" in a Sunday School lesson for adults: "It is a direct contradiction of the idea that a new order evolves from the old or that man came from beasts."[37] In the same genre of thought, Herschel H. Hobbs declared, "Man is to have dominion over, not evolve from, the creeping things. The Bible clearly declares that man is a direct, special creation of God."[38] As to the historicity of the Garden of Eden story, he was equally emphatic: "I see the story as a real historical event. There were two actual trees, the tree of knowledge and the tree of life, in a real garden of Eden."[39]

On the other extreme, some commentators openly embrace biological evolution while holding to the truth they see symbolized in the Genesis story. Joseph A. Callaway's analysis in Volume I of the *Broadman Bible Commentary* epitomizes the view of many. In his opinion, one must allow for prehistoric man existing at the time of Adam.[40] Callaway raised the question of whether or not this falsifies Adam and concluded that in the symbols of Genesis one finds the essences of historical substance and ultimate meaning.[41]

Other writers try to take a mediating position between the two, holding to the historicity of Adam while leaving the door open for biological evolution. Fisher Humphreys seems to follow that road. He implies that the Genesis story is historically accurate when he grants that Genesis portrays God as making the first man from dust. He sees this as teaching the lowly origin of the human race.[42] As to the truth of biological evolution, Humphreys equivocates. He professes to see no necessary incompatibility between it and the belief that the human race is a creation of God.[43]

If, however, one does not believe God created from the dust a historical personage named Adam, inerrantist evangelicals, prone to a more literal interpretation of Genesis, fear drastic implications for related doctrines. Luke 3:38 traces the genealogy of Jesus through Adam to God. Paul treats Adam as a historical figure in Romans 5:14; I Corinthians 15:22, 45; and I Timothy 2:13-14. He erects doctrinal edifices on the assumption that Adam, the man, lived.

Biblical statements about cosmological structures continue to create problems. Many Southern Baptists side with Rudolph Bultmann who rejected belief in a "three-storied universe" as being incompatible with modern man's knowledge about the universe. John M. Lewis called the biblical cosmology pre-scientific, citing references to the three-storied universe and a flat earth.[44] Nevertheless, these pre-scientific beliefs reflected in the Bible do not impugn the authority of the Bible in other matters. Lewis believed that God used pre-scientific views to communicate his authoritative revelation and will.[45]

Inerrantist evangelicals in the current controversy, however, fear that the adoption of higher critical methodology runs a high risk of undermining on subjective grounds the authority of the Bible, and they are not alone. Long before inerrantists gained a position of authority in the convention, several Southern Baptist authors raised a similar warning flag. Ray Summers feared the outcome if critics impugned the Gospel accounts about Jesus as creations of the early church. Extreme subjectivism could undermine the effectiveness of historical studies.[46]

Eric Rust perceived the same danger because investigators might explain away the eternal dimension.[47] Clyde T. Francisco in 1950 saw a similar danger:

> Although it is the custom in some circles to denounce loudly anyone who reads Christian truth into the Old Testament, those same scholars are guilty of a far greater sin, imposing their *own* notions upon a scriptural passage. They go to the Bible with their minds already convinced as to what they shall find there. If their suspicions are not confirmed, the passage is branded as suspicious. . . . It is quite possible that when a passage disagrees with our opinion that the error is not in the passage but in our theory.[48]

What guarantee is there, then, that unbridled subjectivism will not erode confidence in the Bible? Inerrantist evangelicals see one answer as being a clearly defined statement about the inerrancy of the Bible.

HINDRANCES TO DEFINING INSPIRATION

The inerrantist evangelical and neoorthodox evangelical wings of the convention differ in their assumptions about biblical inspiration. Dale Moody in 1970 foresaw the need for a definition by Southern Baptists. To quote Moody:

> Briefly put, Southern Baptists may turn in the direction of the widely publicized *New Scofield Bible* of 1967, which defends the Mosaic authorship of all the Pentateuch to the point that it considers it possible for Moses to write in advance the account of his own death (p. 257). Another direction is indicated by the *Oxford Annotated Bible* that attempts to make constructive use of the conclusions of Biblical criticism. Many colleges and seminaries make this approach.[49]

So far, finding an acceptable definition has proved to be elusive. Inerrantist evangelicals, for their part, come at the problem of definition from two directions, one theoretical and the other practical. Adrian Rogers illustrates the theoretical approach when he notes that all of the autographs of the Bible are lost, but argues that they nevertheless were inerrant. In his President's Address to the Southern Baptist Convention in 1980, he preached:

> Now every serious student of the Bible knows that there are words and phrases found in the King James Version which do not appear in the oldest and best manuscripts of the Bible. These were added by copyists as they copied new manuscripts from older ones, at times copying into the text comments that other students had written on the margin. The Holy Spirit no more protects a copyist from error than He does a typesetter. So when we

speak of the Bible as "truth, without any mixture of error," we are referring to the original manuscripts. The Holy Spirit guarded the original writers from error.[50]

If the autographs are not extant, how can one prove their inerrancy? Furthermore, pulpit expositors and classroom teachers alike observe that when someone says, "The Bible says," some particular version must be quoted. One could ask, To what degree is it meaningful to speak of the infallibility of a particular version, even of the King James Version?

The question suggests the second way that inerrantist evangelicals look at the question of authenticating the biblical text. Two are cited here. W. A. Criswell, the long-time pastor of the First Baptist Church in Dallas and an eloquent spokesman for the view of many inerrantists in the convention, defended the practical approach to defining the authority of the Bible. He saw the benefits derived from textual, or lower, criticism, as establishing the reliability of the scriptures. Researchers compare the ancient manuscripts and identify the variations which have crept in through the centuries. Little by little, they amass evidence for the authenticity of the biblical text.[51] Clark H. Pinnock, a former professor at the New Orleans Baptist Theological Seminary, went even further, calling the Bibles of today as virtually infallible in themselves.[52]

Unquestionably, many Southern Baptist leaders are attempting to give new meaning to what is meant by the infallibility of the Bible. Writers dissatisfied with the inerrantist evangelical concept of infallibility come at the issue from a different angle. Henlee H. Barnett questioned whether one can use the term *infallible* at all. Harking back to the Bultmannian complaint about biblical cosmology, Barnett saw use of the term infallible as misleading if one implies that the Bible is without minor errors.[53] He further doubted that infallibility can mean that the Bible is always scientifically true and that all true science can be found in the Bible. He asked rhetorically, "Who now holds to the cosmology of the Bible setting forth the universe as a three-storied structure with heaven on top, the world in the middle, and flat at that, while hell is beneath the earth?"[54]

William E. Hull stated three problems inherent in the theory of those advocating the infallibility of the original texts. To begin, he noted that no original texts of the Bible have survived. Further, if they had, they would need translating into the language of the people. Hull then argued that an infallible text, if it existed, would have to be explained by fallible interpreters.[55]

Formulating a definition of biblical infallibility has proved elusive for several reasons. The first hindrance arises from what is meant by the Word of God. Two answers have been given: Jesus Christ and the Bible. Baptists, since the time of the Second London Confession in England, have spoken about the Living Word (Jesus Christ) and the Written Word (the Bible). Neoorthodoxy picked up the first term, Christ, the Word, but de-emphasized the second. The Bible points to the Word of God, but properly speaking, it is the Word of God when it bears testimony to God's supreme revelation in Jesus. When the Southern Baptist Convention voted to adopt a new confession in 1963, *The Baptist Faith and Message*, the two new sentences added to the basic document adopted in 1925 reflect the impact of neoorthodoxy. The first refers to the Bible as "the record of God's revelation of Himself to man" and the second adds that "the criterion by which the Bible is to be interpreted is Jesus Christ." Elucidating how the criterion, Jesus, relates to the Bible highlights one side of the rift between neoorthodoxy and inerrantism.

Almost all Southern Baptists hold to a conversionist theology. They believe that one comes to a point of salvation by repenting of sin and professing faith in Jesus Christ. In this encounter, the sinner comes to know Christ in an intimately personal way as Savior and Lord. In the light of this experience, Southern Baptists have little difficulty in accepting the proposition that Jesus, the Word, is the criterion by which the Bible is to be interpreted. In spite of the fact that the concept has deep emotional and spiritual significance, however, one must still give it doctrinal content. On what basis can one pronounce a given statement about Christ, either sound or unsound? There are but three objective sources for learning about the person of Jesus.

The first possibility, natural revelation, provides no help because it says nothing at all about Jesus. Because the data to be interpreted derives from the evidence revealed in the created order, the most it can do is indicate in a general way the existence of God. The traditional arguments for God's existence usually are classified as the Cosmological, Teleological, Anthropological (or Moral), and the Ontological. These strongly indicate the existence of God, but they say nothing about the historical Jesus.

A second independent testimony to Jesus comes from non-Christian writers of the New Testament era. At best, these but corroborate the New Testament claim that a man named Christ lived. Earle E. Cairns identified four "pagans" whose extant writings mention Christ: Tacitus (55-117), Pliny, Suetonius, and Lucian (ca. 125—ca. 190), but none had personal contact with Jesus.[56] Cairns also cites Josephus, the Jewish historian, who names James as the "brother of Jesus, the so-called Christ"; Josephus further called Christ a "wise man" condemned by Pilate to die on the cross.[57] Although these references are invaluable corroborations to the fact that Jesus was a historical figure, they offer almost no help in the formulation of a Christological doctrine.

The third witness of Jesus is the Bible itself, and it is the only definitive witness to his character and work. To say that Jesus is the criterion by which the Bible is to be interpreted can lead into circular reasoning: Jesus is the criterion by which biblical truth is judged, but nearly all that is known about Jesus comes from the Bible. Russell H. Dilday, Jr., in speaking of the pattern of authority for the believer, notes this ambiguity as it relates to the work of the Holy Spirit. The authority of the Bible is an objective check against unbridled subjectivism. The inner witness of the Holy Spirit enlightens and enlivens the written word, preventing it from becoming a collection of historical documents.[58]

In an ultimate and philosophical sense, Jesus Christ is the authority, but on a practical, doctrinal, and day-by-day basis, one must go back to the Bible. The question yet remains, If nearly everything one knows about Jesus comes from the Bible, how can he be the criterion by which the Bible is judged?

The second hindrance to formulating an acceptable definition comes from what is meant by the expression "the Word of God" as used by those not satisfied with the emphasis on the inerrancy of the autographs. They generally reject the notions that the Bible is only partially inspired or that it only becomes the Word of God as it speaks to receptive minds. The Word of God is more definitive and historical to them, as the following frame of reference demonstrates.

To bring the present debate into clearer focus, it may be helpful to posit five groupings of biblical texts. Group I has to do with those passages dealing with specifically religious subjects. These include teachings about such subjects as God, salvation, sin, morality and Christian living. Almost all Southern Baptists could agree that these teachings are infallible, authoritative, without error, reliable, inerrant, or whatever word one prefers. Group II texts include those with textual differences which have crept in through the centuries as the Bible was transmitted from generation to generation. These encompass texts with variant spellings in names, differences in numbers, grammatical changes, and obvious scribal errors. Generally, this class of text poses no insurmountable problems. Textual criticism helps resolve these discrepancies. In Group III texts, biblical references to natural phenomena are couched in the language of the times, such as allusions to the four corners of the earth, sunrise, and the like. These are usually explained on the basis of accommodating to the everyday language of the people. Group IV verses, those relating to the figurative language of the Bible, are more controversial. Nearly everyone admits that the Bible has a wide spectrum of figurative language, such as exhortations to the floods to clap their hands with joy in Psalm 98.8, but some verses are taken literally by some interpreters and figuratively by others. Not even the most fervid inerrantist evangelical would insist that figurative, apocalyptic, and allegorical language be interpreted literally.

Group V texts are the most controversial. They relate to supposed conflicts between biblical concepts and scientific maxims. Four are readily observable. First, a three-storied universe is widely cited as being out of harmony with science. However, the problem with the biblical cosmological problem probably has more to do with the doctrine of hell than with the description of heaven as above the earth. The idea of a literal, fiery hell has lost favor with many expositors. Clark Pinnock, no longer teaching in a Southern Baptist school but a vociferous opponent of theological liberalism when he taught at the New Orleans Baptist Theological Seminary, now believes in the annihilation of the wicked. In a recent article in *Christianity Today*, he argued that the fire of God destroys the lost because God does not raise the dead just to be able to punish them forever.[59] Pinnock raised the question of whether his belief was heretical and granted that some conservative Christians could think so.[60]

Southern Baptists who object to descriptions of hell as literal fire prefer to speak of hell as a "state of being," although they usually do not make clear how anyone can be in a state of being without being somewhere. After all, the center of the earth is large enough to accommodate the damned, whatever that number might be. Nevertheless, the complaint may have less to do with cosmology than with the nature of eternal punishment.

Biological evolution presents a second area of conflict between the Bible and science as seen by many. If one believes that humankind evolved from lower species, it is virtually impossible to keep intact the Genesis account as recorded. If God created Adam from the dust of the earth, literally, not even by a process of allegorizing can one make this refer to humanity's lowly origin.

A third conflict arises from studies in psychology. For researchers seeking causes of mental illness which are explicable in medical terms, demon possession does not fit readily into their scheme of explanations. Consequently, allusions to demon activities in the Bible frequently are taken as primitive explanations of mental illness no longer acceptable to the modern age. The difficulty arises when one tries to reconcile these maxims with the Bible.

A fourth area of conflict between the Bible and science comes from the biblical accounts of miracles. The advent of the scientific revolution with the discovery of the laws of nature led gradually to the concept of a closed universe in which the amount of energy in it is believed to be constant. This conviction gave birth to Deism with its claim that God created the universe, withdrew from it, and left it to its inevitable and necessary laws of cause and effect. It is not that God cannot interfere; he *does* not. In his remoteness, God does not intervene in events in the world. When holding to this assumption, expositors of the Bible seek natural explanations for miraculous events. For example, Jesus did not miraculously feed the five thousand, they say. Probably the multitude, seeing the lad with his five loaves and two fishes, uncovered their own provisions which they had held secret.

Group V passages provide most of the material for the present debate over inerrancy. How are these to be treated? Must they be interpreted literally, or is there latitude allowable at this point? The inerrantists insist that to spiritualize (or allegorize, or see these as saga or myth) is to begin a slippery slide away from biblical authority, which, if left unchecked, will ultimately destroy confidence in the Bible. This slide, they fear, will result in dire consequences for the convention in years to come, especially in a decline in evangelistic fervor. Their opponents see the inerrantist position as authoritarian and creedalistic, tending to undermine the cherished Baptist axioms of soul freedom and the priesthood of believers. They theorize, in affect, that Group V texts should be treated the same way as those in Group III or Group IV. As they see the problem, the controversy revolves around differing interpretations of certain kinds of texts.

There is yet a third hindrance toward formulating an acceptable definition of biblical inspiration, the existentialist mood of neoorthodoxy which focuses on the encounter between God and man. Correspondingly, existentialists view with deep suspicion the advocacy of propositional truths about the divine-human encounter as tending to detract from the dynamism of the divine-human relationship. Just how important are words in initiating the encounter? The existentialist fear of an overemphasis on words occurs in the thought of Theodore R. Clark. He alluded to lessons learned from the Council of Trent in the sixteenth century to demonstrate the difficulties in understanding faith as mental assent. To codify revelation to a set of propositions is to reduce faith to assent to revealed doctrines.[61] Rather, he understood faith as communion with God Himself.[62] Since the Bible itself contains words, statements, and propositions about God, they must not be given an excessive authority. Clark approvingly quoted John Dillenberger and Claude Welch. Fundamentalists, argued Clark, fall into the grievous error of exalting the finite and fallible to a place reserved for God alone.[63]

A fourth hindrance comes from the language of evangelicals who demand acceptance of the proposition that the autographs of the Bible were inerrant. This requirement has aroused scathing denunciations from many academics. Most of their complaints fall into three broad categories.

There are some who see the word *inerrant* as a recent addition to the Southern Baptist theological vocabulary which somehow is foreign to traditional thought. They prefer the word *infallible*. That counterattack seems forced, however, when one notes that *Webster's New World Dictionary*, second edition, lists *infallible* as a synonym for *inerrant*, and defines *infallible* as "incapable of error in setting forth doctrine on faith and morals." Something deeper than semantics is at stake.

A second cluster of objections to enforcing belief in inerrant autographs revolves around the hub of academic freedom. Is that cherished American ideal jeopardized by dogmas set by the controlling body? Although lay people have little concern, it does not appear that accreditation with regional accrediting agencies would be adversely affected. If the school purpose is clear, if the teaching reflects the purpose, and if the academic standards are met, the theological bent of the school does not affect accreditation.

The third objection is the charge of creedalism, the assertion that inerrantist evangelicals, in the drive to force their views on the seminary teachers and the writers of the Sunday School Board, violate such basic Baptist beliefs as soul freedom and the priesthood of the believer. Even though the entire thrust of this argument has been highlighted in the media, one crucial fact is often ignored. These resolutions and mandates passed by the convention in its annual sessions have no binding power at all on the local churches, associations, colleges, and state conventions. All of these are autonomous entities independent of the convention. Its declarations apply only to those boards, commissions, and agencies which it owns and controls, including the six seminaries. The fear that the convention's actions are a violation of the doctrine of the priesthood of the believer can have objective substance only if the convention attempts to impose its doctrinal stance on individuals or agencies not under its control. It has the right to adopt ethical and theological standards for its missionaries, writers, teachers, and other employees. Southern Baptists have a right to expect conformity to those guiding principles by convention employees, just as a local church expects its members to abide by doctrines distinctively Baptist. Baptists have fought for the right of the individual to be free to interpret the Bible for oneself and to address God directly without intermediaries, but they also have championed the rights of churches, associations, and conventions to establish their own doctrinal standards. Southern Baptists never have taught that a person has the right to believe as one wishes and remain in good standing in a Baptist fellowship, whether it be church, association, or convention. Neither have they understood the enforcement of those doctrines to be a violation of soul-freedom or the priesthood of the believer.

Regardless of how deeply one fears the threat of creedalism, debates on the subject may inadvertently mask the fact that committed neoorthodox evangelicals frequently cannot accept the premise of inerrant autographs. First, many do not believe that autographs ever existed for the Pentateuch, Gospels, and certain other books of the Bible. To agree to a statement affirming the possible existence of those autographs will strike at the heart of many assumptions of historical criticism. Second, many do not believe that the original messages referring to scientific data were necessarily inerrant. When the redactors compiled the biblical accounts, neoorthodox evangelicals generally believe they incorporated the pre-scientific world views of the day. Even if an autograph attributed to one of the apostles were discovered, the writing would still require demythologizing unless it were devoid of those elements common to a pre-scientific world view.

COMMON GROUNDS

In spite of the hindrances, what common grounds exist for the formulation of an acceptable definition of biblical inspiration? One possible avenue is suggested by James Leo Garrett. He studied the use of the word *infallible* in the Second London Confession, compared this with other confessions, and concluded that, historically, Baptists have differentiated between functional and model infallibility. In the former, they saw the Bible as authoritative in matters of faith. In the second, they emphasized the inspiration and words of the Bible, almost to the point of being dictated by the Holy Spirit. Neoorthodox evangelicals likely can accept functional infallibility, but not modal.[64] Garrett's differentiation probably represents the only basis upon which the neoorthodox evangelicals are willing to discuss the subject of inspiration. For convenience sake, this could be called the Neoorthodox Requirement.

A second attempt at a definition, in what is being called the Glorieta Statement, resulted from a meeting in October of 1986 when the presidents of the six Southern Baptist seminaries met in Glorieta, New Mexico, with representatives of the inerrantists. Among other statements agreed on, they issued one which affirms that "the 66 books of the Bible are not errant in any area of reality."[65] There were charges that the presidents had "caved in" to the inerrantists, probably because the words "not errant" appear, but the qualifying phrase "in any area of reality" is not without its ambiguities. Metaphysically, philosophers from the time of the Greek Milesians of about 585 B.C. have been trying to define the nature of reality. Speculations about it have ranged all the way from the *Infinite* of Anaximander (6th century B.C.), the *Being* of Parmenides (6th-5th century B.C.), the *Forms* of Plato (428-348 B.C.), the *Idealism* of George Berkeley (1685-1753), and the *Vitalism* of Henri Bergson (1859-1941), to the *Dialectical Materialism* of Karl Marx (1818-1883). Epistemologically, when applied to the story of Adam and Eve, for example, one can legitimately ask: Is the reality of Adam found literally in the belief of his creation out of dust by God, or is it to be found metaphorically in a process over which God presides? Taken in this sense, the Glorieta statement may provide the basis for a definition acceptable to all. The Glorieta Statement significantly left out any mention of inerrant autographs. That was a wise move if a definition acceptable to both factions is to be composed.

SUMMARY

Deep rifts exist in the convention over the issue of biblical authority. Name-calling, posturing, charges, and countercharges have become frequent enough that nearly everyone, by common consent, has suffered sufficiently. Is there a power struggle? Probably. Is there a semantic problem? Without a doubt. But these admissions must not obscure the fact that profound differences separate the inerrantist evangelical and neoorthodox evangelical factions. The Peace Committee, appointed by the convention in 1985 to study the present controversy, confirms these differences. In regard to the diversity of opinion about the Bible, it reported:

> Examples of this diversity include the following which are intended to be illustrative but not exhaustive: (1) Some accept and affirm the direct creation and historicity of Adam and Eve while others view them instead as representative of the human race in its creation and fall. (2) Some understand the historicity of every event in Scripture as reported by the original source while others hold that the historicity can be clarified and revised by the findings of modern historical scholarship. (3) Some hold to the stated authorship of every book in the Bible while others hold that in some cases such attribution may not refer to the final author or may be pseudonymous. (4) Some hold that every miracle in the Bible is intended to be taken as a historical event while others hold that some miracles are intended to be taken as parabolic.[66]

Most Southern Baptist professors, pastors, and leaders doubtless consider themselves a part of the mainstream of Southern Baptist life. All factions impute too much insight to the average church member, who views the present controversy with dismay, confusion, and disgust. But differences, real differences, do exist in the way Southern Baptists see biblical authority. No lasting benefits can evolve unless these differences are faced openly and honestly.

NOTES

1. Theodore R. Clark, *Saved By His Life* (New York: The McMillan Company, 1959).
2. James C. Hefley, *The Truth in Crisis: the Controversy in the Southern Baptist Convention* (Dallas: Criterion Publications, 1986); vol. 2 *The Truth in Crisis: Bringing the Controversy Up-to-Date*. Foreword by Larry Lewis (Hannibal, Missouri: Hannibal Books, 1987).
3. Carl F. H. Henry, "Conflict Over Biblical Inerrancy," *Christianity Today* 20 (May 7, 1976):23.
4. Harold Lindsell, *The Battle for the Bible* (Grand Rapids: Zondervan Publishing House, 1976), p. 104.
5. Russell H. Dilday, Jr., *The Doctrine of Biblical Authority* (Nashville: Convention Press, 1982), pp. 74-75.
6. *Baker's Dictionary of Theology*, s.v. "Evangelical," by Loraine Boettner.
7. *Baker's Dictionary of Theology*, s.v. "Neo-orthodoxy," by Paul K. Jewett.
8. Deane William Ferm, *Contemporary American Theologies: A Critical Survey* (New York: The Seabury Press, 1981), p. 14.
9. Jewett, "Neo-orthodoxy."
10. Page H. Kelly, "Confessions of a Higher Critic," *Florida Baptist Witness* 102 (December 5, 1985):9.
11. G. Henton Davies, "Genesis," in *The Broadman Bible Commentary*, vol. 1, ed. Clifton J. Allen (Nashville: Broadman Press, 1969), p. 198.
12. *SBC Annual*, 1970, pp. 63, 76-78.
13. Clifton J. Allen, "The Book of the Christian Faith," in *The Broadman Bible Commentary*, vol. 1, ed. Clifton J. Allen (Nashville: Broadman Press, 1969), p. 7.
14. Burlan A. Sizemore, Jr., "The Canon and Text of the Old Testament," in *The Broadman Bible Commentary*, vol. 1, ed. Clifton J. Allen (Nashville: Broadman Press, 1969), p. 50.
15. Clyde T. Francisco, "Genesis," in *The Broadman Bible Commentary*, vol. 1 (Revised), ed. Clifton J. Allen (Nashville: Broadman Press, 1973), p. 105.
16. Roy L. Honeycutt, Jr., "Exodus," in *The Broadman Bible Commentary*, vol. 1, ed. Clifton J. Allen (Nashville: Broadman Press, 1973), p. 308.
17. Ronald E. Clements, "Leviticus," in *The Broadman Bible Commentary*, vol. 2, ed. Clifton J. Allen (Nashville: Broadman Press, 1970), p. 2.
18. John D. W. Watts, "Deuteronomy," in *The Broadman Bible Commentary*, vol. 2, ed. Clifton J. Allen (Nashville: Broadman Press, 1970), pp. 175-176.
19. Clyde T. Francisco, "The History of Israel," in *The Broadman Bible Commentary*, vol. 1, ed. Clifton J. Allen (Nashville: Broadman Press, 1969), p. 57.
20. John I Durham, "Contemporary Approaches in Old Testament Study," in *The Broadman Bible Commentary*, vol. 1, ed. Clifton J. Allen (Nashville: Broadman Press, 1969), p. 92.
21. Eric C. Rust, "The Theology of the Old Testament," in *The Broadman Bible Commentary*, vol. 1, ed. Clifton J. Allen (Nashville: Broadman Press, 1969), p. 74.
22. John Joseph Owens, "Daniel," in *The Broadman Bible Commentary*, vol. 6, ed. Clifton J. Allen (Nashville: Broadman Press, 1971), pp. 374, 376.
23. Page H. Kelly, "Isaiah," in *The Broadman Bible Commentary*, vol. 5, ed. Clifton J. Allen (Nashville: Broadman Press, 1971), pp. 159-163.
24. John T. Bunn, "Ezekiel," in *The Broadman Bible Commentary*, vol. 6, ed. Clifton J. Allen (Nashville: Broadman Press, 1971), p. 231.
25. B. Elmo Scoggin, "Micah," in *The Broadman Bible Commentary*, vol. 7, ed. Clifton J. Allen (Nashville: Broadman Press, 1972), p. 187.
26. A. J. Glaze, Jr., "Jonah," in *The Broadman Bible Commentary*, vol. 7, ed. Clifton J. Allen (Nashville: Broadman Press, 1972), p. 155.

27. Ray Summers, "Contemporary Approaches in New Testament Study," in *The Broadman Bible Commentary*, vol. 8, ed. Clifton J. Allen (Nashville: Broadman Press, 1969), pp. 48, 51.

28. Frank Stagg, "Matthew," in *The Broadman Bible Commentary*, vol. 8, ed. Clifton J. Allen (Nashville: Broadman Press, 1969), p. 73.

29. William E. Hull, "John," in *The Broadman Bible Commentary*, vol. 9, ed. Clifton J. Allen (Nashville: Broadman Press, 1970), pp. 197, 200.

30. L. D. Johnson, "An Introduction to the Bible" vol. 1 in *Bible Survey Series* (Nashville, Convention Press, 1969), p. 60.

31. Ibid, p. 61.

32. Page H. Kelly, "A Nation in the Making," vol. 3 in *Bible Survey Series* (Nashville: Convention Press, 1969), pp. 10-14.

33. Joe H. Music, "Anticipating a New Beginning," *The Adult Teacher* 21 (October-November-December 1974), p. 115.

34. William L. Hales, "The Steadfast Love of God," *Sunday School Adults* 75 (April-May-June 1975), pp. 21-24.

35. Robert W. Kicklighter, "God's Glory in Creation," *The Adult Teacher* 21 (April-May-June 1975), pp. 48-55.

36. G. Henton Davies, "Genesis", p. 198.

37. Robert E. Naylor, "In the beginning, God," *Sunday School Adults* 56 (7 October 1956), p. 6.

38. Herschel H. Hobbs, *The Origin of All Things: Studies in Genesis* (Waco: Word Books, 1975), p. 28.

39. Ibid, p. 46.

40. Joseph A. Callaway, "Archaeology and the Bible," in *The Broadman Bible Commentary*, vol. 1, ed. Clifton J. Allen (Nashville: Broadman Press, 1969), p. 47.

41. Ibid.

42. Fisher Humphreys, *Thinking About God*, (New Orleans: Insight Press, 1974), p. 74.

43. Ibid, pp. 74-75.

44. John M. Lewis, "Revelation, Inspiration, Scriptures" in *Layman's Library of Christian Doctrine*, vol. 3 (Nashville: Broadman Press, 1985), p. 26.

45. Ibid., p. 129.

46. Ray Summers, "Approaches in New Testament Study," p. 51.

47. Eric C. Rust, *Salvation History: A Biblical Interpretation* (Richmond: John Knox Press, 1962), pp. 51-52.

48. Clyde T. Francisco, "Things New and Things Old," *The Review and Expositor*, 47 (July 1950), p. 314.

49. Dale Moody, "Whither the Winds of Doctrine?" *The Baptist Program* (January 1970), p. 9.

50. Adrian Rogers, "The Decade of Decision and the Door of Destiny," *Florida Baptist Witness*, 97 (June 19, 1980), pp. 4-5.

51. W. A. Criswell, *Why I Preach That the Bible Is Literally True* (Nashville: Broadman Press, 1969), p. 67.

52. Clark H. Pinnock, *Biblical Revelation-The Foundation of Christian Theology* (Chicago: Moody Press, 1971), p. 89. After leaving the convention, Pinnock moved decidedly away from this view.

53. Henlee H. Barnette, "Southern Baptists and Theological Semantics," *The Baptist Program* (March 1966), p. 15.

54. Ibid.

55. William E. Hull, "Shall we call the Bible infallible?" *The Baptist Program* (December 1970), pp. 17-21.

56. Earle E. Cairns, *Christianity Through the Ages-A History of the Christian Church*, Revised and Enlarged Edition (Grand Rapids: Zondervan Publishing House, 1981), pp. 45-46.

57. Ibid., p. 46.

58. Russell H. Dilday, Jr., *The Doctrine of Biblical Authority* (Nashville: Convention Press, 1982), p. 30.

59. Clark Pinnock, "Fire, Then Nothing," *Christianity Today* 31 (March 20, 1987), 40.

60. Ibid., p. 41.

61. Theodore R. Clark. *Saved By His Life* (New York: The McMillan Company, 1959), p. 128.

62. Ibid., p. 129.

63. Ibid., p. 125.

64. James Leo Garrett, "Biblical Infallibility and Inerrancy According to Baptist Confessions," *Search* (Fall 1972), pp. 44-45.

65. Dan Martin, "Seminary Presidents Repudiate claims of Capitulation," *Florida Baptist Witness* 103 (November 20, 1986):20.

66. "Theological Diversity Statement," *Florida Baptist Witness* 104 (June 11, 1987):4.

CHAPTER 11

THE LAST STAGES OF CALVINISM

Since the beginning of the last third of the twentieth century, economic, social, political, and religious upheavals have coalesced sufficiently to assault the bastions of orthodox Christianity. One of the most pervasive, liberation theology, began taking shape in the social unrest in Central and South America. As to origin, it came from the sociology departments of some of the universities, from the liberal wings of Roman Catholicism, and from mainline Protestantism. Methodologically, liberation theologians apply Marxist presuppositions to the structures of society to determine its exploitative content. They look to such works as Karl Marx's three-volume work, *Capital*, and the oppressor-oppressed factor as found in the *Manifesto of the Communist Party*. Whereas Jewish writers may divide the world into the Jewish-Gentile camps, and evangelical Christians divide it into saved-unsaved, liberationists differentiate on the basis of exploiter-exploited and oppressor-oppressed. Emphasizing that theology is a verb and not a noun, they believe that God works among those who defend the rights of the exploited-oppressed against the exploiters-oppressors irrespective of whether the defenders are radical revolutionaries or even atheistic. Their paradigm biblical model is that of Moses freeing Israel from Egyptian bondage. Black liberationists and women liberationists have adapted economic, social, and political liberationism to their own circumstances. Integral to the liberation analysis is the assumption of Jean-Jacques Rousseau that people, basically good, can only reach their fullest potential in a society freed of its present structures.

In Central and South America the movement becomes heavily anti-imperialistic and anti-colonialistic, which usually translates into rhetoric and action directed principally against the United States. Liberation theological terms only rarely occur in Southern Baptist writings, but features of the women's liberation goals are manifesting themselves in the present controversy over the role of women in Southern Baptist life.

At the same time that liberation theology began developing, neoorthodoxy declined as a movement but permeated the major denominations in unobtrusive ways. Southern Baptists are experiencing that intrusion. Also, the charismatic movement has had a direct effect on the convention. On the other hand, fads such as the Death-of-God theology aroused only derision among Southern Baptists. At the same time, Calvinism has found a few advocates, but it, along with Landmarkism, is dead as a vital force in Southern Baptist theology.

JESUS AND THE TRINITY

Southern Baptists remain in the mainstream of orthodox, trinitarian theology. They continue to believe in the deity of both Jesus and the Holy Spirit, as well as the conception of Jesus in the womb of a virgin. The charismatic phenomenon with its focus on the Holy Spirit occasionally touches a local church, but its appeal on a large scale is waning. Also, the Calvinistic preoccupation with God's sovereignty and decrees rarely absorbs much attention.

Southern Baptists remain trinitarians. Clifton J. Allen wrote: "God is not divided—he is one God. This means that the Spirit is as truly and fully God as the Father is God and the Son is God. . . . Father, Son, and Holy Spirit are one God. They are each God, they are together God."[1] Clayton K. Harrop asserted that Jesus is fully man "in every sense of the term," having been "conceived through the action of the Holy Spirit," born of a virgin.[2]

The doctrine of the virgin birth has not been contested seriously. During the 1950s, it was debated in *The Review and Expositor*. Dale Moody used the argument of A. T. Robertson that "Miraculous Conception" was a more accurate expression than "Virgin Birth."[3] The former expression emphasizes the act of conception apart from a human father whereas the latter emphasizes the birth of Christ nine months later. Even so, Moody never voiced doubts that Jesus was born of a virgin: "The context of Luke 1:27, as in the case of Matthew 1:23, makes it clear beyond any doubt that Mary had no sex relations whatsoever before the birth of our Lord."[4]

Robert E. Naylor voiced similar thoughts in 1956. He wrote in the *Sunday School Adults* quarterly that Christ was conceived of the Holy Ghost and was born of a virgin.[5] Herschel H. Hobbs and Malcolm O. Tolbert,[6] to cite representative writers, made similar statements. Apparently, the doctrine has been debated by many but doubted by none.

Southern Baptist writers continue to defend the deity of Christ on the grounds that no less a Being could redeem from sin. "Human experience has shown," wrote Dallas M. Roark, "that man is incapable of redeeming himself. Anything less than God as Redeemer is to make a mockery of the idea."[7] Dale Moody pursued the same theory, stating, "The humanity of Christ apart from deity is not sufficient for a true and perfect mediator. Only one who is truly God as well as truly man can save men from their sins. If he is not God, he has no power to save; and if he is not man, he has no right to save."[8] Albert McClellan said: "Before the world existed, Christ existed. He was face to face with God, he was with God, and he was God. Just how this can be nobody knows."[9] Hudson Baggett somewhat inelegantly stated that "the claim that Jesus made no claim to divinity is 'hogwash.' Throughout the gospels, Jesus Himself claimed that He was divine and others claimed it for him."[10]

The reality of the divine incarnation is affirmed in the analysis of John 1:1 as given by William E. Hull. In commenting on the final two phrases of that verse, he noted two carefully balanced truths: Jesus and God are distinct persons; yet, Jesus revealed God himself and not just something about God.[11] Billy E. Simmons in *Adult Bible Teacher*, H. H. Hobbs in *The Origin of All Things*, and Joseph F. Green in *Baptist Adults* interpreted the passage similarly.[12]

Deviations from belief in the deity of Jesus fall more in the category of aberrations from the norm than harbingers of a trend. Two are noteworthy. Theodore R. Clark, showing the influence of Tillich's panentheism and belief that any attempt to particularize God amounts to idolatry, cited the statements about Jesus in several hymns such as "Jesus Saves" and "Living for Jesus." These songs, Clark believed, suggest that a kind of Jesusolatry or Jesus Cult has appeared which distorts the doctrine of the atonement in a sentimental, but irrelevant, worship of Jesus.[13] As noted in the previous chapter, the trustees of the New Orleans Baptist Theological Seminary fired Clark in 1960.

Robert S. Alley, former chairman of the department of religion at the University of Richmond, also differed with Southern Baptists in reference to Christ's deity. Speaking to a group of atheists December 6, 1977, Alley stated that Jesus did not claim to be God or even related to Him.[14] A tenured professor, Alley was transferred out of the department of religion to another position in the university.

The one who is God in the flesh and was crucified under the rule of Pontius Pilate yet lives. That the Crucified One rose from the dead very few Southern Baptists doubt. They hold to Paul's statement in I Corinthians 15:19, "If in this life only we have hope in Christ, we are of all men most miserable." To pick up the chain of thought from the beginning of this century, when Adolph Harnack argued that only the Spirit of Jesus lives after the crucifixion, A. T. Robertson of Southern Seminary met Harnack's argument squarely. To base Christianity on the conviction of the disciples that Jesus was merely immortal was "gratuitous, antiscriptural, and a wholly incompetent explanation."[15] A Christianity which has no basis in fact has a slim foundation indeed, according to Robertson. If Jesus came out of the grave, everything can be explained, especially in light of the coming of the Holy Spirit at Pentecost. He concluded, "If we reject the supernatural, once more we are at sea and fail to explain the situation."[16]

The cruciality of the resurrection of Christ is still held by the vast majority of Southern Baptists. Hugh R. Peterson called it the cornerstone of the Christian faith.[17] Roland Q. Leavell said of it, "The Christian church . . . is not founded on a falsehood."[18] Eric C. Rust contended that the physical resurrection of Jesus was necessary to establish the identity of the risen Christ with the significance and mission of the historical Jesus.[19] Frank Stagg noted that only the personal appearance of Christ convinced anyone that he was alive because an empty tomb could convince neither friend nor foe.[20]

The observation by Stagg suggests another aspect of the resurrection: its significance for believers. The proof that Jesus was alive added new authority to the witness of the Christians. James L. Sullivan noted that the resurrected Jesus fed the disciples and ate with them by the seaside. No spirit could have performed these acts. The witnesses to his resurrection no longer needed to be timid in confirming it.[21]

W. T. Conner listed three further benefits of the resurrection. Because the risen Christ indwells believers, they can now live victorious lives. The resurrection of Christ insures that death is not the end and gives assurance of the triumph of the kingdom of God.[22] In the thoughts of Wayne E. Ward, Christ entered death, the last stronghold of the evil one, and opened a doorway of hope by his resurrection.[23]

THE HOLY SPIRIT REDISCOVERED

Southern Baptist Christology correlates with the doctrine of the Holy Spirit. Intensive studies in the person and work of the Holy Spirit have coincided with the rise of the charismatics in the 1960s. Even prior to the sixties, however, Southern Baptists saw the Holy Spirit as the source of spiritual power for the Christian. W. T. Conner, a representative writer, ascribed personal growth and Christian character to the power of the Holy Spirit.[24] In a lesson for the *Baptist Young Peoples Quarterly* in 1957, Dotson M. Nelson dealt with the source of spiritual power. Using the events of Pentecost as the guide, he noted that the early Christians were commanded to wait for the promise of the Father. Further, they were commanded to pray.[25]

Other writers in the mid-fifties expressed the need for a rediscovery of the ministry of the Spirit. Henlee H. Barnette delved into the necessity of the Holy Spirit for ethical living.[26] Eric C. Rust pointed out the need for a fresh understanding of the work of the Holy Spirit if Christians are to be delivered from the word that kills to the Word who makes alive.[27]

The rise of glossolalia in the sixties forced Southern Baptists to give greater consideration to the doctrine of the Holy Spirit. Since then, there has been an avalanche of materials dealing with the subject. The movement transcended denominational barriers as Roman Catholics, Episcopalians, Baptists, and others professed to have received a post-conversion experience with Christ. In most cases, the "filling of the Spirit" expressed itself in ecstatic utterances. Southern Baptists, like other denominations, have re-evaluated their doctrine of the Holy Spirit. When the movement first began, they viewed the issue with a benign indifference, but as members of some Baptist churches began to claim the "second work of grace," pastors and theological teachers wrote books and articles on the subject. Very few Southern Baptists forthrightly condemned the experience as being unscriptural, preferring rather to reach a practical accommodation with the charismatics. Dale Moody's analysis typifies the spirit of conciliation. He understood speaking in tongues as a form of ecstatic praise addressed to God, which, he believed, Paul permitted.[28] Tongues should not be prohibited in private prayer. In a similar vein of thought, J. Morris Ashcraft explained that Paul distinguished between the public exercise of tongues and its use in private. Paul, Ashcraft wrote, endorsed its private use as a form of prayer.[29]

In the event of an outbreak of speaking in tongues in a local congregation, the pastors frequently take a stronger stance. They often understand the biblical gift as that of being able to speak a language not previously learned. The gift of languages, but not that of ecstatic utterance, was given to the disciples so that the gospel could be preached among all peoples. This interpretation goes back more than a century and a half. An article originally published in the *London Evangelical Magazine* and reprinted in the *Christian Watchman* in 1823 states that the gift was the "very thing wanted by illiterate men, who were about to start on a mission to all the nations of the world, with all its Babel of various confused tongues."[30] The author of the article gave no suggestion that the gift of tongues was ecstatic utterance.

Gradually, some of the Baptist associations stiffened their dealings with churches that allow ecstatic utterances. The Lake County Association in Florida, citing evidence of glossolalia, voted thirty-six to one in 1974 not to include Westside and Lady Lakes churches in the formation of the fiftieth annual session of the association.[31] The Dallas Association excluded the Beverly Hills and Shady Grove Baptist churches in 1975; the Cincinnati Association refused to seat messengers from two charismatic churches that same year.[32] The Union Baptist Association, meeting in Houston, Texas, branded the charismatic movement as "being of the devil."[33] The Baptist General Convention of Texas in 1976 refused to seat messengers from two charismatic churches in Dallas.[34] Except for an occasional flare-up in local churches, the charismatic problem is muted among Southern Baptists on both the national and state levels.

ELECTION BASED ON FREE WILL

As Southern Baptists have kept themselves in the main stream of evangelical trinitarianism, they have placed further distance between themselves and their earlier commitment to the doctrine of election. Whereas W. T. Conner and many of his generation assumed the truth of election and tried to reconcile it with free will, Baptists now take for granted free will and then try to reconcile election with it. Herschel H. Hobbs listed four errors implicit in the older view of election: (1) Basing it on God's will or good pleasure ignores other attributes of God such as his love and righteousness. (2) It overlooks the teaching that God wishes as many as possible to be saved and not as few as possible. (3) It arbitrarily destines some to damnation. (4) It "tends toward fatalism."[35] In words reminiscent of those of W. T. Conner, he saw election as referring to a *plan* rather than to *individuals*.[36]

Two variations on the theme of election as a plan seem to summarize adequately what most Southern Baptists who have written on the subject understand election to mean: Election is in Christ and election is to service. Wayne E. Ward voiced those two basic themes in Sunday School materials published in 1958.[37] Ward concluded that salvation and service go together.[38] The same two themes were sounded by R. W. Kicklighter in a symposium edited by Duke K. McCall, *What Is the Church?*[39] These understandings of election contrast sharply with the older discussions of election based on God's decrees.

BODY AND SOUL VERSUS BODY-SOUL

The psalmist studied the heavens centuries ago and raised a question that still perplexes when he inquired of God, "What is man, that thou art mindful of him?" Southern Baptists traditionally have taught the belief that a person has a body which contains a separable entity variously called soul or spirit. Some believe that the complete person composed of body and soul somehow was contained seminally in Adam (traducianism). Others hold to the idea that the body comes from Adam but that God creates a new soul for each person (creationism). Traditionalists agree with the dualism described by Herschel H. Hobbs, who said: "Man is twofold in nature. He is both spirit and body. Man is not a body and has a soul. He is a soul and has a body. The body is mortal; the soul is immortal."[40]

Both of the theological terms, traducianism and creationism, are losing by default to a psychology in secular universities which is moving inexorably toward seeing human personality in behavioristic categories. Soul, in some schools of psychology, has become an unpopular term. John W. Drakeford of Southwestern Baptist Theological Seminary cited the history of the demise of the soul. Psychologists first abandoned distinctions between body and soul, this gave little attention to the soul, and finally left to the theologians the task of giving it meaning.[41]

One of the theological responses to the troublesome concept has been the psychosomatic unity view of personhood in which one does not *have* a soul; one *is* a soul. In the unity view, the person is frequently described as body-soul. Thus Frank Stagg speaks of the "essential" or "whole" person. The terms flesh (*sarx*), Spirit (*pneuma*), body (*soma*), and soul (*psuche*) in the New Testament may seem to assume a dichotomous or trichotomous view, but Stagg thinks this is not the case. Each term describes the whole person from its particular perspective. One may be described as flesh, spirit, body, or soul. Each term is highly serviceable in the analysis of personality or for emphasis of some aspect of human existence, but this never becomes, to Stagg, a thoroughgoing dichotomy or trichotomy.[42]

Other writers have attempted, with varying degrees of success, to explain how a person can be a unity. William W. Stevens said that both the dichotomous and trichotomous theories are inadequate "when viewed from the whole New Testament."[43] Dallas M. Roark wrote that, traditionally, a human being is described as body and soul, but biblically speaking, he or she is a living soul.[44] Francis M. Dubose, in *Source for Leaders*, called the idea of the separation of soul from person a Greek heresy.[45] In the view of Morris Ashcraft, the belief that the body has a soul which can be detached from the body originated in Greek thought. He believed Christians should not think of the soul as an entity separate from the body.[46]

The charge that belief in a spiritual entity separable from the physical body is a Greek heresy, or at least reflects Greek dualism, comes up frequently in Southern Baptist theological works. It is unfortunate for the reader that the meaning is not more explicitly defined because Greek philosophers differed widely on the constituent parts of human personality. Materialists like Leucippus (5th century B.C.) and Democritus (460-360 B.C.) theorized that all reality is comprised of atoms—fiery atoms for the soul and rough atoms for the body. Aristotle (384-322 B.C), except for a few scattered references, had little to say about a soul as a separable entity. Plato (427-347 B.C.) did believe in the soul as a separable entity, but his teachings differed radically from traditional Christian dualism in at least three areas. (1) He pictured the soul as consciously existing prior to its inhabiting a body. In education, therefore, the teacher extracts from the pupil information previously known. The Christian writer Origen (ca.185-ca.254 A.D.) believed in the pre-existence of the soul, but evangelical Christians do not. (2) Greeks like Plato and Socrates did not understand the flesh to be evil in a moral sense. Socrates, the interlocutor in Plato's writings, was a homosexual, and homosexual love is celebrated in Plato's *Symposium*. (3) Plato had no place in his system for the resurrection of the body. These kinds of differences are bothersome when the blanket charge of Greek dualism is made.

But if the soul is not separable from the body, what does this redefinition portend for theology? It will bring about new directions in both evangelism and in understanding the doctrine of the end-time. It will affect evangelism because *soul-winning* is at best a figure of speech if one has no soul. Francis M. Dubose questioned pointedly in *Source for Leaders*, "Is personal soul-winning biblical?"

He concluded, "We have fostered an evangelism which has been indifferent to the basic needs of the whole man."[47] One may object to this criticism of traditional evangelism, but it emphasizes the desire to interpret evangelism as "person-winning" rather than mere "soul-winning," to use current terminology. This broader definition of evangelism probably will be given greater prominence in the convention in the years to come. Seeing the person as a body-soul will help lead Southern Baptists into a wider area of ministry in which the traditional evangelistic concept of soul-winning will be supplanted by attempts to minister to the whole person. If so, then the evangelistic thrust so characteristic of Southern Baptist life will give way to a more pronounced emphasis on social ministries.

The theory that a person is a psychosomatic entity profoundly influences one's view of what happens at death. The doctrine of a visible coming of Christ as a climax to history becomes a moot issue if one believes in a continuous resurrection. Those possibilities are explored below in the section on eschatology.

Belief that a human is a body-soul and not a body with a non-material entity separable from the body also necessitates a new look at the doctrines of inherited depravity, regeneration, and atonement. The strength of the dogma of inherited depravity depends in part on the historical reality of Adam and his fall into sin. If the human race resulted from a process of gradual change from other animal species as some believe, depravity as a constituent element of inherited characteristics does not, cannot, carry the moral necessity of a new birth to counteract it. It then becomes a lack of social and moral adjustment to one's total environment. Not surprisingly, contemporary neoorthodox writings have much to say about the terrible plight of the human condition, but nothing to say about a depraved nature in the Calvinistic sense. Further, substitutionary atonement undergoes radical redefinition.

SUBSTITUTION VERSUS EXAMPLE

Theologians customarily divide doctrines about the death of Christ into two categories, objective theories and subjective theories. Objectivists see the atonement as being objective to the human race and in some sense objective to God the Father because Christ effected salvation, or at least the basis for it, on the cross. The benefits are subjectively appropriated by believers. Objectivists come in many varieties, such as governmental theorists (Hugo Grotius), satisfactionists (Anselm), and federal representationists (Charles Hodge). Subjectivists do not believe it is possible for the Innocent (Christ) to suffer in the place of the guilty (sinners). Instead, believers are to follow Christ's example in living a life of self-sacrifice. This is usually called the Moral Influence theory. Fundamentalism made the substitutionary death of Christ one of its cardinal doctrines in its fight against liberalism. Basic to inerrantist evangelicalism, it is one of the doctrines Southern Baptist inerrantists strive to preserve.

There is no such thing as *the* Southern Baptist doctrine of the cross, and any suggestion that there is would be misleading. Beginning with the Second London Confession, however, trends are discernible and pivotal concepts reoccur. Four of these stand out.

The first dominant theme was that of the Calvinistic belief in limited atonement. The death of Christ was an actual—and not just a potential—payment for the sins of the redeemed, without which they could not be saved. Believing also that none of the payment effected by Jesus could be wasted, and neither could God collect twice (as would be true if some were lost for whom Jesus died), Calvinists developed the closely knit and interlocking system of doctrines. They are popularly known as the five points of Calvinism, i.e., total depravity, unconditional predestination, limited atonement, irresistible grace, and the perseverance of the saints.

The second dominant theme in the evolution of the doctrine of the atonement among Baptists came with the modified Calvinism of Andrew Fuller. He placed the efficacy of the work of Christ in the decree or will of God rather than in the death of Christ. Although the Fuller doctrine softened Calvinism to the extent that it preserved the doctrine of free will, it also breached the defenses of Calvinism and opened the way ultimately for the denial of objective atonement. If the death of Christ *potentially* atoned for sinners, or if the death of Christ is efficacious only by divine decree, an element of arbitrariness is injected into the discussion. If God willed to save by one method, he could have willed to do it some other way.

The third change among Southern Baptists was begun by the personalistic emphasis of E. Y. Mullins in his modified moral influence, or existential, explanation. Mullins still preached the objectiveness of the death of Christ, but he described the efficacy in human experience terms. He dropped entirely the penal satisfaction aspects of the death of Christ. In so doing, he moved Southern Baptists in a giant step toward subjective atonement.

The fourth trend in the Southern Baptist view of the atonement is exemplified in the existential emphasis of Frank Stagg for whom substitution becomes "alongside of" rather than "instead of." He states his view clearly in his *New Testament Theology*, the symbolism of a sports event. A new player does not replace another. Instead, he plays the game alongside of the other. Substitution means that Jesus plays the game of life alongside of, or in, the believer.[48]

The completeness of Stagg's break with the inerrantist evangelical doctrine of substitutionary atonement can be discerned in a more recent work of his entitled *The Doctrine of Christ*. In the chapter on the work of Christ entitled "The Salvation of Christ," he bases his study on the healing of a lame man by Jesus as recorded in John 5:1-18 and 7:10-24, developing the theme of salvation as healing.[49] At no point does he discuss the theories of objective atonement. Two related concepts partially account for this omission.

First, Stagg sees a person as an entity, a whole person, who needs healing physically and spiritually, but he does not see these as facets of separate entities within the person, i.e., body and soul. He believes that soul in biblical usage represents the whole person and not some ghostly self.[50] He ascribes to Plato the idea of a soul trapped in a human body, freed at death. Such a concept, he wrote, contradicts the biblical teaching beginning with Genesis.[51] What, then, is salvation? It is the work of God in Christ in which he heals the total person and makes one truly human.[52] To be lost is to be self-centered and self-serving. The essence of being saved is having the direction reversed.[53] Stagg says nothing about the necessity of an ontological change called the new birth as the beginning of the experience of taking up one's cross to follow Christ.

Second, Stagg's understanding of the Trinity allows no room for the propitiatory death of the Son who appeases God or overcomes any problem in God.[54] The deity of Christ refers to God revealing himself in human form, but Stagg does not see the deity of Christ as implying rigid distinctions in the Godhead. That perception, he believes, does not find explicit exposition in the New Testament.[55] In reference to the saving work of Christ, Jesus is God himself in human form, but the second Person of the Godhead does not save one from the first Person. Jesus is not one Person of three because the totality of God was manifested in him.[56] Neither is the Holy Spirit one Person among three. He is the Spirit of God.[57]

To buttress his contention that there are no personal destinations within the Godhead, Stagg enunciates a relational explanation in which he depicts himself, for example, as a professor, son, brother, husband, father, and fisherman. He is each of these at the same time.[58] He uses this relational model to indicate that God is Father, Son, and Holy Spirit; he then adds that God is also Shepherd, Judge, Savior, and Strength.[59] The cry of Christ on the cross arose from his humanity, thinks Stagg, but one part of God was not praying to another.[60]

Stagg's existentialist-neoorthodox interpretation of the atonement finds a counterpart in the convention among those reasserting the particular redemption or limited atonement beliefs of their Calvinistic forefathers. Thomas J. Nettles is one of the younger men reaffirming the Calvinism of a by-gone generation.[61] Ernest Reisinger and others have been reprinting Calvinistic Classics and making these available to college and seminary students.

The views voiced by Nettles and Stagg represent the polarities of Southern Baptist beliefs about the death of Christ for sin. Theodore R. Clark was close to Stagg's existentialism when he stated the principle by which the cross becomes operative. One dies in Christ through self-denial and by faith enters into the new Being in Christ.[62] Eric C. Rust attempted to make the cross relevant by invoking the concept of contemporaneity. That is, what Christ did on the cross is contemporaneous with all of history. At this point, however, Rust added a concept which placed his view close to traditional Southern Baptist thought. Christ's death and resurrection are made immanent in history by the Holy Spirit.[63] Thus Rust preserved the objective significance of the work of Christ as an event in time and space.

Fisher Humphreys has attempted to maintain the salient features of the substitutionary theories and the moral influence theories by combining them into a synthesis he calls *cruciform*. One can speak of the sufferings of Christ as objective, Humphreys says, because the cross was objective to the life of God. As to the nature of the suffering, Humphreys has little to say beyond its being costly, taking the form of a cross.[64] The cross is objective to humanity in that what God did in Christ was irrespective of any anticipated response from humanity.[65] Humphreys falls short of saying that the cross is strictly substitutionary. Instead, he falls back on the costliness of the event as measured by the experience of Christ.[66] Humphreys takes his model from the realm of interpersonal relationships in that when one is wronged, the wronged person does not suffer in order to earn the right to forgive. Once again, even forgiveness finds its measure by what it costs the one wronged.[67]

In summary, limited atonement—that Christ died only for the sins of the elect—was to be the most prominent position held until the middle of the nineteenth century. Through the influence of Andrew Fuller and others, limited atonement was supplanted by general atonement. The trend since the beginning of the twentieth century has been toward an experiential interpretation at the expense of the legalistic. This does not mean that Baptists are polarized on the issue. Instead, all views are often seen as making a significant contribution to the total understanding of the atonement. For example, when discussing expiation and propitiation, Boyd Hunt saw truth in both concepts.[68] In a broader sense, Eric Rust said that preaching ought to reflect the sacrificial, juridical, and dramatic views of the cross.[69] These citations illustrate the reluctance some have to be identified with any one view. Humphreys doubtless expressed the attitude of many Baptists when he declined to decide whether the death of Christ was either subjective or objective. It was both.[70] The problem as seen by inerrantist evangelicals is the incomplete presentation of neoorthodox evangelicals who see the cross only as a subjective principle which preempts objective, substitutionary atonement.

ETERNAL SECURITY

Four of Calvinism's five basic points—total depravity, unconditional predestination, limited atonement, and irresistible grace—have been either rejected or modified by Southern Baptist theologians as they have restructured their theology along Arminian lines. The fifth basic point, the perseverance of the saints, has an uncertain future. One occasionally hears a doctrinal sermon at associational meetings devoted to the subject, and the doctrine sometimes gains attention in convention literature as in Thomas E. McCullough's topic "Salvation Is Eternal,"[71] and in a recent book by Perry Lassiter, *Once Saved . . . Always Saved.*[72] However, the decline in interest in theology in the convention contributes to a poorly indoctrinated membership. Personal conversations with local Southern Baptists will reveal numbers of them who have serious problems with the doctrine. On the convention-wide level, Dale Moody has stated his belief that salvation can be lost in some exceptional instances. He is the first acclaimed Southern Baptist to embrace publicly the possibility of apostasy or falling from grace. His views are enunciated in his book *The Word of Truth: A Summary of Christian Doctrine Based on Biblical Revelation*.[73] Calvinism's last great fortress in the convention is taking opening shots in what may turn out to be its fall.

POLITICAL LIBERATION

As a kind of footnote to their beliefs about salvation, Southern Baptists continue their foreign mission policy of working toward a personal, spiritual salvation by deliberately avoiding foreign liberation movements. Under no conditions should missionaries become involved in political activities. Keith Parks, president of the Foreign Mission Board, stated emphatically:

> Baptists have protested, gone to prison and died for the cause of religious liberty. Separation of church and state has always been an unquestioned identifying mark.
> . . . .
> Our missionaries overseas and the Foreign Mission Board as an organization must strongly protest any blurring of this distinction. Any implication of political connections compromises our singular spiritual ministry to a lost world.[74]

Parks adds further that missionaries serve as guests under foreign governments and therefore have no right to intervene in the local political processes. He concludes that the convention will change its nature if it begins to support any specific political position.

Virulent liberationism of any variety has no overt proponents among Southern Baptists and only rarely do they speak its language. One of the few examples comes from a recent study found in a publication prepared for church use. Speaking in the context of human rights, church-state separation and social justice, William M. Tillman, Jr., wrote: "The biblical view of justice may contradict our common understanding of justice. For example, God's justice favors the oppressed. Imagine a balance scale. As God sees the oppressors weighing things in their favor, He pushes down the other side, bringing balance. There is a bias or partiality on the part of God toward the oppressed."[75] Only obliquely does Tillman hint at the ethical implications for life. In looking at the political world he suggested, "We will wonder about support for governments which are infamous for their human rights violations."[76] Social commentators familiar with the writings of revolutionaries in underdeveloped countries could raise an eyebrow. Those code words usually express opposition to the imperialism and colonialism of the capitalistic nations. It is extrememly doubtful that Tillman intended any such revolutionary connotations.

Although the Foreign Mission Board never has embraced the tenets of the women's liberation movement, its procedures for appointing missionaries creates a preponderance of female missionaries. The Foreign Mission Board proudly pointed to its 3,350 foreign missionaries under appointment in 1984, to cite a representative year, but 1,825 of these, or 54.48%, were female. The percentage was even higher than the 1,775 women of 3,306 missionaries under appointment in 1983 when it was 53.69%.

The Foreign Mission Board also leans heavily on missionary appointees whose immediate tasks relate to medicine, teaching, and ministries other than full-time evangelism. Statistics released by the board show that in 1983 only 573 males, or 17%, carried the title of general evangelist. Add to this number 120 (3.5%) theology teachers, 53 (1.6%) English language pastors, 39 (1.2%) agricultural evangelists, and 15 (.01%) college teachers, and Southern Baptists still had at the most, no more than 800 (24%) men giving full-time attention to evangelism. This relatively small number of evangelists under appointment should not be interpreted as a policy by the FMB to engage primarily in social actions at the expense of evangelism. The FMB can only appoint those who volunteer for missions. Large numbers of pastors willing to give themselves in evangelistic missionary service have not stepped forward as volunteers for appointment. Until they do, others must carry the load.

SUMMARY

Southern Baptists have divested themselves of most of their Calvinistic heritage. No longer do they feel obligated to explain how God's sovereignty conflicts with free will. Nevertheless, they remain evangelical in their commitment to trinitarian theology inclusive of the deity of Jesus and the Holy Spirit. Neither have liberalizing trends altered drastically the related doctrines of the incarnation, death, and resurrection of Jesus.

Their understanding of human nature is changing. Acceptance of biological evolution and the body-soul entity concept of personality has led some of their theologians to renounce the inerrantist evangelical definition of substitutionary atonement as they lean toward an existential understanding of the death of Christ. The bulk of Southern Baptists, however, remain committed to belief in the substitutionary death of Christ, however naively they may formulate it.

NOTES

1. Clifton J. Allen, "Understanding the Spirit," *Outreach* 5 (May 1975):3.
2. Clayton K. Harrop, "Explaining His Coming," *Adult Bible Study* 5 (October-November-December 1974):65.
3. Dale Moody, "The Miraculous Conception, Part II, *The Review and Expositor* 52 (January 1955):5.
4. Ibid., Part I, (October 1954)51:4.
5. Robert E. Naylor, "The Word Became Flesh," *Sunday School Adults* 56 (December 23, 1956):44.
6. Herschel H. Hobbs, *Fundamentals of Our Faith* (Nashville: Broadman Press, 1960), pp. 44-45; Malcolm O. Tolbert, "Luke," in *Broadman Bible Commentary*, vol. 8 (Nashville: Broadman Press, 1969), p. 21.
7. Dallas M. Roark, *The Christian Faith* (Nashville: Broadman Press, 1969), p. 37.
8. *Encyclopedia of Southern Baptists*, s.v. "Christology," by Dale Moody.
9. McClellan, *The Faith We Hold*, p. 23.
10. Hudson Baggett, "Editorials and Comments," *Alabama Baptist* 142 (July 21, 1977):2.
11. William E. Hull, "John," in *Broadman Bible Commentary*, vol. 9 (Nashville: Broadman Press, 1970), p. 213.
12. Billy E. Simmons, "The Meaning of Christ's Coming," *Adult Bible Teacher* 5 (October-November-December 1974):134; H. H. Hobbs, *The Origin of All Things: Studies in Genesis* (Waco: Word Books, 1975), p. 23; Joseph F. Green, "Beliefs About Jesus," *Baptist Adults* 6 (April-May-June 1977):11.
13. Theodore R. Clark, *Saved by His Life* (N. Y.: The MacMillan Press, 1959), p. 11.
14. "Alley to Chair New Program," *Florida Baptist Witness* 95 (February 2, 1978):4
15. A. T. Robertson, "Expositions," *Review and Expositor* 30 (October 1933):32.
16. Ibid.
17. Hugh R. Peterson, *A Study of the Gospel of Mark* (Nashville: Convention Press, 1958), p. 134.
18. Roland Q. Leavell, *Studies in Matthew: The King and the Kingdom* (Nashville: Convention Press, 1962), p. 138.
19. Eric C. Rust, *Salvation History: A Biblical Interpretation* (Richmond: John Knox Press, 1962), p. 81.
20. Frank Stagg, *Studies in Luke's Gospel* (Nashville: Convention Press, 1967), p. 135.
21. James L. Sullivan, *John's Witness to Jesus* (Nashville: Convention Press, 1965). p. 134.
22. Walter T. Conner, *Christian Doctrine* (Nashville: Broadman Press, 1937), pp. 178-179.
23. Wayne E. Ward, "The Roaring Lion," *Baptist Young People* 61 (February 21, 1960):28.
24. Conner, *Christian Doctrine*, p. 110.
25. Dotson M. Nelson, "How Does Power Come?" *Baptist Young Peoples Quarterly* 58 (February 10, 1957):19.
26. Henlee H. Barnette, "The Significance of the Holy Spirit for Christian Morality," *Review and Expositor* 52 (January 1955):5-20.
27. Eric C. Rust, "Theology and Preaching," *Review and Expositor* 52 (April 1955):152.
28. Dale Moody, "Speaking in Tongues," *The Baptist Program* (July 1967), p. 8.
29. J. Morris Ashcraft, "Glossolalia in the First Epistle to the Corinthians," *Tongues*, ed. Luther B. Dyer (Jefferson City, Missouri: Le Roi Publishers, 1971), p. 75.
30. "Gift of Tongues," *Christian Watchman* 4 (November 8, 1823):192.
31. "Association Excludes Charismatic Churches," *Florida Baptist Witness* 91 (December 5, 1974):7.
32. "Dallas Association Excludes Charismatic Churches," *Florida Baptist Witness* 92 (October 30, 1975):5.
33. "Associations in Louisiana, Houston Lash Charismatics," *Florida Baptist Witness* 92 (November 6, 1975):3.
34. "Texas Convention Refuses to Seat Charismatics," *Florida Baptist Witness* 93 (November 4, 1976):3.
35. Herschel H. Hobbs, *Fundamentals of Our Faith* (Nashville: Broadman Press, 1960), p. 90.
36. Ibid., p. 93.
37. Wayne E. Ward, "Elected by ONE Vote," *Baptist Young People* 59 (February 16, 1958):21.
38. Ibid., p. 22.
39. Robert W. Kicklighter, "The Origin of the Church," in *What Is the Church?* ed. Duke K. McCall (Nashville: Broadman Press, 1958), pp. 34, 41.
40. Hobbs, *Fundamentals of Our Faith*, p. 51.
41. John W. Drakeford, *Psychology in Search of a Soul* (Nashville: Broadman Press, 1964), p. 3.
42. Frank Stagg, *New Testament Theology* (Nashville: Broadman Press, 1962), p. 25.
43. William Wilson Stevens, *Doctrines of the Christian Religion* (Grand Rapids: William B. Eerdmans Publishing Co., 1967), p. 136.
44. Dallas M. Roark, *The Christian Faith* (Nashville: Broadman Press, 1969), p. 193.
45. Francis M. Dubose, "Is Personal Soul-Winning Biblical?" *Source for Leaders* 1 (October-November-December 1970):18.
46. Morris Ashcraft, *Christian Faith and Beliefs* (Nashville: Broadman Press, 1984), pp. 159, 160.
47. Dubose, "Is Personal Soul-Winning Biblical?" p. 18.
48. Stagg, *New Testament Theology*, p. 145.

49. Stagg, *The Doctrine of Christ* (Nashville: Convention Press, 1984), pp. 67-76.
50. Ibid., p. 71.
51. Ibid.
52. Ibid., p. 75.
53. Ibid., pp. 128-129.
54. Ibid., p. 74.
55. Ibid., pp. 90, 96.
56. Ibid., p. 97.
57. Ibid.
58. Ibid., p. 99.
59. Ibid.
60. Ibid.
61. Thomas J. Nettles, *By His Grace and for His Glory: A Historical, Theological, and Practical Study of the Doctrines of Grace in Baptist Life* (Grand Rapids: Baker Book House, 1986), p. 298.
62. Clark, *Saved By His Life*, p. 35.
63. Rust, *Towards a Theological Understanding*, pp. 68-69.
64. Fisher Humphreys, *The Death of Christ* (Nashville: Broadman Press, 1978), p. 125.
65. Ibid., p. 128.
66. Ibid., p. 116.
67. Ibid.
68. *Encyclopedia of Southern Baptists*, s.v. "Expiation," by W. Boyd Hunt.
69. Rust, "Theology and Preaching," *The Review and Expositor* 52 (April 1955):156.
70. Humphreys, *Thinking About God*, p. 121.
71. Thomas E. McCullough, "Salvation Is Eternal," *Baptist Adults* 5 (October-November-December 1975):31-34.
72. Perry Lassiter, *Once Saved . . . Always Saved* (Nashville: Broadman Press, 1975).
73. Dale Moody, *The Word of Truth: A Summary of Christian Doctrine Based on Biblical Revelation* (Grand Rapids: William B. Eerdmans Publishing Co., 1981).
74. Keith Parks, "Caesar and Missions," *The Commission* 45 (September 1982):2.
75. William M. Tillman, Jr., "Justice: God's Demand," *Baptist Adults* 16 (July-August-September 1987):20-21.
76. Ibid., p. 22.

CHAPTER 12

THE CHURCH ALIVE

The doctrine of the church in Southern Baptist theology shows evidence of widespread rejection of its Landmark heritage and acceptance of an existentialist understanding of the meaning of the church. The analysis offered originally by Ernst Troeltsch and then modified by Howard Becker is instructive. Troeltsch saw two distinct ways in which Christians confront the world. The *sect-type* is culture-denying in that believers maintain an aloofness from a world of sin. The *church-type* is culture-affirming in that it tries to establish a dialogue with the world. David O. Moberg, quoting Becker, posits an intermediate stage between the two, the denominational. Southern Baptists usually are described as having originated in the sect-type, but they are moving on a continuum through the denominational stage toward the church-type.

Moberg cites evidences by which to identify the shift from the sect-type as it moves through the denominational stage toward the church-type. He points to a declining church membership, a trend toward open membership and open communion, community churches, liturgical worship, and baptism at younger ages.[1] In contrast to these leveling forces, Moberg sees in fundamentalists a different mentality. They have little interest in the church in its universal dimension, preferring their own mores and symbols. Their "cultic orthodoxy" leads them into individualized applications of historic doctrines.[2]

Adopting Moberg's terms, one might observe that the cultic orthodox and their adherence to the sect-type mentality prevailed among the founders of the Southern Baptist Convention. This was evident when they deliberately placed the headquarters of the Home Mission Board in Marion, Alabama, and the headquarters of the Foreign Mission Board in Richmond, Virginia, to prevent centralization of power. When the Sunday School Board was placed in Nashville, Tennessee, and the Annuity Board in Dallas, Texas, the sect-type mentality manifested itself. In short, Southern Baptists scattered their boards across the land to insure that any attempt to dominate the local church would be prohibitive. Diversification also guaranteed, practically speaking, that no one person would have access to the centers of denominational power.

THE CHURCH, A SPIRITUAL ENTITY

The breaking up of the sect-type mentality, especially of Landmarkism, has taken decades, but the emphases of Moberg's "classical orthodoxy" in the form of neoorthodoxy now hold sway. Precursors of change go back to H. E. Dana, who sought to understand the concept of the body of Christ as Paul presented it in Ephesians and Colossians. He saw no ascending order of ecclesiastical links to a hierarchical head in Paul's teachings, but "an ideal, spiritual body in sacred and vital connection with Christ its divine founder as its head."[3] The emphasis is significant for what it portends. "Church" gradually becomes vital, rather than organizational, and subjective, rather than objective, in Southern Baptist teaching.

W. O. Carver also agonized over the relationship between the church as local and yet universal. He felt constrained to note that in Ephesians the church was represented as a local fellowship, even though that fact is not explicitly stated in Ephesians.[4] He saw in the New Testament no general, organized Christian institution of which the local churches were units.[5] The local church was described as a local, regional, social expression, counterpart, and embodiment of the universal church.[6] There is no mention of baptism as a prerequisite to church membership. Carver's thrust was in a different direction. Such key phrases as fellowship of disciples,[7] nurturing environment, organic instrument, and ethical society[8] came closer to revealing his concept. However, the church as the body of Christ was his focal point. As the body of Christ the church is a new humanity, the continuing incarnation of Christ.[9] Carver thus began with the local church, but shifted to the perspective of the church universal whereas earlier Baptists began with the local church and appended thoughts about the universal.

The mystical emphasis exemplified by Carver's thought is gaining strength in literature produced for the churches. One never finds definitions of the church in terms that excluded non-Baptist groups from being considered New Testament churches, as was done in Landmarkism. Contemporary definitions are broad enough that almost any Christian group may be considered a valid church as long as certain identifying characteristics are included. Gone are the polemics against the improper administration of the ordinance of baptism. The method followed by Albert McClellan in *The Faith We Hold* is typical. He quoted H. C. Vedder who defined the church as a spiritual body, composed of regenerate persons.[10] Of the true nature of the church, McClellan called it a fellowship, local, and free.[11]

The absence of the polemical spirit marks the definitions of church given in the *Encyclopedia of Southern Baptists*. Garland Hendricks described it as a community of believers.[12] In discussing "church" as opposed to "churches," Theron D. Price saw it as being formed wherever the Holy Spirit's presence is manifested in regenerating power which effects changes in the believer.[13] *The* Church becomes embodied in *a* church in situations characterized by their gathering together and disciplining of members. He did not mention the subject of immersion.[14]

Frank Stagg's analysis of *ekklesia* is representative of the contemporary emphasis. He alleged that a study of the Greek usage can be misleading. The pagan idea of a local assembly is present, thought Stagg, but the New Testament thrust is upon ownership, not assembly. The New Testament church points to God's own people, not to places and times of assembly.[15]

Stagg pointed the direction that Southern Baptist Sunday School and Discipleship Training writers would take. The theme of the church as the people of God can be seen in an *Adult Bible Study* lesson for adults, written by A. Douglas Aldrich.[16] Albert L. Cardwell pursued the theme of mission in describing the church. His article is typical of current literature. Under the topic of "What a Church Is," he makes no definitive statement. God calls people; buildings and the like become secondary to the idea of the church as the people of God.[17]

Fisher Humphreys summarized the reality of the church in the following way: The Father chooses, and the church is his people; the Son atones, and the church is his body; the Spirit gives life, and the church is his fellowship.[18] *People*, *body*, and *fellowship* best epitomize present-day discussions about the church. The days of the Landmark exaltation of the local church is probably gone forever from Southern Baptist literature.

THE ORDINANCES: FREE OF LANDMARKISM

Southern Baptists consistently have maintained that Christ established two ordinances to be observed by his followers, baptism and the Lord's Supper. They occasionally observed footwashing in former days, but it never had the popularity of the other two. The meaning they ascribed to baptism and the Supper came much as a reaction against the prominence given to the sacraments in Roman Catholic theology. They considered the Roman interpretation a gross violation of the plain teachings of the New Testament, and consequently they carefully avoided even the language used by sacramentarians. Only in the last twenty years or so have Southern Baptists described the event as a communion service, preferring the simpler term *Supper*. Almost never do they call it a sacrament.

The meaning of baptism receives scarcely more attention because they see it as a sign and little more. Indications of a softening in their doctrinal stance on both baptism and the Supper can be discerned as Southern Baptists wrestle with the doctrine of the church and the role it and the ordinances should play in society. They incline more perceptibly in the direction of community worship services, such as joint Thanksgiving services, but they are not yet ready to participate in joint communion services with other denominations. The Supper, like baptism, they still view as a church function.

As far as formal ecumenicity goes, Southern Baptists show little interest in discussing the subject at all. Gone is most of the acrimony generated between Baptists and the "pedobaptists" in their debates over which fellowship best exemplified the biblical teachings, but neither do the Baptists make much of an issue over who participates in the local observance of the Supper. They often practice a de facto open communion which leaves to the communicant whether or not to participate in the rite.

Confessionally, it would appear that nearly all Southern Baptists believe in and practice closed communion. Such is not the case practically. The Research and Statistics Department of the Sunday School Board polled 361 representative churches in the convention in 1960 to determine their attitude toward participation in the Supper.[19] The percentages are as follows: restricted to members of their own church, 18.3%; permit only Baptists, 8.6%; open communion, 12.2%; and, no restrictions at all, 40.4%. Thus, 47.2% practiced de facto open communion. The trend then and now is to leave to the individual worshiper whether or not to participate, regardless of denominational affiliation.

Most of the materials produced for general use in the churches follow a predictable pattern of interpretation. Whenever the Lord's Supper is interpreted in Sunday School and Discipleship Training materials, at least three themes are almost always sounded. The Supper is a testimony to what Christ accomplished in his death on the cross. Representative statements may be seen in articles by Fred D. Howard in 1966[20] and James F. Eaves in *Adult Bible Study* in 1973.[21] Also, the Supper usually is depicted as a reminder of the future coming of Christ; it looks *forward* to the consummation. Finally, the Supper speaks of the fellowship of believers, of their mystical union with Christ. All three of these are cited in a typical summary statement given by Joseph F. Green in 1977.[22]

Frank Stagg is among those who see in the Supper a meaning which transcends the symbolic. Stagg points out that the meal may be used to symbolize truths, but the meal as given in Acts and I Corinthians was a real meal, not just a symbolic act, because it met material needs.[23] Food and drink for sustenance were served. In another context of thought, Stagg explained the Supper as more than symbolic, but less than sacramental. It should be a time of joyous participation of the believers with each other and Christ in a mood of shared memory, worship, obedience, and the like.[24] Beyond those limits, most Southern Baptists are loath to go.

The Southern Baptist Landmark version of baptism also is now an anachronism. It has experienced a change in defining the source of the authority to baptize. To grasp the significance of the metamorphosis in thought, one may go back to W. T. Conner. In answer to the question, Who has the authority to baptize? he saw three possible sources of authority—the clergy, an individual Christian, or the local church. Of church authority he said, "This we believe to be the correct position."[25] Neither did he favor receiving those who had received alien immersion.[26] Albert McClellan[27] and William Wilson Stevens[28] also believed the right to baptize should be by church authorization.

In the sixties, however, alien immersion and open communion became issues in many churches. The problem surfaced at the 1966 meeting of the Southern Baptist Convention. One messenger protested the seating of a group of other messengers whose church practiced open communion and accepted alien immersion. President Wayne Dehoney ruled the motion out of order because the constitution and bylaws of the convention do not make such issues a requirement for membership.[29]

The problem also has been aired on the floor of state conventions. Messengers from four churches were denied seats in the Arkansas convention in 1965 because their churches accepted alien immersion and practiced open communion. The convention reversed itself in 1971 and seated such messengers.[30] That same year North Carolina Baptists refused to amend their constitution "to exclude churches which have members who have not been baptized by immersion."[31] Some of the North Carolina churches accept long-time Christian candidates for membership who were sprinkled as children, but all the churches administer baptism only by immersion. What brought about this radical reversal of Baptist practice?

Dale Moody highlighted the issues in 1967. Churches face practical as well as theological problems when mature Christians from pedobaptist assemblies wish to unite with a Southern Baptist church. The common policy among Baptists, he noted, is to baptize, but to require it of prospective members coming from pedobaptist churches creates theological ambiguities. The other churches become churches without baptism.[32] He suggested that those coming on profession of faith be immersed, but that those coming from other denominations might be accepted without immersion.[33] Under that arrangement, Baptist churches continue immersing new Christians upon profession of faith while receiving by statement mature Christians who had been sprinkled as a member of a pedobaptist church. Moody admitted that his novel approach is not acceptable to many Baptists, and the issue is far from being settled. The Saluda Baptist Association in South Carolina in 1976 expelled the First Baptist Church of Clemson for receiving from other denominations members who had not been immersed. Such a practice, it argued, was not in accord with the doctrines spelled out in the association's bylaws.[34]

One of Moody's colleagues, G. R. Beasley-Murray, took a more sacramental view toward water baptism. Titus 3:5 and John 3:5 clearly teach that regeneration does not come by the agency of water. However, the Spirit uses baptism as the occasion when he brings new life to the believer.[35] God's saving grace thus comes in the context of baptism.[36]

Beasley-Murray's emphasis is exceptional. Southern Baptists are more comfortable with the sentiments expressed by Joseph F. Green and William L. Lumpkin. In Green's view, "Baptism as taught in the Scriptures is always by immersion and administered to those who already believe."[37] Lumpkin was equally emphatic. The baptism of the believer is both a declaration of faith and a pledge of loyalty to Christ.[38] Southern Baptists seem to be comfortable with their belief in the necessity of requiring immersion of all members, but not with requiring immersion by a Southern Baptist. That phase of Landmarkism has almost vanished.

GRUDGING ACCEPTANCE OF PREMILLENNIALISM

Southern Baptists have had mixed feelings about the doctrine of the second coming of Christ. In the pulpit and pew, the *Scofield Reference Bible* and other "premillennial Bibles" are popular, but the popularity of premillennialism has flourished in spite of Southern Baptist teaching in publications produced for the churches. Until 1984, amillennialism was the unofficial but de facto stance fostered by the Sunday School Board. Throughout Southern Baptist publications, the Kingdom of God has been spoken of as a spiritual reality, almost exclusively. The prevailing sentiment is highlighted in a Sunday School lesson written by Wallace S. Green, Jr. The Jews of Jesus' day, he wrote, expected a nationalistic Messiah who would free them from Roman bondage and establish the Jews as the dominant world power. They never comprehended his intention to establish a kingdom of love, mercy, and judgment.[39]

Understanding the Kingdom of God as the moral and spiritual reign of truth and righteousness in the hearts and lives of believers comported well with the amillennial trend of Southern Baptist publications at the beginning of the twentieth century. The subject matter which dealt with the end-time quickly developed into a pattern. The content of the lessons can be summarized as follows: Arguments about the order and events of the end are fruitless. Baptists should limit themselves to those fundamental points agreed upon by all. Jesus is coming personally and visibly. He may come at any moment. Therefore, one should prepare himself spiritually now. One selection from the *Adult Quarterly* in 1936 illustrates the point. In commenting on Jesus' admonition to seek first the Kingdom of God, the writer saw in it a splendid picture of Christian watchfulness. Since each day could be one's last day, every day should be lived accordingly.[40]

Until the seventies, millennialism of any sort was studiously avoided in Sunday School materials. Note the following titles covering a period of three decades: "Bible Teaching About the Future Life,"[41] "Requirements for Citizenship in the Kingdom,"[42] "The Glorious Consummation,"[43] "The Coming of Our Lord,"[44] and "Apocalyptic Literature in the Bible."[45] In not one lesson was millennialism discussed.

Gradually, writers for Sunday School and Discipleship Training literature became more venturesome. Although none of the lessons for these materials was ever written without apology from a postmillennial or premillennial point of view, the two began to be mentioned. Janet Burton discussed all three millennial views in *Youth in Search Teacher*.[46] Also, Ray Summers authored an undated series of millennial studies for adults in 1973.[47] George E. Ladd took a premillennial stance in his article "Revelation 20 and the Millennium."[48] Robert G. Witty's article "Promises, Power, and Program,"[49] published in *People* in 1970, took a premillennial point of view. Also, many prominent leaders held to some form of premillennialism. Just a few of those who have published their stand are R. G. Lee, W. Herschel Ford, W. A. Criswell, Robert G. Witty, Joe T. Odle, Dale Moody, and George H. Beasley-Murray.[50]

The Sunday School Board's strong bias toward the amillennial view created resentment. Dale Moody complained in 1979 that, of the seven commentaries on Revelation published by Broadman Press, all followed the amillennialism of Augustine.[51] However, change was soon to come. The turning point came in 1983 when the Baptist Sunday School Board called a two-day "Millennial Consultation" to hear differing views of Southern Baptists on that subject.[52] Policies were developed to guide writers who produced materials for the board. The trustees of the board met in 1984 and confirmed guidelines to ensure that the three millennial views prominent among Southern Baptists—dispensational premillennialism, historic premillennialism, and amillennialism—be given "equitable treatment in church literature and Convention Press materials."[53] The effect was dramatically rapid. D. Waylon Bailey, writing in *Sunday School Adults* in 1985[54] and John A. R. Goodwin, writing in *Sunday School Young Adults* in 1986,[55] carefully followed the guidelines. Commenting on Zechariah 2:10-13, Bailey gave equal and impartial treatment to both views, as did Goodwin, in his comments on 2 Peter 3:1-4.

The amillennial bias of the literature and the disdain for premillennialism in many college and seminary classrooms has disfranchised multitudes of Southern Baptists. For decades, those interested in speculation about the end-time, especially prophecy, have had to find sources of information outside convention literature. Further, holding to a premillennial persuasion sometimes has been a liability for prospects seeking a college teaching position. Further, the timidity with which eschatology is dealt in the convention has prevented Southern Baptists from developing a viable cosmology of the relationship between time and eternity and between history and the future life.

John P. Newport is one of the Southern Baptist rarities who has tried to develop such a scheme from the perspective of historic premillennialism. He contends that a necessary key to interpreting the Bible must recognize the importance of eschatology. A combination of holy history and the eschatological can be combined into an eschatalogical-holy history.[56] It is possible that

Southern Baptist theology is now on the threshold of developing a rich cosmology transcending facile statements limited to the bare essentials of the second coming of Christ. If so, writers like Newport must lead the way.

CONTINUOUS RESURRECTION VERSUS FUTURE EVENT

On the problem of the "immortality of the soul," the traditional belief of a person with a soul has raised questions. As discussed above, those who believe a person is a psychosomatic entity are gaining adherents. How one interprets 2 Corinthians 5:8 (KJV), which says, "We are confident, I say, and willing rather to be absent from the body, and to be present with the Lord," can be governed by whether one views a person as body-soul or body with a soul. In his comment, Frank Stagg understood the verse to teach the gaining of a new body at death, an interpretation which does not include the idea of a soul existing in a disembodied or intermediate state following physical death.[57] William L. Blevins was equally emphatic in a *Collegiate Bible Study*. Commenting on 2 Corinthians 5:8, he saw nothing in the text which implies a disembodied state between one's death and resurrection.[58] Morris Ashcraft, addressing the question of the intermediate state, projected the possibility on a misunderstanding arising out of the human view of time and eternity. Once one is in eternity, it may turn out that no such place is necessary. One apparently enters a state of timelessness in which concepts of past and future no longer apply. However, Ashcraft blunted the implications of his statement by noting that many believe in an intermediate state and a future return of Christ to conclude history.[59]

Eric Rust took the premise of a psychosomatic entity, looked at the implications for the doctrine of the resurrection of the body, and saw the value of the doctrine in the message it conveys. Acceptance of the idea implied in Greek dualism, he believes, destroys the unity of body and soul. In Christian thought, one survives as a corporeal whole.[60] Rust believed that resurrection seems to be future from a creaturely point of view, but at death one sees it as already accomplished. It may seem to be required when seen from creaturely time, but it may be an accomplished event in the eternity of God. There one must leave it.[61] He hinted strongly that resurrection is a continuing event. It only appears to be future for those yet alive.

The bulk of Southern Baptists differ sharply with Rust's version of the resurrection. Billy E. Simmons discussed 2 Corinthians 5:8 and concluded that being with the Lord at death interferes in no way with one's participation in the final resurrection.[62] Ray Summers described Paul's view of resurrection in similar language but, instead of seeing dualism, contrasted it with the Greek idea of mere immortality of the soul. The resurrected and transformed body is the final dwelling place of the spirit.[63]

Are the advocates of an indissoluble body-soul entity theory correct when they deny the separation of the soul from the body at death? Concerning the allegation that the New Testament knows nothing of the existence of a disembodied soul at death, Dale Moody retorted, "It is simply not true that the New Testament knows nothing of a disembodied human spirit."[64] To Moody, those who argue for resurrection occurring at the death of the body imply a discontinuity between the physical body and the spiritual body with no real relation between them because the physical body is cast aside.

It may be helpful at this point to summarize the options about death available to those holding to the theory that humans have no separable, non-material entity known as a soul or spirit. What happens to the body-soul entity at death? No longer can one define death as the separation of the soul from the body if the body does not contain a non-material entity. Three possibilities present themselves. First, in the annihilationist view, death is the end of human existence, and there is no life beyond this one. It is doubtful that any Southern Baptists believe in that way. Second, the person remains in the grave, i.e., in death, until a resurrection at the consummation of history. This doctrine, known popularly as "Soul-sleep," has no professed adherents among Southern Baptists. Third, resurrection occurs every time a redeemed person dies. This possibility, popularly called realized eschatology or continuous resurrection, seems to be the most popular option among Southern Baptist advocates of the psychosomatic entity description of human personality. Apart from many biblical texts which seem to contradict it, the theory ultimately succumbs to the Greek dualism its proponents denigrate. If resurrection occurs at death, the physical body, *sarx* (flesh), remains behind while the spiritual body, *soma* (body), experiences eternity. The resurrection of the fleshly body never comes about at all. The body remains in the grave. In one sense the dualism between soul and body is overcome because the "body" is resurrected at death, but another dualism results, that between body (*soma*) and flesh (*sarx*).

Closely related to belief in continuous resurrection is the theory of conditional immortality, that only the redeemed survive death; the unsaved suffer extinction. As already cited, Clark Pinnock has now arrived at that position.[65] Theodore R. Clark also taught it. In his view, the whole person is mortal and subject to final and total destruction.[66] Morris Ashcraft apparently holds to belief in conditional immortality. Couching his language in the thoughts of G. C. Berkouwer, he rejected the traditional view of a body inhabited by an immortal soul. One does not automatically live forever. That state is reserved for those whom God raises from the dead and grants life as new creations.[67] In another context of thought, he wrote that powers beyond human control threaten them with nonexistence.[68] He seems also to reject belief in hell as a place of conscious punishment. Defining death as separation from God, he believes the Bible teaches the fearful possibility of an ultimate and final separation from God, an event called the second death.[69]

EXISTENCE BEYOND THE GRAVE

Descriptions of the future state have varied. Note examples. E. Y. Mullins described heaven as relief from all the trying and hard conditions of earthly life, coming as reward, realization, appreciation, and endless growth.[70] Conversely, he believed hell to be the negation in the soul of all that is meant by heaven.[71] Even though Mullins granted that language describing hell may be symbolic and figurative, the figures do not express all that is meant about the reality of hell.[72] Further, there are degrees of punishment in hell.[73] W. T. Conner understood heaven to be primarily a state of character.[74] Heaven also includes perfect environment; a complete deliverance from sin; freedom from natural evil such as sorrow, sickness, and death; ceaseless service to God; and a place or state of endless development.[75] He argued for the certainty of future punishment on four premises.[76] First, the Bible teaches it. Second, punishment of the sinner is demanded by the moral order. Third, one's sinful nature guarantees punishment as an outcome. Fourth, sin against a holy God must be punished. He concluded that punishment will be suited to the nature of the sin for which it is a punishment;[77] it is endless.[78]

Statements about the future state generally have followed themes exemplified by Boyce, Mullins, and Conner. Of hell, Tribble averred that it is a state, a place, and it is everlasting.[79] Robert E. Naylor believed the thrust of the biblical revelation shows it to be a place of conscious suffering.[80] Herbert C. Jackson voiced essentially the same belief about the certainty of a place of indescribable agony as punishment for evil deeds.[81] The overwhelming consensus among Southern Baptists affirms the fact of heaven and hell as places of conscious existence.

SUMMARY

Southern Baptists are well on their way to a complete break with their Calvinistic and Landmark heritage. The local church, defined in terms of regenerate members, baptismal requirements, disciplinary responsibilities, and evangelistic outreach, is losing out to an understanding that is more existential, personal, non-divisive, and universal. The widespread practice of open communion, and the beginning stage of accepting other modes of baptism than immersion, reenforce that conclusion.

The picture in regard to the second coming of Christ is not as clear because of the resurgence of the inerrantist evangelicals in the convention. The de facto acceptance of amillennialism has been checked in Sunday School literature, but whether that change is more than a temporary respite awaits future developments.

The inroads made by biological evolution and the psychosomatic entity view of human nature is more pervasive. Doubtless, there are those in teaching-preaching positions who no longer believe in the existence of hell as a place of everlasting punishment. Those so believing must take the option of the annihilation of the wicked or the ultimate restoration of everyone. That kind of universalism probably cannot overtly manifest itself in the foreseeable future because of the inerrantist evangelical pressures placed on the convention. It is also doubtful that the convention can ever return to its former dogmatic commitments.

NOTES

1. David O. Moberg, *The Church as a Local Institution: The Sociology of American Religion*, 2nd ed. (Grand Rapids: Baker Book House, 1982), pp. 101-102.
2. Ibid., pp. 292-293.
3. H. E. Dana, *A Manual of Ecclesiology* (Kansas City, Kansas: Central Seminary Press, 1941), p. 53.
4. W. O. Carver, *The Glory of God in the Christian Calling: A Study of the Ephesian Epistle* (Nashville: Broadman Press, 1949), p. 56.
5. Ibid.
6. Ibid., p. 34.
7. Ibid., p. 48.
8. Ibid., p. 34
9. Ibid., p. 48.
10. Albert McClellan, *The Faith We Hold* (Nashville: Broadman Press, 1954), p. 74.
11. Ibid., p. 75.
12. *Encyclopedia of Southern Baptists*, s.v. "Church and Community," by Garland Hendricks.
13. *Encyclopedia of Southern Baptists*, s.v. "Church," by Theron D. Price.
14. Ibid.
15. Frank Stagg, *New Testament Theology* (Nashville: Broadman Press, 1962), p. 181.
16. A. Douglas Aldrich, "What Is a Church?" *Adult Bible Study* 2 (April-May-June 1972):30.
17. Albert L. Cardwell, "A Church on Mission," *Source* 5 (January-February-March 1975):42.
18. Fisher Humphreys, *Thinking About God: An Introduction to Christian Theology* (New Orleans: Insight Press, 1974), p. 171.
19. *Encyclopedia of Southern Baptists*, s.v. "Lord's Supper, Close Communion," by James E. Tull.
20. Fred D. Howard, *Interpreting the Lord's Supper* (Nashville: Broadman Press, 1966), pp. 23-44.
21. James F. Eaves, "In Fellowship at the Lord's Table," *Adult Bible Study* 3 (January-February-March 1973):78.
22. Joseph F. Green, "Beliefs About the Lord's Supper," *Baptist Adults* 7 (October-November-December 1977):16.
23. "Southern Baptist Theology Today: An Interview with Frank Stagg," *The Theological Educator* 8 (Fall 1977):22-23.
24. Frank Stagg, "The Lord's Supper in the New Testament," *Review and Expositor* 66 (Winter 1969):14.
25. W. T. Conner, *Christian Doctrine* (Nashville: Broadman Press, 1937), p. 284.
26. Ibid., p. 285.
27. Albert McClellan, *The Faith We Hold* (Nashville: Broadman Press, 1954), p. 103.
28. William Wilson Stevens, *Doctrines of the Christian Religion* (Grand Rapids: William B. Eerdmans Publishing Company, 1967), p. 336.
29. *Southern Baptist Convention Annual*, 1966, p. 47.
30. "Arkansas Convention Seats Ousted Church Messengers," *Alabama Baptist* 136 (2 December 1971):4.
31. Ibid.
32. Dale Moody, *Baptism: Foundation for Christian Unity* (Philadelphia: The Westminster Press, 1967), p. 301.
33. Ibid.
34. "Association Expels Church Over 'Alien Baptism' Issue," *Florida Baptist Witness* 93 (November 11, 1976):5.
35. George R. Beasley-Murray, *Baptism in the New Testament* (Grand Rapids: William B. Eerdmans Publishing Company, 1962), p. 278.
36. Ibid., p. 273.
37. Joseph F. Green, "Baptizing Disciples Is Not Optional," *Baptist Adults* 6 (April-May-June 1977):24.

38. William L. Lumpkin, *Meditations on Christian Baptism* (Nashville: Broadman Press, 1976), p. 15.
39. Wallace S. Green, Jr., "With a Fixed Purpose," *Adult Bible Study* 5 (January-February-March 1975):64.
40. "How to Put the Kingdom of God First," *Adult Quarterly* 35 (March 22, 1936):36.
41. "Bible Teaching About the Future Life," *Adult Bible Class Quarterly* 18 (September 14, 1919):31-34.
42. "Requirements for Citizenship in the Kingdom," *Adult Quarterly* 35 (March 29, 1936):37-39.
43. "The Glorious Consummation," *Adult Quarterly* 41 (September 28, 1941):31.
44. "The Coming of Our Lord," *Adult Quarterly* 44 (March 5, 1944):24.
45. "Apocalyptic Literature in the Bible," *Adult Quarterly* 48 (Fourth Quarter 1948):25.
46. Janet Burton, "God's New Heaven and Earth," *Youth in Search Teacher* 1 (July-August-September 1971):92-96.
47. Ray Summers, "The Millennial Question," *Source* 3 (April-May-June 1973):47-51, 53-60.
48. George E. Ladd, "Revelation 20 and the Millennium," *Review and Expositor* 57 (April 1960):167-183.
49. Robert G. Witty, "Promises, Power, and Program," *People* 1 (November 1970):5, 7-8.
50. Robert Green Lee, "Comments Concerning Christ's Coming," *The Second Coming*, ed. H. Leo Eddleman (Nashville: Broadman Press, 1964), pp. 49-52; W. Herschel Ford, *Seven Simple Sermons on the Second Coming of Christ* (Grand Rapids: Zondervan Publishing House, 1945); W. A Criswell, *These Issues We Must Face* (Grand Rapids: Zondervan Publishing House, 1953), pp. 124-128; Robert G. Witty, *Signs of the Second Coming* (Nashville: Broadman Press, 1969), p. 65; Joe T. Odle, *Is Christ Coming Soon?* (Nashville: Broadman Press, 1971), p. xiii; Dale Moody, *The Hope of Glory* (Grand Rapids: William B. Eerdmans Publishing Company, 1964), p. 137; George R. Beasley-Murray, *Highlights of the Book of Revelation* (Nashville: Broadman Press, 1972), p. 68.
51. Dale Moody, "The Shaping of Southern Baptist Polity," *Baptist History and Heritage* 14 (July 1979):9.
52. "Pastors Present Views on Millennium," *Florida Baptist Witness* 100 (October 20, 1983):3.
53. "BSSB Trustees Approve Millennial Guidelines," *Florida Baptist Witness* 101 (August 16, 1984):10.
54. D. Waylon Bailey, "God Will Not Forsake His Own," *Sunday School Adults* 86 (August 11, 1985):28-31.
55. John A. R. Goodwin, "A Hope Worth Living For," *Sunday School Young Adults* 28 (January-February-March 1986):45-48.
56. John P. Newport, "Biblical Interpretation and Eschatological-Holy History," *Southwestern Journal of Theology* 41 (October 1961):88.
57. Stagg, *New Testament Theology*, p. 322.
58. William L. Blevins, "Motives for Ministering," *Collegiate Bible Study* 5 (October-November-December 1974):34.
59. Morris Ashcraft, *Christian Faith and Beliefs* (Nashville: Broadman Press, 1984), p. 330.
60. Eric C. Rust, *Towards a Theological Understanding of History* (New York: Oxford University Press, 1963), pp. 262-263.
61. Ibid., pp. 263-264.
62. Billy E. Simmons, "Motive for Ministering," *Adult Bible Teacher* 5 (October-November-December 1974):70.
63. Ray Summers, "First Corinthians: An Exposition," *Review and Expositor* 62 (October 1960):420.
64. Moody, *The Hope of Glory*, p. 72.
65. Clark Pinnock, "Fire, Then Nothing," *Christianity Today* 31 (March 20, 1987):40-41.
66. Theodore R. Clark, *Saved By His Life* (New York: MacMillan Company, 1959), p. 176.
67. Ashcraft, *Christian Faith*, p. 160.
68. Ibid., p. 138.
69. Ibid., p. 199.
70. E. Y. Mullins, *The Christian Religion in Its Doctrinal Expression* (Philadelphia: The Judson Press, 1917), pp. 485-488.
71. Ibid., p. 488.
72. Ibid., p. 489.
73. Ibid., p. 491.
74. Conner, *Christian Doctrine*, p. 321.
75. Ibid., pp. 322-326.
76. Ibid., pp. 326-328.
77. Ibid., p. 329.
78. Ibid., p. 330.
79. Harold W. Tribble, *Our Doctrines* (Nashville: Convention Press, 1936), pp. 131-132.
80. Robert E. Naylor, "The New Heaven and Earth," *Sunday School Adults* 56 (December 30, 1956):47.
81. Herbert C. Jackson, "How Shall We Be Judged?" *Sunday School Adults* 57 (March 31, 1957):48.

CHAPTER 13

WHENCE AND WHITHER

Strife about the nature of biblical inspiration has plagued the Southern Baptist Convention since 1962. Since 1979, the convention has been embroiled in a state of theological and procedural warfare engendered by the doctrinal dissension. Amid all the charges and counter-changes, the majority of Southern Baptists probably find themselves in a state of confusion. What is happening to Southern Baptist theology? One might even go further and ask, Is there such a thing as Southern Baptist theology? The evidence contained in this book suggests a qualified affirmative answer. There has been a Southern Baptist consensus about theology at any given stage, but it is fluid, dynamic, and changing. Nevertheless, the core of beliefs common throughout their history places them in the evangelical camp.

THE BIBLE

Their attitude toward the Bible has remained rather constant until the sixties of this century. Insofar as their earlier pronouncements in pamphlets, books, sermons, and confessions speak, they have held the Bible in high esteem. In matters of faith, morals, and practice, probably all Southern Baptists doubt not its utter reliability nor question its infallibility in those matters. However, in those passages where the Bible speaks on subjects of a scientific nature, consensus about the nature of those teachings crumbles, at least on the professorial level. The insistence by the inerrantist evangelicals that the autographs of the Bible were inerrant in every respect cannot be reconciled with the concept of infallibility espoused by neoorthodox evangelicals. The cease-fire recommended by the Peace

Committee and voted at the 1987 convention proved to be a coerced peace not based on a resolution of the underlying conflicts. Contending factions continue to organize and depict themselves as the true Southern Baptists. Apparently, all others are thieves and robbers.

Basic assumptions have changed. New discoveries by scientists about the nature and structure of the universe do not alter drastically cosmological structures assumed to be true a hundred years ago. Except for implications drawn from Einstein's story of general relativity (which postulates a curved universe), inferences drawn from quantum mechanics, and speculations about Heisenberg's Indeterminacy Principle relating to the random motion of subatomic particles, biblical cosmology as such is not seriously affected. On the contrary, it could be reenforced because the postulate of a universe locked into a closed system of cause and effect is no longer assured. The problem lies not so much with scientific discoveries as much as with the fact that many Southern Baptist scholars have changed their assumptions. If one assumes the truth of biological evolution from lower species to the higher, the acceptance of God's creation of Adam from dust and Eve from Adam's rib as historical fact is untenable. If one no longer believes that hell is a place, assumptions about hell, and not biblical cosmology, is the issue. The changes in assumptions, not the discovery of new scientific data, create the differences in interpreting crucial texts.

HUMAN NATURE AND SIN

The doctrines about human nature and sin remain unsettled. To refer once again to biological evolution, if humanity represents a stage in evolutionary development from microscopic organisms through the invertebrates, vertebrates, mammals, and primates, the idea of an Adamic fall into sin must be redefined radically. Related doctrines such as the image of God, inherited depravity, and the new birth as an ontological change will be anachronistic dogmas of a bygone era. When one adds emphases from psychological studies which see non-demonic causes for all personality disorders, much biblical language on the subject of Satan and demons will be understood metaphorically or rejected outright as being prescientific. Additionally, widespread acceptance of the psychosomatic entity theory also impacts on the related doctrines of the new birth and belief in a literal resurrection of the body at the end of the world as it is presently constituted.

The leavening effects of such doctrines seep into sermons, Sunday School classes, and other convention media. Preachers must adjust their sermonic presentations if they are to communicate the gospel in a rapidly changing culture. Further, what kind of delivery constitutes "good preaching" can vary from region to region and even from church to church. Nevertheless, biblical injunctions against sin abound, and no amount of psychological equivocations can lessen one's accountability for acts committed against God and neighbor, nor should they. Yet, sermons against a "hot hell" in a "long eternity" seem to be dropping from favor. In some sermons, there is little to be converted from or to. It is doubtful that additional pastoral classes on counseling procedures will be sufficient to turn the tide of indifference and rekindle lost fervor. The churches need a recommitment to the lostness of sinners and the availability of salvation in Jesus Christ.

THE CHURCH

Since the founding of the convention in 1845, the doctrine of the church metamorphosized from the rigidly defined dogmas of Landmarkism to the amorphous description of the church as the people of God. The breakdown in stressing denominational distinctiveness more or less characterizes much of American Christianity, by no means being limited to Southern Baptists. Among Southern Baptists the doctrine of the local church is not being challenged as much as it is being ignored.

Ernst Troeltsch theorized that Baptists originated as a sect-type religion; if so, they have developed beyond that stage. As they emerged from the sect stage in the antebellum South, denominationalism gripped them for more than a century, holding them aloof from ecumenical dialogues and trans-denominational social activities. Their fervid denominationalism, however, shows signs of wear as internal tensions and external influences combine to break up whatever homogeneity there was in their doctrines, polity, and outlook on life.

The multifarious sources of tensions within the denomination defy simple classification, but at least three are evident. First, sect-type religion constitutes a vital element in many parts of the Southern Baptist constituency. As did their forefathers, they are suspicious of ecclesiastical hierarchies that threaten the autonomy of the local church. Any hint of encroachment from "denominational headquarters" will cause them to attend conventions to vote down resolutions regardless of advertised merit.

Second, some of the internal tensions come from the denominational theoreticians. They are graduated from the colleges and seminaries with a thorough commitment to such Baptist distinctives as freedom of conscience, the priesthood of all believers, and the separation of church and state. When resolutions like the so-called prayer amendment are brought before the convention, the theorists argue eloquently that its adoption could help destroy the wall of church-state separation. But many in the larger constituency believe that the state has forfeited its neutral stance in regard to religion in its mandates. Similarly, the denominational theoreticians remain aloof from direct political involvement, but thousands of Southern Baptists on the local level feel no such compunctions. The disparity between the way the theoreticians and the people on the local levels understand the role of believers in society shows no evidence of being bridged.

The third factor in the decline of denominational loyalty arises inadvertently from the publications of the Sunday School Board. In its desire to enlarge its appeal to millions of Southern Baptists as well as to many churches not affiliated with the convention, it gives a low profile to doctrines and practices that may lead to discord. In offending none it satisfies few, but neither does it build strong denominational ties. When writers who often reflect the ecclesia-type concept produce materials for people whose perspective more closely approximates the sect-type, confusion results. For the present, however, Southern Baptists see the local church as the arena of both spiritual and social action. External influences also impact upon Southern Baptists. Billy Graham, one of the most visible of Southern Baptists, charted new avenues of race relations in the South with his refusal to sponsor crusades if the meetings were segregated. The charismatic movement also has turned attention to theological vistas unknown to Southern Baptists a generation ago. The "electronic church" which comes via radio and television exposes Southern Baptists to points of view diverse from their own.

EVANGELISM AND MISSIONS

Change comes slowly to Southern Baptists, but it is coming. On paper they are committed to take the gospel of Christ to all nations by the year 2,000. Whether they can resolve their internal conflicts, identify causes of apathy, and achieve that goal is problematical. What they perceive the gospel to be and what they perceive their role in society to be will bear directly on the outcome of their evangelistic zeal.

The gradual acceptance of neoorthodox existentialism with its suspicion of propositional truths will probably manifest itself in two other areas of Baptist life. First, baptisms will continue to decline among those churches which neglect conversionist theology in favor of a nurturist approach. Even churches outwardly exalting soul-winning often invest more time, money, and attention to character personality development through Christian education than in evangelistic outreach. The decline in baptisms will also be exacerbated by the demographic change coming over the American populace. There is a decreasing number of youth resulting from the crest in the post World War II baby boom. The loss of the segment of the population that supplied Southern Baptists with their main source of converts will profoundly affect every facet of church life.

Pastors experience frustration at the low level of commitment to the local church by the members. Loyal Baptists move from one community to another and frequently join a church of some other denomination. Doctrinal ties are broken in favor of friendly churches or churches better able to minister to the social needs of the family. What can be done to strengthen loyalty to the denomination? The emphasis on Baptist distinctiveness promoted by the convention in 1989 may be too little too late to staunch the hemorrhage. It will be a drastic mistake, however, to blame all the ills in the convention on the confusion created by the inerrantist evangelical and neoorthodox evangelical battles.

Second, there is a saying among teachers of evangelism that a church must decide whether it wishes to minister to the classes or the masses. There is also a discernible trend on the part of churches in the convention to move away from their humble roots among the masses to become class-oriented churches. Erudite sermons, high church music, stylized worship, and stately cathedrals do not appeal to the masses, whether they be in the United States or elsewhere. The seminaries—and colleges to some degree—must launch intense on-the-field studies of how to win the masses to Christ, giving special attention to the ethnic groups. Hispanics, Haitians, and Koreans, even when bound together by their brotherhood in Christ, nevertheless have different patterns of worship. Golden Gate Theological Seminary is making strides in that direction. More, much more, is needed.

Third, missionary expansion requires financial commitment by the supporting churches. The financial crises at all levels in the convention cannot be traced solely to the present controversy. That kind of reductionist thinking is facile and erroneous. In spite of the healthy economy in the United States, young couples have a hard time financially even though both husband and wife are employed. High interest rates reduce useable income for businesses. On what basis can church leaders make appeals for financial support of church and convention needs? Teaching about tithing is already experiencing a loss in popularity on the grounds of its being too legalistic. Church Discipleship Training lessons can be cited which, although devoted to the subject of stewardship, never speak about tithing as an option. Instead, Christian stewardship is being placed in the context of the totality of life. Whether promoting the stewardship of one's time and self will produce a greater financial commitment than the older approach based on tithing remains to be proved.

THE ORDINANCES

The old Landmark dogmas about the ordinances are practically dead. The enforcement of closed communion rarely occurs among Southern Baptists. In spite of the fact that most Southern Baptists still believe that immersion is the only proper mode of baptism, the doctrine has little practical significance beyond restrictions placed on church membership. That is, immersion is not seen as a requirement for participation in the Supper.

The whole question of ordination represents a relatively new field of thought for Southern Baptists. To illustrate, the July, 1988, issue of *The Baptist Faith and Heritage* was given to the subject of what is happening in the churches, especially in regard to the ordination of women. First, it can be observed that many Southern Baptist churches see no biblical reasons for not ordaining women to the office of deacon and are doing so. Second, few Southern Baptist churches are inclined to extend a call to a woman to become the pastor. Probably fewer than a dozen women served as pastors in 1988, and many of those work as co-pastors with their husbands or with another male minister. The drive among Baptists to have women serve as pastors is a phenomenon unique to the seventies and eighties of the twentieth century. Even in the sixteenth century among New Light Baptists with their volatile services, women never served in the capacity of pastors. Third, in filling staff positions other than preaching, women are finding a wider acceptance. Many churches which formerly allowed a woman to direct choirs, but refused to permit her to direct the congregation portion of the worship services, have now removed that restriction.

Questions about the meaning and recipients of ordination have been opened up by the increase in the number of church staff members with their specialized ministry roles. Are only deacons and preaching ministers to be ordained, or should ordination include others devoted to full-time ministries? Further, many staff members and college-seminary teachers see an inequity in governmental laws which grant tax breaks to part of the faculty—those who are ordained—while excluding others who perform essentially the same kinds of tasks. Positions such as institutional chaplaincies also require ordination in some cases. Women who are otherwise qualified for these counseling ministries may find themselves barred from being hired. These practical problems are placing new pressures on Southern Baptists to take a new look at their beliefs about ordination.

THE END TIME

Two actions by the Sunday School Board reflect the abandonment of the exclusive promotion of amillennialism in its literature. The board authorized a new commentary on the Bible to be written from the inerrantist point of view. Also, exclusive promotion of amillennialism is no longer acceptable. Sunday School lessons dealing with disputed passages having to do with the end time now give interpretations from the other two principal theories popular among Southern Baptists, dispensationalism and historic premillennialism, without making a commitment to either one. A special edition of *The Theological Educator*, published by the faculty of New Orleans Baptist Theological Seminary, carried an article by Jerry Vines, who took the premillennial side against amillennialism.[1] Herschel H. Hobbs defended amillennialism.[2] Postmillennialism has no discernible following in the convention.

Those people in the convention who desire studies about the order, signs, and nature of the second coming of Christ will not likely find those expositions in Sunday School and Church Discipleship Training materials in the next few years. In spite of the richness of biblical teaching about the end of time and the profound way it permeates nearly all other doctrines (e.g., note the point of view given by John P. Newport in the previous chapter), editors may not yet be ready to launch these investigations. Of all the major biblical doctrines, eschatology and the doctrine of the Holy Spirit have received the least attention by Southern Baptists. Both are ripe for intensive study.

LIVING WITH THE CONTROVERSY

If the past is but prelude to the future, does the convention face the prospects of acrimony and dissension into the twenty-first century? There are signs that the worst is over as both sides cool off and the level of political intensity diminishes. On the one hand, the inerrantists claim that the battles are over and are offering assurances of no widespread witch hunts or summary firings of neoorthodox professors. On the other, the opposition does not have the capability of marshalling a convention-wide momentum to oust the inerrantists. For example, Daniel Vestal's portrayal of himself in 1989 as a centrist who could heal the convention did not convince the messengers when the convention met in Las Vegas. His purchase of TV advertisement, although indicative of his frustration at not having access to a suitable forum, offended many messengers. Further, the Southern Baptist Alliance is sputtering. Whether fundamentalist in origin or otherwise, protest organizations tend either to fade away or else take on a life of their own without regard for their original purpose. In any case, its impact on the controversy is negligible. What does the future hold?

First, not only are the two factions in the convention not reconciled theologically, but they cannot be. The chasms between contrasting doctrines like inerrancy on the one hand and biblical authority the other, between body and soul versus body-soul, between a literal hell and no hell at all are unbridgeable. Differing beliefs on other vital doctrines are equally intense. Despite these differences, however, the convention at large is uninformed as to the depth of the diverging views. Further, many of them, including seminary graduates, seem unable to grasp the nuances of the debate. Whereas the spokesmen for both sides see the issues clearly, the masses are befuddled. As tragic as it sounds, the broadest base for healing lies in the ignorance of Baptists at large.

Second, both sides genuinely believe that the theories and attitudes of the other side, if not checked, will strip the convention of its dynamism and reduce it to a lifeless monument to former glories. One need not impugn the sincerity of fifteen seminary professors who published and appeal for reconciliation in 1981.[3] They are Robert A. Baker, William R. Estep, Timothy George, G. Thomas Halbrooks, E. Glenn Hinson, Dan Holcomb, Claude L. Howe, Jr., Bill Leonard, Leon McBeth, Glenn T. Miller, W. Morgan Patterson, Walter B. Shurden, Penrose St. Amant, John E. Steely, and G. Hugh Wamble. They unquestionably expressed their deepest concern that the course of action being followed by the inerrantists was leading to creedalism, an erosion of the doctrine of the priesthood of the believer, and a threat to soul freedom.

Neither should one question the sincerity of James T. Draper, Jr., when he addressed the SBC evangelism directors in San Juan, Puerto Rico. Painting a dismal picture of the decline in evangelistic fervor which always accompanies liberal theology, he warned that the jobs of the missionaries were at stake.[4] In another context of thought, he expressed one of the bases for his concern. Once one compromises belief in the authority of the Scriptures, one inevitably "cuts the nerve of evangelism and missions in the biblical sense."[5] The apprehensions each side harbors against the other transcend personal pique and perverse desires to control the convention bureaucracy. They are rooted in years of studying, praying, preaching, and lecturing. They also preclude any facile solutions to the divided spirit in the convention.

Third, the convention is not likely, after this many years of contention, to experience a major split. Some analysts view the situation pessimistically, especially those who view with alarm the ascendancy of the inerrantists. E. Glenn Hinson typifies many who see the convention as irretrievably divided. He went so far as to suggest that a formal divorce could be in order, even to the extent of a division of the control of some property.[6] Nevertheless, a split of any magnitude is unlikely to occur. To begin, the rank and file members do not perceive the inerrantists to be an unholy force eroding the purposes of the convention. When they listen to sermons by inerrantist pastors like Adrian Rogers, Charles Stanley, and Jerry Vines, the theology sounds like the theology being preached in the average Southern Baptist pulpit Sunday after Sunday. Conversely, when they learn the neoorthodox wing allegorizes the Genesis account of creation, explains away the miracles in the Bible and then equivocates over words like infallible, inerrantist, and authority, they are ready to do battle. Esoteric arguments about threats to cherished Baptist doctrines such as the priesthood of the believers and soul-freedom are lost on them. Opponents of the inerrantists have neither an emotional issue to rally the people nor a national forum from which to proclaim it.

There is a practical, down-to-earth reason why a split is unlikely to occur. One sometimes hears the half-jesting statement made by church leaders, "If the convention splits, I'm going with the half that has the Annuity Board." The point is well taken. A person who has invested money for decades in the convention retirement program cannot afford to be cut off from those investments.

If the inerrantist and neoorthodox factions cannot compromise their doctrinal positions without capitulating to the other, can the convention expect additional years of spiteful warfare? A definitive answer is impossible because of two conflicting developments. The inerrantists are declaring that the conflict is resolved and are calling for a recommitment by Southern Baptists to soul-winning and missionary fervor. Public assurances that there would be no witch hunts nor faulty firings may help assuage suspicions about their intentions.

On the other hand, many of the advocates of the tenets of neoorthodoxy remain secure in their academic fortresses. Neither are the inerrantists likely to dislodge them even if they make the attempt. The reason for such a conclusive statement lies in the seminary trustee-administration relationship and duties.

From the side of the trustees, they meet in small committees at various times and places but assemble on the seminary campus only once a year. The seminary administrators mail to them, in advance of the meeting, a thick packet of materials related to the school. When the trustees arrive from across the nation, immediately they are rushed into a frenetic pace of committee meetings and conferences. There is little personal contact between them, the teaching faculty, and the students. Except for attending worship services and visiting a class in session, they are isolated from the seminary family. Almost everything they know about the functioning of the school is filtered through the administration. They have little knowledge of what is being taught and almost no mechanism for obtaining it. The faculty and students, who know what is being taught, posses no effective procedure for presenting the information to the trustees.

From the school administration side, nearly all of the power resides in the office of the president in matters concerning faculty employment. Faculty committees are free to make recommendations for new faculty when vacancies occur, but the president makes the final decision about which nominees to present to the trustees for approval. The trustees rarely reject the recommendations from the president.

What doctrinal qualifications should prospective faculty possess? The extensive recommendation of the Peace Committee in its 1987 report is explicit in some respects, but ambiguous in others. Part of the report reads:

> We, as a Peace Committee, reaffirm the Baptist commitment to the absolute authority of Scripture and to the historic Baptist position that the Bible has "truth without any mixture of error for its matter." We affirm that the narratives of Scripture are historically and factually accurate. We affirm that the historic accounts of the miraculous and the supernatural are truthful as given by God and recorded by the biblical writers.[7]

The Peace Committee found that most Southern Baptists believe the Bible contains "truth without any mixture of error for its matter." This implies four truths, said the committee:

> (1) They believe in direct creation of mankind and therefore they believe Adam and Eve were real persons.

> (2) They believe the named authors did write the biblical books attributed to them by those books.

> (3) They believe the miracles described in Scripture did indeed occur as supernatural events in history.

(4) They believe that the historical narratives given by biblical authors are indeed accurate and reliable as given by those authors.[8]

The next two paragraphs composed by the committee asserted:

> We call upon Southern Baptist institutions to recognize the great number of Southern Baptists who believe this interpretation of our confessional statement and, in the future, to build their professional staffs and faculties from those who clearly reflect such dominant convictions and beliefs held by Southern Baptists at large.
>
> However, some members of the Peace Committee differ from this viewpoint. They would hold that "truth without any mixture of error" relates only to faith and practice. They would also prefer a broader theological perspective. Yet, we have learned to live together on the Peace Committee in mutual charity and commitment to each other.[9]

Note carefully the last paragraph. If the presidents interpret it to imply a balanced faculty of both inerrantists and neoorthodox professors, the seminaries face disruption as long as the inerrantists are in power. The inerrantists ultimately gained control by controlling the Committee on Committees. They may well lose out in the long run because the seminary trustees cannot break through the administrative wall. The intensity and extent of the controversy now rests on what each of the six presidents decides his role to be. The presidents can insure a gradual elimination of neoorthodoxy if they recommend as prospective faculty and staff only those who meet the theological guidelines adopted in 1987. If the trustees sense an adversarial spirit on the part of the presidents, mutual distrust and public displays of rancor will continue. In a sense, then, the ultimate outcome of the controversy, as well as the future of the Convention, may rest in the hands of its educators, especially of those in the seminaries.

NOTES

1. Jerry Vines, "Eschatology: Premillennial or Amillennial?" *Theological Educator* 37 (Spring, 1988):134-144.
2. Herschel H. Hobbs, Ibid., pp. 145-153.
3. "Historians Appeal to SBC to Protect Heritage," *Baptist Standard* 93 (3 June 1981):9.
4. James T. Draper, Jr., "No Evangelism If Liberals Take Over SBC," *Florida Baptist Witness* 99 (16 December 1983):3.
5. Draper, *Authority: The Critical Issue for Southern* Baptists. Old Tappan, N.J.: Fleming H. Revell Company, 1984, p. 96.
6. "Seminary Professor Calls for 'Divorce' within SBC," *Florida Baptist Witness* 104 (9 April 1987):6.
7. *Southern Baptist Convention Annual*, 1987, p. 237.
8. Ibid.
9. Ibid.

INDEX

Abelard, 25
Adams, J. McKee, 86
Aldrich, A. Douglas, 201
Alien Immersion, 71, 72, 108, 109, 203
Allen, Clifton J., 169, 184
Alley, Robert S., 185
Amillennialism, 204-205, 208, 216
Analytical Repository, 74, 75
Anglicanism, 5, 6, 26
Anselm, 25, 57, 93
Apostles, Baptist, 31
Arminianism
    Dargan, 97
    defined, 8-9
    Dewees, 58
    eroded, 126-127, 193
    Fullerism, 56
    ridiculed, 13-14, 52
Arminius, Jacob, 9
Armitage, Thomas, 31
Armstrong, Annie Walker, 115, 116
Ashcraft, J. Morris
    body-soul dualism, 189
    conditional immortality, 207
    intermediate state, 206
    tongues-speaking, 187
Astruc, Jean, 19
Atonement, Theories of, 190
    Fullerism, 55-56, 124, 191
    limited-general, 9-11, 45, 51-52, 58, 191
    propitiation-expiation, 153, 192
    ransom, 155
    salvation of infants, 129
    subjective-objective, 25, 156, 193
    substitutionary, 131-132, 143, 191
    sufficiency-efficacy, 57-58, 126

Backus, Isaac, xi, 7-8, 17-18, 20-30, 73-79, 108-110
Baggett, Hudson, 185
Bailey, D. Waylon, 205
Baker, Robert A., 217
Barnes, W. W., 107, 133
Barnette, Henlee H., 186
Barth, Karl, 123, 151, 152
Baur, Ferdinand C., 86
Beasley-Murray, G. R.
    baptism, 203
    premillennialism, 205
Becker, Howard, 199
Beissel, John Conrad, 11
Benedict, David, 12, 18, 36, 49-52, 72, 78
Biggs, Joseph, 26
Blevins, William, 206
Body-Soul Relationship, 188-190, 195, 206-207, 217
Boettner, Loraine, 166
Bogard, Ben, 107
Bonhoeffer, Dietrich, 151
Boone, William C.
    eschatology, 136
    inspiration, 147
    satisfaction, 131
    soul, 130
Botsford, Edmond, 34-36
Bowne, B. P., 143, 154
Boyce, James P.
    atonement, 131
    Calvinism, 52, 85, 92
    covenant theology, 73
    depravity, 96-97
    hell, 208
    Holy Spirit, 49

inspiration, 87
intermediate state, 113
millennialism, 111, 135
salvation of infants, 129
slavery, 78
soul, 97, 130
Toy, 88, 142
Trinity, 92
Brantly, William T., Sr.
   depravity, 51, 97
   efficacy, 56-57, 94
   infant baptism, 73
   Fullerism, 56
   Trinity, 50
Brinkley, A. R., 68
Broadman Bible Commentary, 2, 163-172, 205
Broaddus, Andrew
   alien immersion, 72
   Baptist antiquity, 68
   Campbellism, 54
   general atonement, 58
   holy tone, 80
   inspiration, 47
   visible kingdom, 77
Broadus, John A.
   amillennialism, 110-111, 135
   inspiration, 87
   resurrection, 93-94
   Toy, 88, 142
Brown, J. Newton, 64
Brunner, Emil, 151, 152
Buck, W. C., 55, 68
Bunn, John T., 169
Bultmann, Rudolph, 140, 151-153, 172
Burnett, J. J., 35, 58, 69, 79, 102, 106
Burton, Janet, 205
Busher, Leonard, 6

Cairns, Earle E., 20, 175
Callaway, Joseph A., 172
Campbell, Alexander, 50, 53-55, 66-78, 96, 110, 135,
Cappellus, Ludovicus, 19
Cardwell, Albert L., 201
Carey, William, 34, 113
Carnes, Clinton S., 147
Carroll, B. H.
   inspiration, 145
   postmillennialism, 136
   soul, 129
Carroll, J. M., 107
Cartwright, Thomas, 5
Carver, W. O., 90, 136, 200,
Childs, James, 7
Chiliasm, 32, 33, 37
Christian, John T., 107
Church of England, 5, 6, 26
Clark, Theodore, R., xii, 121, 163
   immortality, 207
   Jesusolotry, 185
   revelation, 178
   self-denial, 192
Clarke, John, 10, 14
Clarke, Samuel J., 21
Clements, Ronald L., 169
Colson, Howard P., 136
Communion, Closed, 70, 92, 134, 136, 202, 215,
Communion, Open, 11, 109-110, 199, 202, 203, 288
Congregationalism, 6, 27, 28, 73
Conkwright, S. J., 70
Conner, W. T.
   baptism, 203
   election, 188
   heaven, 208
   hereditary guilt, 129
   local church, 133, 203
   Lord's Supper, 134
   resurrection, 186
Cooperative Program, 142, 147
Cotton Grove Resolutions, 103
Corbley, John, 7

Corley, B. F., 111, 112
Covenant Theology, 25-28, 73, 107, 133
Craig, Elijah, 7, 31
Craig, Lewis, 7
Crandall, John, 10
Crane, W. C., 68
Crawford, Nathaniel M.
   Campbellism, 54
   limited atonement, 51-52
Criswell, W. A.
   premillennialism, 205
   textual criticism, 174
Critical Movement, 19-20, 46-47, 56, 59, 71, 86-87, 140-144, 164, 167-169, 172
Crosby, Thomas, 66
Culpepper, Robert, 7, 25

Dagg, John L.
   Calvinism, 85
   inspiration, 91
   systematic theology, 92
Dana, H. E.
   church, 133, 200
   infallibility, 147
   Lord's Supper, 134
Darby, J. N., 63, 74
Dargan, Edwin C.
   baptism, 109
   church, 107, 133
   deity of Christ, 93
   depravity, 97, 124
   infallibility, 91
   postmillennialism, 112
   satisfaction, 95
   substitution, 96
   resurrection, 113
Darwin, Charles, 85, 87, 88, 171
Davies, G. Henton, 168, 171
Deacons, 10, 13, 26, 30, 70, 106, 216
Dehoney, Wayne, 203

Deism, 21, 77, 92, 177
Depravity, xi, 24, 37-59, 81-97, 124-130, 190-193, 212
Dermont, J. J., 69
Dewey, John, 128
Dibelius, Martin, 140
Dilday, Russell H., Jr.
   Holy Spirit, 175
   inspiration, 166
Dispensationalism, 205
Dodd, C. H., 95, 153
Dodd, M. E., 147
Dort, Synod of, 9, 56
Drakeford, John W., 188
DuBose, Francis M., 189
Dunster, Henry, 6
Durham, John I, 11, 169

Eaves, James F., 202
Ebenstein, William, 5
Ecclesiology, 43, 115, 124,
Ecumenism, Baptist, 63-65, 213
Edwards, Jonathan, xi, 11
Edwards, Morgan, 28-31
Eichhorn, Johann G., 19, 20
Elder, Office of, 26, 30-37, 70, 71, 106
Elliott, Ralph H., xii,
Estep, William R., Jr., 141, 217
Evolution, Biological, 85-88, 124, 127-128, 143-151, 171-172, 177, 191, 195, 208, 212

Farrar, Frederic W., 19
Ferm, Vergilius, 140
Field, John, 5
Filioque Clause, 22, 48
Footwashing, 29, 73-74, 134-135, 201
Ford, W. Herschel, 205
Foreign Mission Board, 107, 114, 115, 194, 195, 199
Form Criticism, 139-140, 168

Francisco, Clyde T.
  Genesis, 164, 168-169
  subjectivism, 173
Free Will, 127, 155, 161, 187, 188, 191, 195
Freewill Baptists, 10, 11, 126
Freud, Sigmund, 86, 128
Frontier Revival, 3, 52, 59, 79
Fuller, Andrew
  Calvinism, 45
  general atonement, 50, 193
  influence, 55-56, 59, 94, 126, 191
  missions, 113
  sufficiency, 55, 95
Fuller, Richard
  baptism, 72
  covenant, 73
  satisfaction, 95
  succession, 109
Fundamentalism, xii, 110, 121, 124, 139, 141-142, 147-148, 151-155, 157, 161, 168, 190, 217
Furman, Richard
  authority, 20
  camp meeting, 70
  Calvinism, 17
  missions, 81
  religious freedom, 8
Furman, Wood, 49

Gainsborough, 6
Galileo, 21, 171
Gambrell, J. B., 106, 111
Gano, John, 12, 18, 20, 34
Gardner, Robert G., 10, 92
Garrett, James Leo, 58, 179
General Baptists, 3, 6, 9-12, 52
General Six Principle Baptists, 10
George, Timothy, 217
German Rationalism, xii, 85, 92, 156
Glaze, A. J., Jr., 169

Glossolalia, 186, 187
Goodwin, John A. R., 13, 205
Gordon, A. J., 110
Graf, K. H., 86, 87, 143
Graves, J. R.
  church, 77
  Landmarkism, 101, 115, 135
  premillennialism, 110, 112
  successionism, 67
Great Awakening, xi, 3, 11, 34, 37, 52, 64, 78
Green, Joseph F., 185, 202, 204
Green, Wallace S., Jr., 204
Gunkel, Hermann, 139, 140
Gwaltney, L. L., 136

Halbrooks, G. Thomas, 217
Hales, William L., 170
Half-way Covenant, 27, 65
Hall, Robert, 48
Harnack, Adolph, 185
Harrop, Clayton K., 184
Head, E. D., 127
Heavenly Tone, 36, 46, 47, 80
Hefley, James C., 164
Hegel, G. W. F, 22, 92, 143
Helwys, Thomas, 6, 11
Hendricks, Garland, 201
Henry, Patrick, 7
Hinson, E. Glenn, 217
Hiscox, Edward T., 64, 106
Historical (Higher) Criticism, 19-20, 43, 45, 85-87, 139-147, 151, 156, 167-170, 179
Hobbes, Thomas, 23
Hobbs, Herschel H.
  amillennialism, 216
  deity of Christ, 185
  Garden of Eden, 172
  soul, 188
  substitution, 131
  Virgin Birth, 184
Holcomb, Dan, 217

Holcombe, Henry, 64
Holcombe, Hosea, 59, 68, 74, 75
Holy Spirit, 9, 20-25, 72, 89-94, 125, 129, 147, 165-166, 173-175, 179, 184-187, 192, 195, 201, 217
Home Mission Board, 109, 115, 127, 147, 199
Honeycutt, Roy L., Jr. 169
Hovey, Alvah, 27, 50, 95
Howard, Fred D., 202
Howe, Claude L., Jr., 217
Howell, R. B. C., 68, 102
Hull, William E.
   authorship of John, 169
   deity of Christ, 185
   infallibility, 174
Hume, David, 85, 128
Humphreys, Fisher
   Adam, 172
   church, 201
   death of Christ, 193
Hunt, W. Boyd, 146, 193
Hutchinson, James 29

Inerrancy, 46, 141, 146, 155, 161, 163-165, 170, 173-180, 211, 217
Infants, Salvation of, 28, 50-51, 68-73, 97, 129
Ireland, James, 103, 114

Jackson, Herbert C., 208
James I, 5-6
Jefferson, Thomas, 8
Jenkins, Charles A., 89
Jesus, Resurrection of, 4, 131, 144, 186, 195
Jeter, J. B.
   alien immersion, 71
   Fullerism, 55
   holy tone, 80
   plenary inspiration, 89

Jewett, Paul K., 151, 167
Johnson, L. D., 170
Johnson, William B., 75, 79, 108
Judson, Adoniram, 79
Jung, Carl G., 86

Keach, Benjamin, 18
Keithians, 10
Kelly, Page H.
   Deutero-Isaiah, 169
   historical criticism, 168
   Mosaic authorship, 170
Kerfoot, F. H.
   alien immersion, 108
   infallibility, 90-91, 98
   millennialism, 111
Kicklighter, Robert W., 170, 188
Kierkegaard, Søren, 151
Koller, C.W., 129
Kuenen, Abraham, 86-88, 143

Ladd, George E., 205
Lamm, Wilbur C., 134
Landmarkism, xii, 27, 41-43, 63-72, 85, 101-116, 121, 124, 133-136, 184, 199-208, 213, 215
Lane, Tidence, 35
Lassiter, Perry, 193
Leavell, Roland Q., 186
Lee, R. G., 132, 205
Leibniz, G. W., 21
Leland, John, 7, 8, 104
Leonard, Bill, 217
Lewis, John M., 172
Liberation Theology, 183, 184
Lindsell, Harold, 165
Locke, John, 23
Lord's Supper, 26, 28-29, 63, 69-70, 188, 201-202
Lottie Moon Christmas Offering, 115
Lumpkin, W. L., 46, 204

McBeth, Leon, 31, 81, 142, 217
McCall, Duke K., 188
McClellan, Albert, 185, 200
McCullough, Thomas E., 193
McDaniel, George W., 147
McDowell, Edward A., 134
McGlothlin, W. J., 8, 107
Macomber, Job, 30
Madison, James, 7, 8
Manly, Basil, 79
Manly, Basil, Jr., 87, 89
Manning, James, 18
Marsh, William, 7
Marshall, Abraham, 13, 35
Marshall, Daniel, 12, 13, 17, 34, 35
Marx, Karl, 86, 180, 183
Matthews, James, Sr., 13
May, Lynn E., Jr., 114
Mell, P. H., 51, 52
Mercer, Jesse
    atonement, 95
    Calvinism, 51, 57
    ecumenism, 64
    Fullerite, 58
    successionism, 67
Merrill, Daniel, 72
Miller, Glenn T., 217
Miller, William, 77, 135
Moberg, David O., 199-200
Moody, Dale
    alien baptism, 203
    glossolalia, 187
    inspiration, 173
    intermediate state, 207
    millennialism, 205
    Virgin Birth, 184
Moon, Charlotte "Lottie", 115, 116
Moore, Ephraim, 58
Moore, Hight C., 134
Mullins, E. Y., 151
    atonement, 155-156
    deity of Christ, 143, 147
    election, 155

    Fundamentalism, 141
    hell, 208
    millennialism, 110-111
    neoorthodoxy, 154
    Personalism, 153, 191
    revelation, 154
    theism, 22
    traducianism, 128
    Trinity, 125
Murton, John, 6
Music, Joe H., 170

Naylor, Robert E., 171, 184, 208
Nelson, Dotson M., 186
Nettles, Thomas, J., 56, 57, 125, 126, 192
New Light Baptists, 12, 17, 31, 216
New Test Party, 59, 74
Newport, John P., 205, 216
Nietzsche, Friedrich W., 86
Norris, J. Frank, 135, 141, 146, 147

Odle, Joe T., 205
Oglethorpe, John, 114
Old School, 59, 79, 92
Orchard, G. H., 62, 102, 110
Ordination, 30, 31, 37, 215, 216
Owen, R. D., 74

Palmer, Paul, 29
Pantheism, 21, 22, 92, 140
Parker, Daniel, 78
Particular Baptists, 3, 9-13, 18
Paschal, George W., 13
Patterson, Paige M., 161
Patterson, W. Morgan, xiii, 101, 217
Peace Committee, 180, 212, 219-220
Peck, J. M., 68
Pendleton, J. M.
    church, 64

death of Christ, 95
deity of Christ, 93
Fullerism, 55
Landmarkism, 101, 103
postmillennialism, 110, 112
Personalism, 154
Peterson, Hugh R., 186
Pickett, John, 7
Pinnock, Clark H., 174, 176, 207
Postmillennialism, 32-33, 37, 75-76, 111-112, 116, 123, 135-136, 216
Predestination, 9, 10, 24, 43, 51, 54, 59, 125-126, 191, 193
Premillennial Baptist Missionary Fellowship, 135
Premillennialism, 32, 74, 76-77, 110, 112, 116, 135-136, 204-205, 216
Pressler, Paul, 161, 164
Price, J. M., 130
Priesthood of the Believer, 178-179, 217
Providence Plantations, 6
Psychology, Schools of, 85, 127-128, 131, 142, 177, 188
Purefoy, George W., 73, 80

Quakers, 6, 17, 45

Rauschenbusch, Walter, 140-141
Ray, D. B., 105
Redaction Criticism, 168
Randall, Benjamin, 11, 18, 33
Reeve, J. J., 141-144
Regular Baptists, 12, 14, 20, 22, 24, 43, 52, 64, 93-96
Remonstrance, 9, 88
Renan, Joseph E., 86
Reynolds, J. A., 8
Rice, Luther, 79
Richardson, Alan, 21
Roach, Sally Neill, 131

Roark, Dallas M., 184, 189
Robertson, A. T.
  Kerfoot, 108
  higher critics, 145
  resurrection, 185
  theology, 23
  salvation of infants, 129
  satisfaction, 132
  Virgin Birth, 184
Rogerenes, 10
Rogers, Adrian, 164-165
  inerrancy, 173, 218
Rogers, John, 10, 32
Roman Catholicism, 5, 9, 21, 26-27, 66-67, 103-104, 141, 171, 183, 201
Rousseau, Jean-Jacques, 23, 183
Ruling Elders, 30-31, 37
Rust, Eric C., 169, 186, 192

Scarborough, L. R., 125-127, 133
Scientific Revolution, 21, 177
Schleiermacher, Friedrich, 146
Schopenhauer, Arthur, 22, 92
Scoggin, B. Elmo, 169
Second Coming of Christ, 34, 75, 113, 204, 206, 208, 216
Second Great Awakening, 3, 36-37, 64, 78
Semple, Robert B., 7, 29-30, 34, 36, 53-54, 71
Separate Baptists, 10-13, 19, 23, 31, 52, 76, 106, 161, 180, 189, 191
Separatists, 6
Seventh Day Baptists, 10-11, 72
Shannon, Harper, 129
Shurden, Walter B., 78, 101, 217
Simmons, Billy E., 185, 206
Skinner, B. F., 128
Smith, Hezekiah, 17, 26
Smyth, John, 6
Social Gospel, 141
Societal Missions, 113, 115

Sommers, Charles G., 8
Soul Freedom, 6, 14, 177-178, 217
Soul, Pre-existence, 98, 189
Source Criticism, 139, 168
Southern Baptist Fellowship, 135
Southern Baptist Premillennial Fellowship, 135
Spitalfield, 6
Stagg, Frank
    authorship of Matthew, 169
    church, 201
    death of Christ, 191
    intermediate state, 206
    Lord's Supper, 202
    resurrection of Christ, 186
    soul, 189
Stearns, Shubal, 12-13, 17, 31, 35
Stevens, William W., 189
Stillman, Samuel, 18
Stow, Baron, 55
Strauss, David F., 86
Strong, A. H., 94, 107, 109, 112, 128-130, 133
Sullivan, James L., 186
Summers, Ray
    historical criticism, 169
    millennialism, 205
    resurrection, 206
    subjectivism, 172

Taylor, John, 78-79
Tennent, Gilbert, 11
Textual (Lower) Criticism, 91, 167, 171, 176
Thomas, David, 12
Tillich, Paul, xii, 152, 163
Tillman, William M., Jr., 194-195
Tolbert, Malcolm O., 184
Toy, Crawford H., 86-89, 142
Traducianism, 98, 128, 188
Transubstantiation, 27
Trent, Robbie, 136
Tribble, Harold W.
    hell, 208
    Lord's Supper, 134
    Millennialism, 135
    soul, 130
    Trinity, 125
Trinity, Trinitarianism, xi, xiii, 17, 22, 47-48, 81, 92-94, 125, 130, 152, 184, 187, 192, 195
Troeltsch, Ernst, 199, 213
Turner, Gwin T., 168
Turner, J. Clyde
    atonement, 131
    church, 133
    millennialism, 136

Unitarianism, 22, 49-50, 77

Van Ness, I. J., 127, 133, 134, 145
Vardeman, Jeremiah, 80
Vedder, H. C., 56, 200
Voluntarism, 5

Walker, Jeremiah, 13, 30, 55, 80, 89
Waller, John, 7, 31
Wamble, Hugh, 217
Ward, Wayne E., 186, 188
Warne, Joseph A., 50
Watson, John B., 128
Watts, J. D. W., 169
Wayland, Francis, 55
Wellhausen, Julius, 86-88, 140, 143
Wertheimer, Max, 128
Westminster Confession, 11, 18, 20, 37
Wetstein, J. J., 19
White, W. R., 133, 134
Whitefield, George, xi, 11, 13, 34
Whitsitt, William H., xi, 43, 67, 107, 121, 132, 154
Wilcox, Thomas, 5
Willard, Conrad C., 134
Williams, Charles B., 141-142

Williams, Roger, 3, 6-14, 72
Williams, Robert, 12
Williams, William, 87
Witty, Robert G., 205
Woman's Missionary Union, 115-116, 127
Wrede, Wilhelm, 140
Wyley, John, 7